Administrator's Desk Reference on Special Education

Gregory R. Weisenstein, Ed.D.
University of Washington
Seattle, Washington

Ruth Pelz
University of Washington
Seattle, Washington

AN ASPEN PUBLICATION®
Aspen Publishers, Inc.
Rockville, Maryland
Royal Tunbridge Wells
1986

Library of Congress Cataloging in Publication Data

Weisenstein, Gregory R.
Administrator's desk reference on special education.

"An Aspen publication."
Includes bibliographical references and index.
1. Exceptional children—Education—United States—Handbooks, manuals, etc. 2. Exceptional children—Education—Law and legislation—United States—Handbooks, manuals, etc. I. Pelz, Ruth. II. Title
LC3981.W38 1986 371.9'0973 86-10905
ISBN: 0-87189-357-6

Editorial Services: Carolyn Ormes

Library of Congress Catalog Card Number: 86-10905
ISBN: 0-87189-357-6

Printed in the United States of America

1 2 3 4 5

This book is dedicated to our parents, Ralph and Alice, Dick and Kelly, for their continuing and invaluable support and encouragement.

Table of Contents

Foreword

We are in a period of deep renegotiation of relations between "special" and "regular" education. The term "renegotiation" implies that all parties have positive contributions to make in the restructuring of a situation—in this case the restructuring of school programs. A major principle operating in the changes is that of the "least restrictive environment," which in effect calls for the strengthening of regular school programs as a resource for exceptional students. The "two-box" versions of regular and special education, with two distinct sets of pupils, teachers, and classes, have had their day, and the call now is for integration and collaboration. The school principal is the key figure in this renegotiation and will be the continuing leader/administrator of all of the revised programs.

Teachers often are skeptical about changes until they get well past the preliminary rhetoric. They want to see that the special education teacher will, indeed, be more available to regular teachers for consultation and mutual help. "Regular" teachers will need assurance that they will be able to contribute to planning the individualized education programs (IEPs), not just delivering on someone else's plans. Principals face the challenge of making certain that the new policies, expectations, staff functions, and patterns of communication are clear and implemented in fact.

In the recent past a great deal of disjointedness developed in school programs. Much of that occurred because programs were launched in a variety of narrowly framed categories. Each category developed almost as if it were assured that there were no interactions with other programs. An extreme case of this assumption occurred with the passage of the Elementary and Secondary Education Act in 1965 (P.L. 89-10). So-called Title I programs were administered so separately that even overhead projectors purchased with Title I funds sometimes could not be used in other programs. Categorical programs involved much separateness in teacher qualification, entitlements of students, advocacy groups, and more. In truth, these many programs tended to narrow and limit the leadership opportunities of school principals, especially in efforts for schoolwide improvements of instruction.

That situation now is in reverse, however, and there is a readiness among special educators to help build general school programs. There is increased recognition that exceptional students will not be well served until the rich total resources of the school are opened to them. More special education teachers are ready to come to the mainstream, along with their exceptional pupils, to help build a worthy mainstream program to serve all children.

Special educators these days are prepared to contribute generally to the schools their experience in the planning of programs for individual students, in working with parents, in meeting due process requirements, and in the very intensive forms of instruction. Many of the ideas and practices in special education are appropriate for application to all students. On the other hand, special educators can profit from the fuller knowledge of effective group instruction than can be offered by their regular education colleagues. It is the school principal who has the opportunity to lead what can be a creative rejoining of efforts by all school staff members to serve all students.

In this fine text, Weisenstein and Pelz outline some of the basics to be considered from the special education side as the renegotiation goes forward. They cover procedural and policy matters, such as those emerging recently out of law and judicial processes. They review, as well, substantive matters about the nature of the exceptionalities and the instructional and administrative processes found useful in dealing with them.

A point to be emphasized here is that hardly any of these matters are entirely secure, confirmed irrefutably. Indeed, most matters concerning identification, diagnosis, and instruction of exceptional pupils still are widely open to further study and improvement. Principals who now take up the challenge of leading their schools in a coordinated fashion to serve all children will receive much help from this book; it also is to be hoped that this reading will provide stimulus for principals to add their creative leadership in designing even better programs for the future.

Dr. Maynard Reynolds
Professor, Educational Psychology
University of Minnesota
Minneapolis

Preface

This handbook is designed to consolidate, in clear and easily accessible form, the information of most concern to school principals on topics related to special education. Specifically, it is directed toward principals whose training and experience is in regular education but who now find themselves with special education students or programs in their schools. It may be used both as a text for classes and seminars in educational administration and as a desk reference for practicing administrators.

The handbook has three parts: Legal and Policy Issues, Handicapping Conditions, and Administrative Issues. Each part, in turn, is divided into short, topical chapters, alphabetically arranged. Each chapter begins with a summary of key information on relevant legal requirements, current best practices, and critical issues. This can be skimmed as a quick reminder, duplicated, and distributed to staff, or read as an introduction to the chapter.

Within the chapter itself are discussions of problems commonly encountered by school principals and suggested solutions to them; the evolution of federal laws and policies and their implications for schools; key terms and definitions; descriptions of programs, staffing patterns, and service delivery models; and summaries of both commonly accepted practice and continuing controversies in the field.

All elements are designed and prepared with the special needs of the busy school administrator foremost in mind. The information is concise, realistic, direct, and free of excessive professional jargon. The chapters are organized clearly and consistently. Key concepts are highlighted for quick access and easy reading. Overall, the presentation is geared toward providing the background most necessary for formulating policy, preparing for meetings, handling controversy, and managing continuing programs.

Many people, including school principals, district-level special education directors, state education agency staff members, and university faculty were involved in the production and editing of this handbook. We would like to extend special thanks to Barbara Day, Lois Hart, and John Jewell for their careful reading and detailed comments on the manuscript; to Ken Ostrander for helping us get the project started; and to Ralph Julness, Tracy Faust, Sharon Field, Herb Barkaloo, and Jim Pruess, who also provided editorial comments and assistance.

We also wish to acknowledge the support and assistance of Dr. Theodore Kaltsounis who, as principal investigator of the University of Washington Dean's Grant on mainstreaming, contributed so importantly to bringing this publication into being.

Part I

Legal and Policy Issues

Chapter 1

Basic Mainstreaming

SUMMARY

Statement of the Problem

Within little more than a decade, major federal laws have revolutionized treatment of the handicapped in America, with far-reaching effects on the schools. The new requirements for mainstreamed and individualized education of handicapped students place demands on school principals and staff members for which they often have not received adequate professional training.

Legal Issues

The two most important laws governing education of the handicapped are Public Law (P.L.) 94-142, the Education for All Handicapped Children Act (passed in 1975 and implemented in 1977) and Section 504 of the Rehabilitation Act Amendments of 1973 (P.L. 93-112). The latter is a basic civil rights guarantee, prohibiting discrimination against the handicapped in any program receiving federal funds. It is somewhat broader than P.L. 94-142 in that it affects employment opportunities as well as education and includes persons not actually handicapped but regarded as such (e.g., discriminated against because of abnormal, though not disabling, appearance). Although both contain many of the same provisions on educational programs, P.L. 94-142 alone provides funding for such programs. It also goes somewhat farther in spelling out the following basic requirements for special education:

- All school-age children and youth, no matter how severe their handicaps, must be provided a free (no cost to parents), appropriate (corresponding to individual abilities and needs) public education.

- The program must be delivered in the most normal or "least restrictive" environment feasible, to the greatest possible extent in the company of nonhandicapped peers.
- Students and their parents are guaranteed a variety of legal protections, including nondiscriminatory evaluation of the student, parent involvement in the individualized education program (IEP) process, permission for initial evaluation, and prior notice of any changes in identification, evaluation, program, or placement; confidentiality of student records; and the right to call for a due process hearing if necessary to resolve disputes with the school.

Specific interpretations of the laws continue to change, based on judicial decisions, state laws, congressional acts, changes in administrations, and other factors.

Rationale

Current policies in special education are based on constitutional guarantees for equal protection under the law (in this case, equal rights to a public education), on the recognition that every child can learn and has a right to, that integration of the handicapped and nonhandicapped in everyday life is beneficial to both groups, and the acknowledgment that these students, by definition, have exceptional needs that require special, highly individualized accommodations.

Approaches

There are four basic areas in which modifications in school programs may have to be made for individual handicapped students:

1. content (e.g., emphasis on daily living skills rather than preparation for more advanced study)
2. teaching strategies (such as increased repetition, substitution of more appropriate materials, special emphasis on visual or auditory communication, regular use of reinforcers, and so on)
3. physical environment (nonglare lighting for the visually and hearing impaired, wheelchair accessibility, and other needed adjustments)
4. grading and evaluation procedures, including appropriate test construction (e.g., oral testing for the visually impaired, clear presentation, allowances for extraneous factors such as handwriting quality), fair and realistic grading systems and recording of grades (possibilities include separate grades for effort, achievement, etc., student/teacher contracts, group grades for group projects).

The key in each case is arriving at modifications appropriate to the student's individual needs.

Principals are essential to the success of mainstreaming and can contribute by modeling acceptance of special education students and programs: setting a positive tone; assigning equally desirable space, schedules, and school duties to both regular and special education; facilitating cooperation among staff members, acceptance among students, and good relations with the community.

BASIC MAINSTREAMING CONSIDERATIONS

A REVOLUTION IN PROGRESS

Every revolution, it is fair to say, catches a certain percentage of the population unaware, or at least insufficiently prepared. That certainly is true of the sweeping changes in education of the handicapped that were enacted into law in the United States in the mid 1970s. While parents of the handicapped had been aware of problems and had struggled toward solutions for agonized years—sometimes decades—the majority of those in the public education system were unaffected by these struggles.

Most educators—principals and classroom teachers—were not trained to work with handicapped students and did not expect to. Then, in 1977, with the implementation of P.L. 94-142, the situation changed dramatically. Regular class teachers found exceptional children assigned to their classrooms; special educators had to give up ownership of "their" students and routines; new systems had to be set up; parents' doubts had to be quelled; a myriad of smaller changes had to be made; and building principals, it often seemed, had to make it all happen.

Again like other revolutions, this one has not been, and will not be, accomplished overnight. Passage of the law in many ways marked the beginning, not the end, of the process of change. Much has been learned since then, and it is clear that further changes will come.

PURPOSE OF THIS CHAPTER

This chapter serves as an introduction to the general topic of mainstreamed special education as defined by federal law. It is directed primarily toward those with little experience and training in an integrated school setting, although it does include information on grading and curriculum modification not covered in other parts of the book. There is a brief history of special education, followed by a description of basic terms, principles, and procedures described in P.L. 94-142, and examples of the types of modifications that might be needed to accommodate handicapped learners in the regular classroom—modifications in content, teaching strategies, physical environment, and grading procedures.

The information here is extremely brief. Much more detailed discussion of legal topics is given in later chapters (in Part I, especially); the particular needs and suggested modifications for specific handicapping conditions are presented in Part II.

EARLY HISTORY

THE AGE OF ENLIGHTENMENT—AND BEYOND

For much of human history, the treatment of handicapped individuals has been defined by superstitions and fear. Infanticide, expulsion, attributions of witchcraft or divine punishment, and awed respect all have been sanctioned socially. Then, with the rise of scientific understanding and democratic values in the late 1700s (the Age of Enlightenment), attitudes began to change. The handicapped began to be seen as capable of learning, and the earliest special schools were founded for the deaf and blind. In institutions for the mentally ill and retarded (then grouped together indiscriminately), people literally were freed from their chains, and conditions became somewhat more humane.

During the 19th century, reformers campaigned for new and more humane institutions. These generally were based on earlier European residential models, each one accommodating a different categorical population. Some were state operated, some private, some obviously better than others. Their overall capacity was limited, and many children—especially those with severe or multiple handicaps—were not served.

The early 20th century saw the beginning of community-based programs and the first university training of teachers of the handicapped. The movement in this direction grew slowly. In most cases, the public attitude was "at best . . . bare tolerance of exceptional children" (Reynolds and Birch, 1977, p. 17). Programs still tended to be segregated along categorical lines and separate from regular classes and schools. Some students attended classes for only minimal periods a day, and many others were not served at all. Mildly handicapped students who did attend the public schools often were held back, forced to repeat grade after grade.

THE POSTWAR DECADES

Only in the decades since World War II has there been momentum for profound and rapid change. This period was marked by great increases in the number of student enrollments, teacher training programs, and state support for special programs—even before the federal government became fully involved. Spurred in part by the response of wounded war veterans unwilling to accept a segregated, unproductive life, a change in philosophy was under way. While earlier reformers had argued for segregated schools as the most humane and receptive environment for educating the handicapped, the new trend was toward integration, toward "normalization" of handicapped individuals' lives.

This trend was supported by the fusion of two important social elements in pressuring for change: (1) the civil rights movement of the 1950s and 1960s and (2) organizations of parents of handicapped students. Many other 20th century developments contributed to the advancement of special education, including:

- the first standardized intelligence tests and other types of reliable educational assessment
- the development of new professional fields such as psychiatry, speech, pathology, and educational psychology
- advances in medical understanding and treatment of previously mysterious diseases such as epilepsy and polio
- technological developments in such diverse and important areas as public transportation, artificial limbs and braces, and electronic communication aids for the deaf and blind.

By the middle 1970s, these combined forces had resulted in a legalized commitment to educate all the nation's handicapped young people and to do it in the most normal setting possible.

THE NEWNESS OF PUBLIC EDUCATION

To put this in reasonable perspective, it must be understood that public education itself is a relatively recent institution. Not until 1918 did all states in the country have compulsory education laws. Child labor, which had involved a large percentage of school-age children, was not effectively banned on a national level until 1938. Federal government involvement with the special rights and needs of children began in the 20th century also, with the first White House Conference on Children and Youth in 1909.

The concept of universal public education won wide acceptance in this country only after the tremendous influx of immigrants in the late 19th and early 20th centuries prompted concerns that the population be "Americanized." And even then, as is well known, large numbers of the children and youth were seriously underserved (as in the case of many handicapped students, racial minorities, and other groups) or given no education at all (as many as one million handicapped children in the early 1970s). Governmental attention to the needs of all children was a necessary prerequisite for the improvement of special education.

LEGAL ISSUES

All of these 20th century developments—governmental, theoretical, technological, medical, and organizational—formed the roots of the powerful movement for educational change in the 1960s and 1970s. The organizations pushing for improvements in education of the handicapped were inspired and influenced by the successes of the civil rights movement in many ways. The landmark five cases consolidated into *Brown vs. Board of Education* (347 U.S. 483) in 1954, for example, had been brought on racial grounds. But the Supreme Court ruling against "separate but equal" schooling and its affirmation of education as a right of all Americans was seen as relevant to handicapped students. Over the next 20 years, advocate groups led an active, and ultimately successful, campaign to win legal guarantees for education of the handicapped.

IN CONGRESS AND THE COURTS

The efforts toward public awareness received an important boost from President Kennedy, who himself had a retarded sister. In 1961, he called a Presidential Panel on Mental Retardation, and in the ensuing decade, Congress passed several laws that began to address the issue of handicapped education. The Elementary and Secondary Education Act (ESEA) of 1965 (P.L. 89-10) included funding to meet the needs of educationally deprived students, and later ESEA amendments provided state agencies with special funds for the evaluation and education of handicapped students (and later for gifted students as well). The Handicapped Children's Early Education Act of 1968 (P.L. 90-247) provided funds to set up model demonstration programs for preschool children. The federal Bureau for Education of the Handicapped was created in 1966.

Just as the *Brown* decision preceded major congressional acts in the civil rights arena, key court cases helped set the stage for passage of Section 504 of the Rehabilitation Act of 1973 (P.L. 93-112) and P.L. 94-142. The two cases most often cited are *Pennsylvania Association for Retarded Citizens (PARC) v. Pennsylvania,* 334 F. Supp. 1257 (E.D. Pa. 1971), 343 F. Supp. 279 (E.D. Pa. 1972) and *Mills v. Board of Education,* 348 F. Supp. 866 (D.D.C. 1972).

The rulings on these cases included many of the principles that were incorporated later into federal law, including the right of all handicapped children to a free, appropriate education.

Both P.L. 93-112, of which the well-known Section 504 is part, and P.L. 94-142 were passed and implemented in the following five years. They are the most important laws governing special education in the United States and form the basis for legal discussions in each chapter of this handbook. As explained in the chapter summary, Section 504 is essentially a civil rights statement, while P.L. 94-142 defines, and authorizes funding for, educational programs specifically. Some basic aspects of P.L. 94-142 are summarized next.

GENERAL PURPOSES OF THE LAW

P.L. 94-142 AND ITS 5 BASIC PURPOSES

As Shrybman (1982) points out, P.L. 94-142 has the following purposes:

1. to ensure that all handicapped children and youth receive a free, appropriate public education and the related services necessary for them to benefit from it
2. to guarantee protection of student and parent rights (such as those listed in the chapter summary)
3. to provide funds for state and local agencies to carry out these programs
4. to monitor and evaluate those programs
5. to institute the IEP as a written record of commitment to meet individual students' needs.

Important Terms

IMPORTANT DEFINITIONS

A number of key terms are used and defined in the law. They include:

Special education is defined in P.L. 94-142 as specially designed instruction, at no cost to parents or guardians, to meet the unique needs of a handicapped child, including classroom instruction, home instruction, and instruction in hospitals and institutions.

Handicapped children are those who have been evaluated and found to have one of the following handicaps: mentally retarded, hard of hearing, deaf, speech impaired, visually handicapped, seriously emotionally disturbed, orthopedically impaired, other health impaired, deaf-blind, multihandicapped, or having specific learning disabilities.

Related services are referred to in the law guaranteeing free provision of "special education and related services." Related services are defined as:

> transportation and such developmental, corrective, and other supportive services as are required to assist a handicapped child to benefit from special education and includes speech pathology and audiology, psychological services, physical and occupational therapy, recreation, early identification

and assessment of disabilities in children, counseling services, and medical services for diagnostic or evaluation purposes. The term also includes school health services, social work services in schools, and parent counseling and training. (42 Fed. Reg. 42479 [1977], Sec. 121a. 13)

MAJOR PRINCIPLES BEHIND THE LAW

Turnbull and Turnbull (1978) point to six major principles related to parent and student rights that constitute the backbone of this law (all are discussed in detail in later chapters of this handbook):

1. Zero Reject: Every school-age individual must be served, and services must be provided at no cost to families. The state must have a program (often known as child find) for identifying the eligible population.
2. Testing, Evaluation, and Placement: Prescribed methods for nondiscriminatory evaluation and appropriate placement must be followed.
3. Individualized and Appropriate Education: Programs must be individualized to meet the specific needs of each child. This is probably the most critical principle for building administrators and teaching staff. The IEP serves as a record that each student's needs and abilities have been considered and addressed individually.
4. Least Restrictive Placement: This stipulates that handicapped students be educated to the greatest extent feasible in the company of their nonhandicapped peers. It is not required that every handicapped student be placed in a regular class or school.
5. Procedural Due Process: The right of parents to protest state or local school district actions that they find discriminatory, inappropriate, or unfair is derived from the U.S. Constitution and is essential to ensuring that the provisions of the law are carried out.
6. Parent Participation and Shared Decision Making: P.L. 94-142 involves students' parents (or legal guardians or appointed surrogates) at each stage of the legally defined special education process. For example, these elders must give their consent for the process to begin in the first place, they must be notified in advance of key district actions regarding their child's special education, and they must be encouraged to participate in developing the IEP.

OVERVIEW OF THE PROCESS

THE PROGRAM STARTS IN MOTION

Once a child is identified (through individual referral or routine screening procedures) as needing special education and related services, a chain of activities is set in motion, with the three basic steps prescribed by law:

1. A thorough, nondiscriminatory evaluation assesses all areas of possible handicap.
2. The IEP is prepared. This document is based on the evaluation data and is formulated in a meeting involving the student's parent(s), teacher(s), and at

least one other school district representative. It records the pupil's current levels of functioning, educational goals, and special services required.

3. The educational placement is chosen. This must be a setting in which the IEP can be carried out and which meets other requirements of the law. The district must have a continuum of placements available (whether provided by the district itself or under contract through outside agencies) in regular and special schools.

IDENTIFICATION, EVALUATION, AND PLACEMENT

Specific state, district, and school policies can be (and in many cases have been) developed to help each step proceed smoothly. Such policies include preparing for IEP meetings with thorough knowledge of student evaluation data and the programs actually available in the school district, preplacement preparation of the student (assuring that the student has the prerequisite skills necessary for success in the setting), educating and sensitizing the other students in the class, and postplacement monitoring systems involving periodic communication between regular and special education staff.

THE LAW IS SUBJECT TO CHANGE

Although Section 504 and P.L. 94-142 represent extremely important milestones, the legal status of special education in this country still is subject to change. It continues to be influenced by such factors as court decisions, changes in administration, new acts of Congress, and changes at the state and local levels. Some examples include the court cases affecting school discipline procedures and program settings (discussed in Chapter 2 on Discipline and Chapter 6 on Placement) and the Carl D. Perkins Vocational Education Act of 1984, which deals with vocational education programs (Chapter 17 on Budgets and Funding).

Each chapter contains information on legal requirements and trends at the federal level. State laws and school district policies are not covered here, but will have to be consulted since they affect the options available to building administrators in many cases. Congress consistently has affirmed that education is primarily a state responsibility, and although the basic requirements of P.L. 93-112 and P.L. 94-142 are firm, the states still have a variety of options in specific areas as to how they will meet these requirements.

HOW THE LAW MAKES FUNDS AVAILABLE

The Education for All Handicapped Children Act, P.L. 94-142, essentially is a contract between the federal government and the states, whereby the latter agree to follow certain regulations in exchange for federal funds. To qualify for these funds, each state must submit annual program plans, including assurances that the basic principles of the federal law will be followed, copies of related state laws and regulations, counts of handicapped children in the state and where served, monitoring and evaluation activities, use of the funds and accounting systems, facilities available, and other information.

The state, in turn, makes funds available to local school districts upon receipt of their applications, which must include descriptions of facilities, personnel, and services available; guarantees that federal guidelines are being followed; plans for parent participation; accounting systems; and agreement to furnish data required by the state for its reports.

Thus each district is held accountable by the state department of education, which itself is policed by the federal government. To ensure contract compliance, program data and planning information must be collected and delivered to the federal government each year. This, briefly, is the legal and financial reality behind many of the paperwork requirements that go along with special education.

APPROACHES TO COMPLIANCE

IMPLEMENTATION OF THE FEDERAL MANDATES

Two of the chief mandates of federal special education law, as noted, are individualization of programming and integration of the handicapped and their nonhandicapped peers. Both concepts are admirable and philosophically sound. But the question is, how are they accomplished in the reality of the classroom? How does a regular class teacher, who may have no special training in exceptional education, meet the unique needs of two or three handicapped learners in an already demanding class of 25 or more students? And how does the principal/administrator deal with all this?

Part of the answer must be: "With help." In the mainstreamed classroom, teachers need special consideration as surely as do the handicapped students. This handbook includes information on structuring supportive relationships between regular class teachers and special education professionals (Chapter 6, Placement; Chapter 20, Staff Relationships and Staffing Patterns, and Part II). There also is information on setting up volunteer programs and gaining other types of support from the community (Chapter 18, Community Relations; Chapter 19, Interagency Cooperation; and Chapter 21, Student Relationships). And there are tips in every chapter on what the principal can do to establish a positive, cooperative atmosphere, and sound school policy.

Classroom Modifications

Other answers to the question of accommodating exceptional students in the mainstream lie in appropriate modifications of the classroom. These may be in any or all of the four general areas: physical environment, teaching strategies, content, and grading.

Modifications in the physical environment are most straightforward. Special environmental considerations related to each handicapping condition (covered in Part II) include adequate lighting, accessibility, preenrollment classroom orientation, appropriate seating, and testing considerations.

Teaching Strategies

MODIFYING THE MAINSTREAMED CLASSROOM

In mainstreamed settings, principals must assure appropriate modifications in teaching strategies, in both the materials used and the means of presenting information. Some of these modifications are obvious. With a blind student in the classroom, for example, it will not be possible to rely on visual communication exclusively. Assignments may have to be tape recorded; visual and spatial concepts may have to be explained; appropriate tools and materials such as Braille or large print books, typewriters, or Braille writers may be needed.

Other, less obvious, modifications will be required with many exceptional students. These may include the use of concrete examples in explaining new concepts, extra opportunities for rehearsal and repetition, consistent daily schedules, cooperative small group structures, special reinforcers, and so on.

ANALYZING EDUCATIONAL MATERIALS

Familiarity with materials analysis procedures will be helpful both during initial selection of the texts to be used in each class and in locating or preparing materials appropriate to specific students. (Specialists such as physical therapists, special education consultants, and resource room staff should be able to provide assistance in this process.)

Factors to analyze include the following:

- Reading Level: This probably is the most critical, since so many handicapping conditions may affect reading skills. Several formulas have been developed to provide quick estimates of the readability of publications. Those developed by Gunning (1972) and Fry (1977) are two of the most common. They rely on sentence length and number of multisyllabic words in a short sample to produce a grade level score.
- Concept Level: This is more difficult to assess than basic readability (although in a sense, of course, the two are interrelated). Comparison with standard course goals and objectives, and the educator's "feel" for the material, are two methods used.
- Graphic Presentation: Factors such as the following should be checked: Is the print dark and readable? Is it large enough? Are key ideas highlighted through titles, headings, and other graphic means? Are the page layouts too dense and confusing?
- Skills Development: Questions in this area include: Does the material offer ample opportunities for practice and repetition? Are skills presented sequentially, so that necessary prerequisites can be mastered before more complex concepts are introduced?
- Physical Factors: Can the student physically manipulate the materials as necessary?
- Motivation: Will students find the materials motivating and interesting? (In part, this is a result of the appropriateness of other factors discussed.)
- Adaptability: Can the materials be adapted easily to accommodate handicapped students' needs? (Examples of adaptations are underlining key concepts, preparation of a study guide, location or development of additional practice activities, assigning variable amounts of reading/study to students of different ability levels.)

Curriculum Content

Content modifications are most likely to be required with students who have mental handicaps but may also be appropriate with others who for some reason (lack of

MODIFICATIONS IN CONTENT: A BROADER SCOPE

prerequisites, poor reading skills) cannot master the normal curriculum. The need for such modifications should never be assumed but rather should be based on individualized assessments that pinpoint each student's specific needs. The following are examples of such approaches:

- Teaching More Slowly: The emphasis in this approach is on ensuring that prerequisite steps have been mastered before students go on to more advanced tasks. Teachers may use individually paced curricula or modify time requirements for completing regular class materials. Task analysis, and frequent assessments to see that sequential steps are being mastered, are important elements. Coordination is necessary to see that students begin at an appropriate level the following year.
- Teaching Only Essentials: The teacher should either present all content to all students and hold special learners responsible only for the essential key concepts, or allow the learners extra time with basic skills while the rest of the class completes a less essential unit.
- Providing an Alternative Curriculum: Students who lack necessary prerequisites or whose educational goals are very different from the norm may require a totally different curriculum. Specialists should be consulted for help in selecting or developing such curricula.
- Providing a Parallel Curriculum: For students with poor reading skills, it should be possible to locate a text that covers the same general content (U.S. history, for example) at a lower reading level and to prepare individualized assignments. The students still should be included in group activities and class discussions.
- Providing Supplements: These might include separate instruction in study skills, special therapy, or additional opportunities for practicing regular curricular material. Such supplemental services are commonly provided by specialists such as speech therapists or resource room teachers.
- Altering Expectations: Nonpublic agreements can be made with students to hold them responsible, for example, for only odd-numbered items on assignments; standards for writing can be lowered, and so on. The method has problems: these students actually may need more practice, rather than less. Without it, they may never achieve adequate mastery. Extra drill in the resource room may alleviate these difficulties.

Grading

GRADING: HOW TO BE FAIR TO ALL STUDENTS

Suppose that the previously discussed modifications have been made. The classroom is accessible. Appropriate texts have been selected and the curriculum altered to match the handicapped students' abilities. What happens when grading time comes around? What evaluation system can be fair to both the handicapped students (who may be putting forth tremendous effort and still not meeting course goals) and those in the nonhandicapped majority (who may object strenuously to a system they perceive as unequal and unfair)?

This is one of the stickiest issues facing educators in a mainstreamed setting. It has generated persistent and difficult problems among parents, teachers, and students. For example, teachers have been known to refuse to take exceptional students in their classes because of the awkwardness of developing an evaluation system that is fair to all students, one that reinforces effort but also realistically reports performance. This last is important both for its present communication value and for its influence on future planning.

It is possible to develop fair, accurate, and justifiable evaluation systems for integrated classes. (The pages that follow offer several suggestions.) It is to the principal's advantage, clearly, to be aware of these strategies and to assist teachers in implementing them since so many potential problems can be avoided by doing so.

Modifying Tests

Three aspects of evaluation may have to be modified in a mainstreamed class setting: test construction, test grading, and recording of grades.

ADAPTATIONS TO ASSURE TEST FAIRNESS FOR ALL

The same tests that are quite adequate for the majority of students in a class may not yield fair and accurate results for those with special needs. It would be inappropriate, for example, to give an exam to a hearing impaired student in which all instructions and questions were given orally. The following list suggests a variety of testing modifications that principals, in consultation with the teachers, may decide are needed to meet the needs of individual students. Not all modifications will be appropriate or necessary with all students.

- Visual Presentation: The teachers must be sure that the test is clearly printed and easy to read. (Small flaws in print may be extremely distracting and frustrating to some students.) They should type rather than handwrite whenever possible, print on only one side of the page, be sure the duplicating machine is working properly, and use dark ink on white paper.
- Organization: Teachers should number all pages, ask questions in sequential order, group questions of the same format (e.g., multiple choice) together, print all instructions on the page and review these instructions orally before testing begins, allow plenty of space for the students' responses and provide lines for them to write on, and group questions (e.g., matching questions) into small sets rather than long lists.
- Minimizing Stress: Teachers must keep down distracting noise and activity, place the students in a quiet location, try not to give oral instructions while they are taking the test (but be available to quietly answer individual questions). It is preferable to give several short tests rather than one long one. Timed tests should be avoided except where speed is an essential element of the skill. Bonus questions and/or other options for improving grades should be provided for those who perform poorly on exams. Point values should be assigned to each part of the test and noted on the page. Teachers should help students prioritize their time in testing situations.

- Communication Mode: Students should be allowed to take a test orally if needed, or the exam should be structured to minimize writing (for example, they could mark an "x" beside the correct response rather than writing in the entire word). Teachers should give instructions both orally and in writing as needed, assign another student to write down responses, tape record the test, or have the student indicate correct answers by pointing to them, as needed.
- Clarity: Teachers should give simple, clear instructions and questions and avoid asking questions with many parts to the answer. They should walk around the room during the tests, checking the students' work to be sure they all are following the directions accurately.
- Format: Teachers who discern that a student responds much better to one type of test (e.g., multiple choice) than another should consider preparing tests for that student in the format that assures the best performance. Tests can be offered with a balanced selection of formats and point values (e.g., 25 percent essay, 25 percent true/false, 25 percent matching, and so on). Students may also be allowed to demonstrate knowledge or ability using evaluation techniques other than tests.

Modifications in Grading and Recording of Grades

ADJUSTMENTS FOR HANDWRITING, TIMING, GRAMMAR

In grading tests and other class activities, the key issues are fairness and a firm grip on what is being evaluated and what is not. It would be important, for example, that teachers not downgrade students because of poor handwriting or poor grammar if the test really is designed to assess their knowledge of social studies concepts, especially if writing is a skill directly affected by the handicap.

The same may be true of timed tests. Several handicapping conditions may have an adverse affect on students' ability to demonstrate abilities accurately under time pressure, including physiological impairments that make writing slower and emotional problems that exaggerate stress. If time is not a critical part of the behavior being measured, it would be inappropriate to penalize such students' scores because of it. The goal, after all, is to measure students' strengths and achievements, not their weaknesses.

An obvious solution to many of these problems is to assign multiple grades for each task or subject. For example, principals could assure that teachers grade work separately on content and form, effort, and/or amount of time spent; students might receive one grade for individual achievement or improvement and another on their relation to the achievement level of peers. Another possibility is to give a grade that reflects fulfillment of the central intent of the lesson, regardless of specific issues or quality.

EVALUATIONS OF STUDENT PERFORMANCE

Ideally, the concept of multiple grades should be extended to report cards as well, although many computerized systems unfortunately do not offer that potential. The following are alternative means of arriving at reasonable evaluations of student performance.

Contracts: The teacher and student may sit down together and negotiate a specific grade for a specific amount of work at an agreed-upon level of functioning. (For example, the agreement might be that the student will earn a B for completing two spelling lists a week at 90 percent accuracy, on the average, over the course of the grading period, and so on.) The contracted educational goals must be positive (what the student will do, not won't do), measurable, clearly stated, honest, and reasonable, given the student's current ability levels. Student and teacher must understand and agree on each part of the contract, then each must sign it. Progress toward stated goals should be evaluated periodically.

Differing Requirements: The teacher can allow the student to respond in a different communication mode, require different amounts or kinds of work, or allow a longer period of time for completion of an assignment. For example, a one-page rather than a two-page essay can be required, or one chemical experiment rather than two, and so forth. Care must be exercised in using this option for a variety of reasons. Sometimes the handicapped students need more practice, rather than less, to master a skill. Social factors are important considerations, especially for adolescents who do not want to be perceived as different from their peers. Inappropriately low expectations may hinder chances of reaching true potential.

Small Group Assignments: The teacher can divide the class into small, heterogeneous groups and assign a task to the whole group. Handicapped students can be assigned specific, appropriate roles in a cooperative structure. All group members receive the same grade for work completed, or one group grade and one for individual effort. This structure can generate extra benefits in terms of understanding and acceptance of the handicapped classmate and sharing of skills.

NEW CHALLENGES

Past abuses in the education of the handicapped might be summarized with the phrase "failure to individualize." Despite all the legal progress, today's schools are not immune from the impulse to act on prejudice or stereotype rather than to provide supportive understanding of individual students' strengths and needs.

To help combat that impulse, educators (principals and teachers alike) should remember that students' performance problems can be the result of many interacting factors, including inappropriate treatment by the schools. A helpful key to keep in mind when analyzing such problems is the SUM formula (Weisenstein, 1980), where

- "S" indicates skill deficits: necessary prerequisite skills not yet attained that prevent students from completing a given task.
- "U" stands for unrealistic expectations: students' placement in programs where course requirements clearly are beyond their abilities.
- "M" signifies motivational deficits: exceptional learners often require additional motivation to complete a task; the use of appropriate reinforcers may close the performance gap.

Effective implementation of the special education process, as outlined in P.L. 94-142, may require new understanding and awareness, new roles, new flexibility. Meeting these challenges requires information, cooperation, and commitment. But it is worth it. The experience in thousands of classrooms across the country has shown that the process can be successful and productive, not only for the handicapped students but for all those involved.

REFERENCES

Federal Register, 42 (163), Part II, p. 42479, August 23, 1977.

Fry, E. (1977). Fry's readability graph: Clarification, validity, and extension to level 17. *Journal of Reading, 21,* 242–253.

Gunning, R. (1952). *The technique of clear writing.* New York: McGraw-Hill.

Reynolds, M.C., & Birch, J.N. (1977). *Teaching exceptional children in all America's schools.* Reston, VA: Council for Exceptional Children.

Shrybman, J.D. (1982). *Due process in special education.* Rockville, MD: Aspen Publishers, Inc.

Turnbull, H.R., & Turnbull, A. (1982). *Free appropriate education: Law and implementation.* Denver: Love Publishing Co.

Weisenstein, G.R. (1980, August). *Motivating handicapped and disadvantaged students in vocational education classrooms.* Presentation to the National Conference of Cooperative Occupational Education, Phoenix, AZ.

Chapter 2

Discipline

SUMMARY

Statement of the Problem

Schools are prohibited by law, in some cases, from applying to special education students the same disciplinary procedures used with regular students. This problem is compounded by the fact that a small percentage of special education students exhibit unusually difficult and disruptive behavior problems.

Legal Issues

The law on disciplining handicapped students may vary from state to state. Moreover, the relevant state and federal laws are complex and continually reinterpreted, so specific problems should be checked with school legal staff. These are the current trends as of the mid 1980s:

The courts have ruled that a student may not be expelled for behavior directly related to an identified handicapping condition. However:

- Short-term suspensions apparently are legal as a disciplinary technique.
- A pupil who has not been formally assessed as handicapped or identified as a focus of concern probably may be disciplined as a regular student.
- A student may be expelled if the behavior problem concerned is not related to the handicap. (This may require a full hearing to determine.)
- The student may be placed in a more restrictive environment, provided all the due process protections of the law have been followed.

In general, expulsion of a handicapped student—or suspension for more than a very brief period—must be viewed as a change of placement and must be preceded by the standard procedures required for such a change. The burden of proof or justification for the change is on the school district. The courts seem to be taking the direction that schools can apply the same disciplinary standards and procedures to all students, except where that procedure would otherwise require a hearing for a handicapped pupil.

Rationale

Handicapped children are more like nonhandicapped children than they are different. All children need to receive approval and to experience success and self-worth, and all can grow in their mastery of appropriate behavior. Effective disciplinary systems for handicapped children are based on techniques that benefit all students.

Denial of an education to students because of their handicap-related behavior violates four aspects of P.L. 94-142 and the principles behind it: (1) the right to an appropriate public education, (2) the right to remain in the present placement until resolution of the special education complaint, (3) the right to an education in the least restrictive environment, and (4) the right to prescribed procedures for changes in placement.

Approaches

To minimize behavior problems and to avoid unnecessary hearings and unfavorable court decisions, the school system must have the following: (1) a clearly stated and consistently followed disciplinary system for all students; (2) opportunities for all students to achieve a sense of success and belonging in the school; (3) a flexible, cooperative; problem-solving approach involving parents and regular and special education staff members; (4) established disciplinary alternatives short of suspension, such as detention or timeout rooms; (5) commitment to the philosophy that every student deserves and can benefit from an education.

PROBLEMS FOR ADMINISTRATORS

"I was unprepared. It was a real shock." said one assistant principal of his experiences with a behavioral disability (BD) program that was moved into his high school in 1983. "Nobody let me know what kind of problems I was going to have to deal with."

In this case, the high school was a relatively tranquil one in an affluent suburb; the BD program—still separate from other classes—had just been placed in a regular school setting for the first time and the "shocking" problems included several seizures of deadly weapons. A number of factors—the type of students, the isolation of the program, the lack of preparation for both students and staff—helped make this situation extreme. But the fact remains that new responsibilities for educating and disciplining handicapped students often make unfamiliar and stressful demands on school administrators.

NEW AND STRESSFUL DEMANDS

The stresses have two sources: (1) uncertainty about (and in many cases resentment of) the demands of the law; (2) unfamiliarity with the students themselves, with the nature and needs of different handicapping conditions, and with proved methods for solving or preventing their sometimes unique disciplinary problems. At the same time, it is important to emphasize that: (1) the majority of handicapped students do not present discipline problems of a nature different from regular student populations, and (2) disciplining of handicapped youngsters may involve some new knowledge, procedures, and philosophy, but in the end the process is based on the same principles that apply to other students.

SIMILARITIES TO REGULAR STUDENTS

The various handicapping conditions are covered more fully in Part II. This section concentrates on general issues and approaches that apply to all special education students.

LEGAL HISTORY UNDER THE ACT

With discipline, as with other aspects of mainstreaming, the most fruitful approach for administrators generally is an assertive one: they must understand the legal and educational realities involved and plan ahead to minimize problems. The legal realities of disciplining mainstreamed students include the issues discussed below.

The courts can, in some cases, require the school to discipline handicapped and nonhandicapped students differently. They can prevent the school from expelling a handicapped student, no matter how serious the behavioral infraction. They can force readmission of a student to the previous educational placement. Moreover, the decisions may be based more on what seem to be technical or procedural issues than on substantive ones.

WHAT THE COURTS CAN DO

Experience has shown that it pays to develop clear and consistent policies based on the requirements of the law. But that is not always as straightforward as it sounds. The law is not fixed; it is continually being modified by new court decisions, administrative policies, and even new legislation. The information given here, because it has been simplified, is a useful guideline to most situations but cannot be guaranteed

COMPLEX AND CHANGING MEANING OF THE LAW

to predict the legal outcome of every case. It is a good idea for principals to update themselves periodically, either through professional publications or by asking opinions from the school district's legal staff.

In the meantime, here are summaries of some of the more recent and significant cases in this area. None of them can be taken as the final word on the subject; most involve subtle legal issues that may be contradicted in future cases. But together they may help point the way to future trends. The case summaries are adapted from the University of Washington publication, *Focus: A Review of the Law and Special Education*, July 1981 and May 1983, and from a memo from the Washington State Attorney General's Office, September 15, 1982.

Goss v. Lopez

THE CASE THAT SET THE STANDARD

The well-known case *Goss v. Lopez* 419 U.S. 565 (1975) set the standard for due process in student suspensions from school. The Supreme Court ruled that the degree of due process afforded to students in the event of a suspension of 10 days or less need not be as extensive as the degree required if the suspension were to be for a longer period. In the case of a suspension of less than 10 days, the minimum of due process was required—a statement to the student about why the pupil was being suspended and an opportunity to present the youngster's side of the matter. The right to a more formal hearing, the right to have counsel present, etc., are required only in situations where more serious loss of rights is a possible outcome (i.e., longer suspension or expulsion).

Stuart v. Nappi

SCHOOL PREVENTED FROM EXPELLING A HANDICAPPED STUDENT

One of the first judicial decisions concerned with suspension and expulsion of handicapped pupils, *Stuart v. Nappi*, 443 F. Supp. 1235, (D. Conn., 1978), enjoined a Connecticut school district from expelling a handicapped student. Kathy Stuart, a pupil with a history of learning disabilities and emotional disturbance, had been involved with other students in schoolwide disturbances. The school district suspended her for 10 days and had scheduled a disciplinary hearing to expel her. Before the expulsion hearing, her mother requested a hearing and review of her daughter's special education program.

The U.S. District Court judge found that the defendant school district had failed to provide Kathy Stuart with the educational program recommended by its own Placement and Planning Team. Further, the school did not respond adequately to Kathy's failure to participate in the special education program that it had provided. The judge, in granting the preliminary injunction, suggested that the school's handling of the pupil's educational program may have contributed to her problems and ordered that it conduct an immediate review of her special education program. The Court also ruled that expulsion prior to the resolution of the plaintiff's special education complaint would violate the Education for All Handicapped Children Act (EHA), which requires that a pupil remain in the current placement until resolution of a special education complaint.

Blue v. Board of Education

In a similar case, *Blue v. Board of Education*, No. 81-41, (D. Conn., March 23, 1981), a U.S. District Court in Connecticut enjoined a local board of education from expelling a 16-year-old classified as emotionally disturbed. The youth had been suspended because of an altercation involving one of his teachers. After suspending the pupil, the principal recommended to the board of education that the youth be expelled. Before the expulsion hearing, the school's Planning and Placement Team met and recommended that the student receive homebound instruction until the hearing, with continuation of homebound instruction or placement at a special school afterward.

PLACEMENT CAN'T CHANGE WHILE COMPLAINT IS PENDING

The Court ruled that expulsion or change in educational placement while a special education complaint was pending was in violation of EHA. It also held that the pupil's placement should be changed only by the Planning and Placement Team, not through the school district's disciplinary procedures. Finally, the Court stated that homebound instruction or placement at the special school interfered with the pupil's right to an education in the least restrictive environment.

Stanley v. School Administrative District No. 40

In *Stanley v. School Administrative District No. 40*, No. 80-9 D, (D.N.H., Jan. 15, 1980), a U.S. District Court judge in New Hampshire refused to grant a preliminary injunction to prevent the suspension of a learning disabled pupil for disruptive behavior. The pupil involved had used profanity and had failed to report to detention on a number of occasions. The Court found no relationship between the pupil's handicapping condition and the school's handling of the condition and the misbehavior. In this case, the school had followed its regular disciplinary procedures, which included due process safeguards, in suspending the pupil.

STUDENT SUSPENSION UPHELD

Doe v. Koger

Another case dealing with the applicability of normal disciplinary procedures for handicapped pupils, *Doe v. Koger*, 3 EHLR 552:267, (1979), involved a mildly mentally handicapped student who had been suspended and then expelled for disciplinary reasons. After the expulsion, an attorney for the handicapped student requested a special education placement hearing. A U.S. District Court judge in Northern Indiana ruled that (1) using placement procedures required by the EHA, schools must determine whether a child's disruptive behavior is related to the handicap; (2) schools that accept monies under the provisions of the EHA are prohibited from expelling students whose disruptive behavior is related to their handicapping condition; (3) disruptive students cannot be suspended indefinitely, but only until a more appropriate and (possibly) restrictive placement is found; and (4) appropriately placed handicapped pupils can be expelled in the same manner as other children.

RELATION OF BEHAVIOR TO HANDICAP IS KEY

S-1 v. Turlington

APPEALS DECISION AFFIRMS RELATION OF EXPULSION TO EHA

The U.S. Court of Appeals Fifth Circuit affirmed a U.S. District Court decision in Southern Florida granting an injunction to handicapped students who had been expelled from school. The injunction also required the defendant school district to provide the students with procedural safeguards and educational services. The case, *S-1 v. Turlington,* 635 F. 2d 342, (5th Cir., 1981), involved the expulsion of seven mentally retarded pupils for misbehavior and the denial of due process hearings to review the IEPs of two other mentally retarded pupils. The trial court found that the seven expelled pupils had been given procedural safeguards required by the *Goss v. Lopez* decision. However, it also ruled that the expelled students had been denied a free appropriate public education in violation of the EHA. Only one of the seven students had requested a hearing before his expulsion. The superintendent decided that because this student was not classified as seriously emotionally disturbed, his behavior could not be related to his handicapping condition.

In affirming the lower court decision, the three-judge panel in *S-1 v. Turlington* held: (1) a "trained and knowledgeable group" must decide whether a relationship exists between a child's handicapping condition and misbehavior before that pupil can be expelled; (2) expulsion is a change in educational placement and therefore should involve procedural protection required by EHA and Section 504; and (3) expulsion is an appropriate form of discipline in some cases, but complete withdrawal of educational services is not. The Appeals Court also ruled that two of the plaintiffs who had not been expelled but were not attending school were entitled to due process hearings (Leone, 1981, pp. 2-3).

Peoria v. Illinois

FIVE-DAY SUSPENSION RULED LEGAL

Board of Education of Peoria School District v. Illinois State Board of Education, 531 F. Supp. 184 (C.D. Ill., 1982). In this case, a 17-year-old learning disabled student was suspended for five days for verbally abusing a teacher in a mainstream class. The parents claimed that the school district had violated federal law in attempting to terminate educational services without regard to his handicapped status.

The Court distinguished earlier cases as all involving disciplinary expulsion, rather than short-term suspension. The Court held that a short-term suspension was not a change in educational placement or termination of educational services. Procedural protections of the EHA consequently need not be involved. The Court analogized this brief period of enforced absence to that often caused by a common cold.

The state superintendent had thrown out the suspension, holding that there is an assumption that the handicapping condition in some way affected the child's behavior that precipitated the discipline, and as such an exceptional student could not be excluded from special education as a result of that conduct. The court sharply criticized this decision at 531 F. Supp. 150:

> This sophistry in relation to a 17-year-old "exceptional child" with "learning disabilities," who has made it at that age, with school help, through ten previous grades to a mainstream class in the 11th grade, when composed in

> the process of seeking to prohibit a five-day suspension of that student for very shameful verbal abuse to a teacher, rests not on "the courts" but solely on the State Superintendent's own fallacious equating of a brief, temporary suspension, with *expulsion* or *termination of special education.*
>
> It is vividly apparent that there was no expulsion from, or termination of, special education here, but rather a five-day disciplinary interruption for a flagrant offense, which was reasonably calculated to teach the "child," who obviously knew better, in an effort to avoid repetition and a consequent necessity for more drastic penalties.
>
> There is absolutely no social or other value in assuming that the "child's" outburst in these circumstances was due to inadequate placement, i.e., the fault of someone other than the offending student. . . .

LEGITIMATE DISCIPLINARY MEASURE

This case helps to clarify a previously gray area of existing law by indicating that short term nonemergency suspensions may take place without resort to the procedural complexities of the EHA (Moore, 1982, pp. 2-3).

A number of common issues emerge from these cases. Courts have found suspension of handicapped pupils for ten days or less an appropriate disciplinary tool in some instances. Indefinite suspensions and expulsions have been considered changes in educational placement for handicapped pupils. These cases suggest that school districts need to address two questions if they are planning to suspend or expel handicapped pupils or pupils suspected of being handicapped: (1) Is the disruptive child handicapped? and (2) Is there a relationship between the pupil's handicapping condition and misbehavior?

KEY POINTS OF RECENT RULINGS

These seem fairly straightforward. Further examination of each question, however, raises additional concerns. In regard to whether or not a particular child is handicapped, a review of a student's records may indicate that the pupil is eligible for services but has not been placed in a special program. As to whether a relationship exists between a youngster's misbehavior and handicapping condition, courts have ruled that children other than those labeled seriously emotionally disturbed may exhibit disruptive behavior related to their handicapping condition. Finally, it appears that suspension of handicapped pupils whose behavior presents immediate danger to themselves or others is an appropriate response by the schools (Leone, 1981, p. 4).

DECIDING IF THE BEHAVIOR IS RELATED TO THE HANDICAP

APPROACHES TO RESOLVING PROBLEMS

IMPORTANCE OF THE SCHOOL ENVIRONMENT

Behavioral problems, from the most routine to the most extreme, have causes. Many of these causes—family problems, physiological, social, and economic factors—are frustratingly outside the administrator's control. But there are causes that schools can address and preventive measures that administrators can initiate.

The first place to look is the school itself. For handicapped children, especially, the school experience is likely to be one of frustration and can lead to classroom failure.

Resulting feelings of worthlessness, anger, and frustration may be acted out through inappropriate behavior. Students who do not find success and recognition in regular school activities may seek out negative forms of attention through inappropriate behavior. (Even negative attention, such as scolding, may be reinforcing to the student who has little opportunity for positive recognition at home or in school.) The challenge for educators is to create an educational environment that provides all students with feelings of success and self-worth.

IS THE PLACEMENT APPROPRIATE?

With handicapped students, the IEP should be developed and placement decisions made with this in mind. An "appropriate" placement should be one in which the child can develop positive relationships with the school, with peers, and with self. If this is not happening, if the youngster's academic record and behavior point to a lack of success in the program, the law places the burden of responsibility for change (improvement) on the school.

A SUCCESS STORY

Frequently changes in the school environment can have a positive effect on student behavior. The BD program mentioned earlier is a good example. After the initial difficulties, the school made several changes that helped alleviate behavior problems. The program was moved from its first location in an isolated, unattractive wing of the school to a pleasant, wood-paneled classroom. The students have been mainstreamed; they now are enrolled as regular members of the high school population, and they spend part of their day in regular classes. Getting to know each other in class has helped reduce hostility between groups and has provided positive behavior models among the students' peers. Finally, staff members have set high expectations of the students and have stuck with them.

Some Preventive Measures

As this example suggests, preventing discipline problems begins with creating positive, receptive attitudes and relationships among special and regular students and staff. It begins also with the expectation that handicapped students can succeed, with the understanding that appropriate behavior is, and can be, learned. There are proved techniques, adaptable for classroom use, for improving handicapped children's behaviors. In addition, the handicapped benefit from sound classroom management and discipline systems that are appropriate for all students.

Educational Change Associates (1981) suggested that such a system must:

ELEMENTS OF SUCCESSFUL DISCIPLINE SYSTEMS

- pinpoint specific problem areas and keep data on their occurrence
- involve parents, students, school board members, and others in the development of discipline policies
- make just a few clear and simple rules
- make everyone—parents, students, and staff—aware of what the rules are
- apply consequences consistently
- try to understand and treat students' problems, not just their symptoms
- maintain a positive approach.

Stating that "The principal plays a key role in establishing the learning environment; the goal should be to reduce that portion of student disturbance *caused* by a negative school environment" (p. 8), this report suggests that principals can help create a positive learning environment by:

KEY ROLES FOR PRINCIPALS

- being accessible and visible, visiting classrooms and the playground and attending assemblies
- displaying a genuine interest in the students, visiting with them and calling them by name
- fostering respect, not fear, and respecting the students as unique individuals
- establishing a climate of trust by dealing with students and staff in an honest, straightforward manner
- providing appropriate support to teachers; if problems arise, they should be dealt with in private, not in front of parents or co-workers
- encouraging parental visits to the school for nondisciplinary reasons
- encouraging frequent communication with parents; parents should feel free to schedule conferences before serious difficulties arise (p. 6).

The same publication offers a number of suggestions to lessen the chance of discipline problems. Principals and teachers both need to:

TIPS FOR MINIMIZING DISCIPLINE PROBLEMS WITH SPECIAL STUDENTS

- Remember that they are children, with the same needs as other students.
- Learn about handicapping conditions; it will assist teachers in understanding and working with such children.
- Seek information from the parents of the handicapped student; often negative situations can be avoided by prior knowledge.
- Provide an opportunity for the handicapped student and the parents to visit with the teacher in the classroom or school, if possible, prior to attending class on a regular basis.
- Be familiar with the range of normal behavior problems in the other children so that this behavior can be distinguished from behavior associated with the pupil's handicap.
- Be aware of the handicapped student's strengths; keep expectations positive but realistic.
- Don't hesitate to ask for assistance; parents or aides may be a source of help if severely handicapped students require a great deal of the teacher's time.
- Respond honestly to questions other students ask about the handicapped student.
- Be alert for students in the classroom who seem to be cruel or overprotective toward the handicapped student and attempt to discover the source of this behavior.

- Help the handicapped child learn to follow the rules. Adjustment to the group may take time, but the teacher can express confidence to the class and the parents that the pupil will adjust.
- Review the classroom, school, and/or district policies and procedures on discipline; it may be advisable to instigate changes.
- Recognize their own limitations when dealing with handicapped students; don't hesitate to ask for help (pp. 7-8).

Disciplinary Alternatives

CHANGE OF PLACEMENT

There are effective disciplinary alternatives for handicapped students. Where conventional procedures are not successful or are legally barred, a number of possibilities exist. Short-term suspensions generally are legal, for example, although emphasis needs to be placed on disciplinary alternatives that allow the student to remain in school. If relevant legal procedures are followed, the student can be transferred to a different educational program. (See Chapter 6 on Placement.) Other common approaches are described next.

OPERANT CONDITIONING APPROACH

Behavior Modification Techniques: Many educators—among them Affleck, Lowenbraun, and Archer (1980), and Turnbull and Schultz (1979)—point to past successes and the great potential of behavior modification techniques as a means of improving student behavior, especially at the elementary level. Those educators offer guidelines such as the following for the use of behavioral methods in mainstreamed and special education classes.

A behavior modification program for an individual student begins with specific description, careful observation, and recording of the behavior to be addressed. The second step is the selection of reasonable, measurable goals. Next, an appropriate reinforcer and reinforcement schedule must be chosen, and contingencies planned for. While the program is being implemented, it is important to continue to observe the behavior and note how often it occurs (collect data) and also to be sure that other staff members involved with this student are using the same techniques. A program should be maintained for at least five days before considering any alterations.

CHOOSING REINFORCERS

The reinforcer must be something the student actually wants. For example, verbal praise may not be an effective reinforcer for a child who is shy and easily embarrassed. In fact, it may be viewed as a punishment and tend to reduce the behavior. Negative behavior also can be reinforced by teacher attention, peer response, etc. This should be carefully avoided.

The most desirable reinforcers are natural or social ones, such as satisfaction, praise (if appropriate), approval, teacher time and attention, etc. These may not be effective with all children, however. When necessary, other types of reinforcement may be paired with social means and then gradually faded out. The main types are:

- tangible reinforcers: candy, toys, etc.
- tokens: points, checks, or other symbols that can be accumulated and cashed in later for one of the above
- the opportunity to do something the student really likes to do

Reinforcers should be changed if they cease to produce results, and if a certain action is promised as the consequence of negative behavior or positive behavior, the teacher must follow through.

REINFORCERS TO AFFECT POSITIVE AND NEGATIVE BEHAVIOR

Punishment should never be the only means used to control behavior. It is important to work to increase appropriate behavior even while maintaining a program to reduce problem behavior.

Other Disciplinary Measures

In addition to the continuing use of behavior modification techniques and sound schoolwide disciplinary policies, a number of legal measures have been used by schools to deal with disciplinary emergencies.

TIMEOUT

Most schools already use some form of "timeout" to remove a disruptive student from stimuli that may be reinforcing to inappropriate behavior. Some have carried this further by instituting a timeout room staffed by personnel from the guidance program. This room functions both as a means of defusing immediate problems and as a preventive measure: students can go there to talk out problems before they escalate into disciplinary crises. (A related program, staffed by volunteers, is covered in Chapter 18, Community Relations.) Behaviorists caution, however, that timeout should be used as a means of removing students from positive reinforcement (the attention of peers, for example). If the pupils' timeout takes them from situations they do not want to be in anyway, then what is intended as a punitive action becomes itself reinforcing. Timeout also should not be used over extended periods of time (an hour or more) as a form of punishment. This is not the intent of the timeout strategy.

As a substitute for conventional suspension, some schools have experimented with:

SUBSTITUTES FOR SUSPENSION

- In-School Suspension: Students are sent to a supervised room for tutoring and drills. This type of program also has been staffed by volunteers (and is discussed in Chapter 18).
- At-Home Suspension: Called "systematic exclusion," this requires prior agreements and commitment from parents. Students are expected to continue schoolwork at home.
- Respite: Students are sent home but not marked as absent and are given an opportunity to make up work.
- Saturday Campus: Students are required to come in for four hours of supervised labor, such as cleaning and maintenance of the school campus, on weekends. (Educational Change Associates, 1981).

REFERENCES

Affleck, J., Lowenbraun, S., & Archer, A. (1980). *Teaching the mildly handicapped in the regular classroom*. Columbus, OH: Charles E. Merrill, pp. 31–60.

Educational Change Associates. (1981). *Disciplining the handicapped student*. Olympia, WA: The Association of Washington School Principals.

Leone, P. (1981). *Focus: A review of the law and special education. 1*(2), 2–4.

Moore, S. (1982). Memorandum to handicapped education discipline file. Olympia, WA: Office of the Attorney General, September 15.

Romer, L. (1983). In brief. *Focus: A review of the law and special education. 2*(12), 3.

Turnbull, A., & Schultz, J. (1979). *Mainstreaming handicapped students: A guide for the classroom teacher*. Boston: Allyn & Bacon, pp. 311–337.

Chapter 3

Due Process Hearings

SUMMARY

Statement of the Problem

Either parents or the schools may call for an impartial hearing to resolve differences regarding the identification, evaluation, placement, or right to a free, appropriate education of a handicapped student. In practice, these due process hearings usually are: (1) called for by parents, (2) decided in favor of the schools, (3) expensive, time-consuming, and emotionally exhausting for both parties, (4) viewed as a last resort.

Legal Issues

P.L. 94-142 requires that parents receive written notice each time the school proposes or refuses to initiate an action regarding a student's identification or evaluation as handicapped or subsequent educational placement. That notice, in addition to describing and explaining the proposed action, must advise parents of their rights, including the right to call for a due process hearing. If such a hearing is called, both parents and school agency are guaranteed the right to:

- be advised and accompanied by a lawyer and/or experts if they choose
- present evidence, call witnesses, and cross-examine
- have a qualified and impartial hearing officer
- receive a decision, in writing, within 45 days after the hearing was requested (although the hearing officer may grant an extension at either party's request)
- appeal the decision if they believe this is warranted

- have the hearing at a convenient time and place
- have the child present or open the hearing to the public if they choose.

The law does not require due process hearings in any situation, nor does it explicitly define all aspects of the proceedings. There will be variations from state to state and among individual hearing officers. In general, due process hearings can be seen as somewhat like court proceedings, but much less formal. The student's placement remains the same during the due process procedure.

Rationale

The Fourteenth Amendment to the United States Constitution guarantees that no state shall "deprive any persons of life, liberty, or property without due process of law." Yet in the past, millions of handicapped children were systematically denied access to public education. Their parents could protest and negotiate but had no legal recourse if they were unhappy with the school's decisions. The due process hearing guaranteed by P.L. 94-142 provides such a recourse and thus is a key guarantee that the intent of the law will be carried out.

Approaches

Most disagreements between parents and schools can be settled without going into due process hearings, and it is to both parties' benefit to do so. Preventive policies include: Creating a cooperative environment in the school, providing satisfying and meaningful opportunities for parents to become involved in their child's education, and providing and using other problem-solving procedures such as arbitration by a mutually agreed-upon mediator.

THE SHADOW OF DUE PROCESS HEARINGS

The possibility of due process hearings hangs over most mainstreamed school environments like a mysterious and ever-present threat. Few regular staff members know exactly what the hearings entail, but everyone knows they have a bad reputation. "What makes these hearings happen?" "What goes on in them, anyway?" and especially, "How can I avoid them?" are haunting questions in the back of many an educator's mind.

Where has the overwhelmingly negative reputation of due process hearings come from? Not from frequency of occurrence. The number of disputes between parents and schools that actually end up going to hearings is relatively small. Jacobs (1979) has estimated that only one-half of one percent of the population served is involved. In a 1980 survey (Smith, 1981), only five of the most populous states responding had held more than 200 hearings, while 13 states reported 20 or fewer. The onslaught of hearing requests that many educators feared had failed to materialize.

FEW DISPUTES END IN HEARINGS

Nor does the reputation result from schools' continued failure in hearings. Although parents initiate more than 90 percent of the hearings, they win only about a third of them (Smith, 1981). One parent advocate (Silberberg, 1979) laments that the "procedures do not give parents equality. In fact, parents continue at a disadvantage. They are facing an adversary who has time, money, resources, and determination on its side. . . . It is amazing that parents, against such odds, even bother to request due process hearings" (p. 89).

MOST CASES ARE INITIATED BY PARENTS AND WON BY SCHOOLS

The fact is, of course, that schools have "time, money, and resources" for hearings only at the expense of other educational programs. And this is where the stigma originates. Due process hearings drain time, money, and emotional energy from the system that would otherwise be directed more positively toward improving children's education. Hearings are expensive (an average state hearing costs thousands of dollars). They require substantial investments in staff time, thus aggravating resentment at the paperwork already demanded by P.L. 94-142. They are damaging to community attitudes, since the implicit content of every hearing is an accusation of wrongdoing—or, at the very least, neglect—on the part of the school. And the outcry and zealous lobbying of dissatisfied parents is rarely matched or compensated by testimony from the majority of parents who are satisfied. This tends to lower staff morale and to increase resentment of mainstreaming.

There are other, more hidden costs, generated not by due process hearings themselves but by fear of them. The avoidance of hearings too often becomes an end in itself, a goal that begins to divert time and attention away from the effort to meet students' needs. As Jacobs (1979) warns:

HIDDEN COSTS

> Constant adversarial pressure cannot help but create in some educators an attitude designed to protect the system rather than the child's best interest . . . to make them reluctant to recommend services which they will be forced to justify at some upcoming hearing. This timidity in professional decision making can . . . place self-protection ahead of concern for the best interest of their client (p. 88).

THE ADVERSARIAL RELATIONSHIP

The key word here is adversarial. A cooperative attitude toward decision making—the sense that both parents and school share the good of the child as a common goal—is difficult to maintain once legal, adversarial procedures have been interjected between the bargaining parties. The situation is similar to that experienced by many divorcing couples who find a relatively amicable separation transformed into a legal war over children and possessions by the lawyers they have hired. It is the unfamiliar and exhausting role of adversaries that participants in due process hearings often find most profoundly distressing. In the quasi-judicial due process setting, educators find themselves suddenly cast in the role of the villains, the accused. And parents are encouraged, by the structure and the proceedings, to view them that way. The child involved cannot help but suffer, no matter what the outcome.

CHALLENGES FOR EDUCATORS

The challenges confronting educators with regard to due process, then, are twofold. On the one hand, it is important to avoid the adversarial setting as much as possible. On the other hand, it is equally important to avoid sacrificing educational quality for institutional safety. The most productive policy is not to focus on the negative aspect (how not to get embroiled in hearings) but rather on the positive (how to create a relationship of cooperation and trust with parents and staff).

LEGAL HISTORY UNDER THE ACT

Many disputes can be resolved before reaching the point of a due process hearing (this is, of course, desirable), but some will not be settled even in such a setting. If a party to the hearing is dissatisfied with the results, the case can be appealed, first to the state level and then to the courts. (The appeals process is discussed later in this chapter.)

CASES APPEALED TO THE COURTS

The following are summaries of a few significant due process hearings that were appealed to the courts. While they are not definitive guides, they do offer insights into the possible content and outcome of such hearings and the experiences that some schools have had. All case descriptions are adapted from the University of Washington publication, *Focus: A Review of Special Education and the Law.*

In re Tredyffrin-Eastown School District

The Pennsylvania state education agency (SEA) ruled that Maureen S., a 5-year-old who is profoundly retarded and suffers from a seizure disorder, can be provided with a Free Appropriate Public Education in the local school district program and does not require a residential placement for educational purposes. Her parents contended that the school district's program would be life-threatening to Maureen because of the travel time and the absence of sufficient medical support in the school. The parents also said she required after-school care such as washing and feeding.

APPROPRIATENESS OF RESIDENTIAL PLACEMENT

The state hearing officer, in agreement with the local decision, held that, where the courts have found a residential placement to be more appropriate than a day program, two conditions were present: (1) the student consistently and over several years had failed to show any progress in various day programs, and (2) the residential placement proposed for the student was a specific behavior modification program that extended into the nonschool hours and was designed to reinforce or to lay a foundation for skills to be learned during the school day. Neither of these conditions was determined to be present in Maureen's case.

Two other findings by the hearing officers are worthy of note. Since the contention that the day placement would be life-threatening to Maureen was made only on the basis of a report from a psychologist who reviewed the records—not by a physician—it was not accepted. Further, the school district would not be liable for the residential portion of the program even if it were found to be more appropriate since it was noneducational. See *In re Tredyffrin-Eastown School District,* 3 EHLR 503:245 (1982).

In re The Riverside Unified School District

The parents of a boy described as both learning disabled and emotionally disturbed refused to accept an IEP developed by the local district that was to be implemented at a private placement. The local and state hearing officers held that the IEP was designed to meet the needs of the student and could be implemented appropriately by the private placement. Since the parents continued to refuse the IEP, and since California law makes no provisions for overriding parental refusal, the hearing officer ruled that the district's only obligation to the student was to offer him placement in a regular class with his age peers. In other words, the parents had to accept the IEP in order for their child to be eligible for special education. *In re The Riverside Unified School District,* 3 EHLR 502:222 (1981).

SCHOOL OBLIGATIONS WHEN PARENTS REFUSE AN IEP

In a similar California case, the parents of a child who is hearing impaired removed him from his placement in a county day program for the deaf and hard of hearing and unilaterally placed him in a regular classroom. The parents then insisted on his continued placement in the regular class, with tutoring three days per week, private speech therapy, provision of an aide two hours per day, inservice training for the deaf for all of the student's teachers, and other services. The school district contended that the child should be returned to the county program or placed in an alternative program more suited to his needs than a regular classroom. But the district could not develop a new IEP for the student because the parents would not consent to an assessment of the child. By refusing to permit the assessment, the parents effectively were blocking the development of an IEP.

The hearing officer held that an IEP could be developed based upon other current information. The preponderance of evidence at the hearing confirmed that the appropriate placement for the student was in a special day class for the hearing impaired. This decision was based on information that the student was performing at least two, and possibly three, years below grade level in the regular class placement, was a discipline problem, and was suffering from low self-esteem. The hearing officer concluded that while California law does allow for overriding a parental decision to order an evaluation, no such override is possible in the case of a parental refusal to accept an IEP.

PARENTS AND THE IEP: IMPACT OF STATE LAW

The hearing officer ordered a new IEP to be developed for the student with placement in a deaf and hard of hearing day class. He cautioned the parents that if they refused this IEP and placement, the school district was obligated only to offer the student placement in a regular class without support services and that he would be treated as a regular student with regard to his discipline problems. *In re Palos Verdes Peninsula Unified School District,* 3 EHLR 502:246 (1981).

P.L. 94-142 regulations defer to state law on the issue of overriding parental refusal to allow evaluations or accept IEPs. Educators should consult with attorneys to determine what the law is in their state (Romer, 1982, p. 4).

In re Stoneham Public Schools

APPROPRIATENESS OF HOME PROGRAM

The parents of a 13-year-old girl who is severely retarded and has a history of susceptibility to upper respiratory infections disagreed with the school district's recommendation that the child attend an educational program in a hospital on a day student basis. They desired a homebound program because it would minimize the risk of infection caused by movement between different environments.

The child's physician testified that placement in the day program at the hospital would constitute a life-threatening situation for her. His opinion was that "no precautions could ensure (the child's) safety as adequately as maintaining her in her home placement." The state hearing officer held that the question of whether the child should be placed in a day program or a homebound program was best left to the child's physician rather than the IEP team. The hearing officer further held that the school was responsible for providing only those parts of the homebound program that were related to her educational needs, i.e., occupational, physical, and speech therapy, but not nutritional therapy or home health care because for this child they did not come within the meaning of special education or related services. See *In re Stoneham Public Schools,* 3 EHLR 503:207 (1982) (Romer, 1983, p. 2).

APPROACHES TO RESOLVING PROBLEMS

ALTERNATIVES TO DUE PROCESS HEARINGS

The law does not require that disputes between schools and the parents of handicapped children be resolved in due process hearings; it provides that format only as a legal recourse. Various less antagonistic and less expensive means of resolving conflicts have been used successfully in schools. More and more school districts are adopting less formal models of mediation as preliminary alternatives for parents—a kind of screening process to ensure that due process hearings are used only for the most difficult or most stubborn problems.

Mediation, or arbitration, should be undertaken only when direct negotiating efforts between staff members and parents (and/or their legal counsel) have failed and only if both parties express willingness to abide by the mediator's decision. The most common problem with arbitration of special education disagreements is that of finding a mediator acceptable to both parents and the schools. The qualifications for the position include knowledge of special education and relevant laws, fairness toward and lack of involvement with both parties, ability to minimize adversarial conduct, and background preparation on the specific case to be mediated. Training and experience in the role are important.

Conduct of the Hearing

If a hearing cannot be avoided, it is important to prepare well for it. Since part of that preparation must include knowing what to expect, this section begins with a description of the hearing process.

The conduct of a due process hearing is less formal than a court procedure and will vary from place to place. It is completely under the control of the hearing officer and usually proceeds through the following steps:

WHAT GOES ON IN A HEARING

1. The hearing officer makes an opening statement, including introductions; describes what due process hearings are and the conduct and procedures to be followed; reviews parent rights; and states the issue to be resolved.
2. Under the direction of the hearing officer, participants resolve any preliminary matters such as absence of a witness, objections to a piece of evidence, whether the meeting will be open or closed, and whether witnesses will be allowed to be present other than while testifying.
3. Each party (the school usually goes first) presents an opening statement.
4. The first party (again, usually the school) presents its evidence, with cross-examination by the other party permitted. (The hearing officer may determine what evidence is relevant.)
5. The other party presents its evidence in the same manner.
6. Both parties are allowed to present brief rebuttal and closing statements.
7. The hearing officer closes the hearing (and must produce written findings within the allotted time period).

Detailed explanations of hearing procedures and related topics may be found in James Shrybman's (1982) book, *Due Process in Special Education.* Other interesting and potentially important points to know include:

GROUNDS FOR A HEARING

- The hearing officer need not decide in favor of either party but may come up with a third solution.
- Grounds for a hearing may include more, but not less, than those spelled out in the law and may not interfere with other legally guaranteed parent/student rights. Parents must be notified of their right to call for a hearing, and may do so at any time, regardless of previous consent.

INVOLVING THE CHILD

- Parents may have the child attend, although Ekstrand (1979) asserts that this generally is not advisable. The child may be called as a witness or may meet with the hearing officer before the session.
- Either party may petition the hearing officer for a delay, with reasonable cause.

BURDEN OF PROOF

- Federal rules do not state whether either party in the hearing has the burden of proof; hearing officers often simply weigh the evidence of both and decide in favor of the stronger or more convincing argument. One exception is least restrictive environment; transfer to a more restrictive program must be strictly justified, and the burden of proof lies with the party proposing greater restriction.

CHOOSE ATTORNEY WITH CAUTION

- Though the parties in due process hearings are quite often aided by lawyers, one must be cautious in making this choice. Few attorneys—not even all school district attorneys—are adequately and currently prepared on the complexities of special education law.

Appeals

APPEALS

Decisions may be appealed to a state hearing officer for review. In most cases, this involves only a review of the records of the original hearing; however, in some cases, it may include the opportunity to present further oral or written argument and additional evidence. (For this reason, it is important that the original hearing be recorded. If a simple tape recording system is used, the hearing officer must make sure that the equipment is functioning properly, that the voices are clearly audible, that adequate blank tapes are available, and that speakers verbally identify themselves before speaking.)

Decisions at the state level may be appealed further through civil suits in the appropriate state or federal courts. This is the source of the court cases summarized earlier in this chapter.

Results

A survey of due process hearings over a 27-month period in Illinois (Kammerlohr, Henderson, & Rock, 1983) showed that:

STATISTICS FROM ONE STATE

- Hearings were held in 314 cases.
- Of these, 159 were decided in favor of schools and 71 in favor of parents.
- In 60 cases, the hearing officer recommended further development of the child's IEP.
- In 95 cases, the decisions were appealed.
- The average time lag between the hearing and delivery of the decision was only 10.5 days but the appeals process averaged four months.
- Preparation by schools for a "typical" hearing required 73 hours of staff time (including both clerical and professional staff).
- The vast majority of hearings involved disputes over placement brought by parents. In many cases, these were based on misunderstanding or misinformation on the parents' part.

Preparation for the Hearing

An excellent summary by Ekstrand (1979) of how to prepare for a due process hearing is reprinted next.

> There are two parties to the local level due process hearing: the local school system and the parents. There is no question that preparation by both parties

is the most important part of the hearing process. If the local school system and the parents are fully prepared, the hearing will flow smoothly and all necessary information will be presented in an orderly fashion, allowing the hearing officer to make a well-informed decision in the best interest of the child.

PREPARATION IS CRITICAL

The federal rules provide that either party has the right to be represented by counsel. While legal representation is not necessary, the parties can often be greatly assisted in the preparation and conduct of a hearing by an attorney who is familiar with special education due process procedures. Although the hearing is much less formal than court and judicial procedures, many legal rights are involved. As a result, both parties often are represented by counsel. The local school system is required to inform parents of any available free and low-cost legal and other relevant services when a hearing is initiated or when the parents request this information.

ATTORNEY'S SERVICES

Preparation for the hearing involves gathering and organizing the relevant information so that it can be presented clearly, completely, and concisely. . . . The evidence presented in such a case will usually be in two forms: documents (such as student progress reports) and testimony (statements made by witnesses).

Preparation should start with a review of the child's entire school file. Those records that appear most informative should be selected as evidence to be submitted at the hearing. So that the hearing officer may easily refer to the documents, it is advantageous to put them in chronological order, with a cover summary sheet identifying each one. And if the records are organized properly, a simple reading of them will give the hearing officer a fairly comprehensive chronological history of the child. Further, each document should be marked as an exhibit. For instance, School Exhibit 1, etc., or Parent Exhibit A, etc., for easy identification during the hearing. . . . The documents [should] provide the hearing officer with an understanding of the background of the child, the handicapping conditions and educational needs, and finally, a description of the program and services which the party believes will appropriately meet the needs of the child.

NECESSARY DOCUMENTS

Once the documentation is properly organized, it is necessary to determine what witnesses will testify at the hearing. The federal rules state that any party to a hearing has the right to be accompanied and advised by individuals with special knowledge or training with respect to the problems of handicapped children. Witnesses are not required but are generally necessary to a sufficiently complete presentation of the position of either party. In

WITNESSES

Source: From "Preparing for the Due Process Hearing: What To Expect and What To Do" by R. Ekstrand, 1979, *Amicus, 4,* pp. 93–96. Copyright 1979 by National Center for Law and the Handicapped, Inc. Reprinted by permission of author.

determining what witnesses will testify, it is recommended, although not necessary and often not possible, that the witness have first-hand knowledge of the child.

The child's school history can be described by any appropriate school representative and by the parent. A specialist . . . can then discuss the handicapping conditions and educational needs of the child. Finally, a representative from the proposed school . . . can describe the programs and services available at that school and explain why those met the child's educational needs. During their testimony, these witnesses should identify any documents or reports substantiating particular aspects of their testimony. . . .

PREPARATION DEADLINE

The preparation for the hearing should be completed at least ten days before the hearing date because the federal rules provide that any party to the hearing may prohibit the introduction of any evidence that has not been disclosed to that party at least five days before the hearing. The meaning of the word "disclosed" is not clear, however. Since both school and parents have free access to the child's school file, it could be said that any document in the child's file is automatically disclosed. Yet a better approach to this issue might require parent and school to inform each other, within the time limit, of each document intended for submission at the hearing. This should be done in writing, and if the other party does not have the document, a copy should be provided. The federal rules require, moreover, that "any evidence" must be disclosed. Because testimony is evidence, a strict reading of this provision would seem to mandate the advance disclosure of any statement or testimony of a witness. Practically, this would of course be unreasonable—if not impossible. It would, however, appear that if the parties disclose the names of the witnesses who will testify at the hearing on their behalf [and the subject matter of the testimony], the intent and purpose of the provision will be met. It is clear that the purpose of this rule is to avoid a "hearing by surprise," which would be contrary to the very purpose of a full and fair impartial due process hearing.

DISCLOSING EVIDENCE

Proper preparation and disclosure of evidence before the hearing will greatly simplify the conduct of the hearing and will provide the complete information necessary for the hearing officer to make a proper decision.

REFERENCES

Ekstrand, R. (1979). Preparing for the due process hearing: What to expect and what to do. *Amicus, 4*(2), 91–96.

Jacobs, L. (1979). Hidden dangers, hidden costs. *Amicus, 4*(2), 86–88.

Kammerlohr, B., Henderson, R., and Rock, S. (1983). Special education due process hearings in Illinois. *Exceptional Children, 49*(5), 417–422.

Romer, L. (1982). In brief. *Focus: A review of special education and the law.* 2(2), 1–2.

Romer, L. (1983). In review. *Focus: A review of special education and the law.* 2(12), 4.

Shrybman, J.A. (1982). *Due process in special education.* Rockville, MD: Aspen Publishers, Inc.

Silberberg, N.G. (1979). Schools have home court advantage. *Amicus, 4*(2), 89–90.

Smith, T.E.C. (1981). Status of due process hearings. *Exceptional Children, 48*(3), 232–236.

Chapter 4

Identification and Evaluation of Students

SUMMARY

Statement of the Problem

School districts must design and maintain systems for identifying all handicapped children within their jurisdiction. These systems must be both effective at finding all those who need special education and at producing evaluations upon which rational educational programs can be based and efficient in terms of the district's financial and personnel resources.

Legal Issues

The law spells out several protections regarding the evaluation of handicapped students, including:

- Materials and procedures used may not be racially or culturally discriminating.
- Evaluation must be administered in the child's native language by trained personnel according to instructions.
- These evaluations must be validated for the specific purpose for which they are being used.
- They must take into account any sensory, physical, or speech impairments and still provide an accurate picture of the child's abilities.

Several provisions are aimed at guaranteeing that the evaluation is based on multiple, rather than single, sources: The evaluation must be made by a multidisciplinary team including at least one teacher or other specialist with knowledge in the suspected disability, the child must be assessed in all areas related to that disability, tests and other materials must be designed to assess specific areas of educational need, and more than one source must be used.

Parents must receive prior notice of the types of identification and evaluation activities proposed and of their rights in the process; they also must give written consent before the initial evaluation can take place. (Should they refuse, the school may call for a hearing unless other state regulations apply.) If dissatisfied with the evaluation results, parents may request an independent evaluation at public expense, unless an impartial hearing officer rules the initial evaluation appropriate. If parents obtain an evaluation at their own expense, it must be considered in decisions regarding the child's educational program.

Rationale

A child's educational program is most appropriate and productive when based on an accurate picture of that child's abilities and the extent of specific constraints on learning. The multiple, nondiscriminatory approach required by law is designed to prevent the recurrence of abuses in which large numbers of minority children, especially, were mislabeled and therefore miseducated.

Approaches

With the severely handicapped in particular, early identification may be critical to educational progress. However, several pitfalls must be avoided. The improper labeling of a child and/or inaccurate recognition of the pupil's abilities can lead to lifelong stigma and denial of opportunities to learn and grow. It is important also to avoid overidentification of handicapped children. Many school districts are working both to improve the effectiveness of their screening and referral systems and to institute prereferral interventions that can identify and resolve some learning problems without formal special education services.

IDENTIFICATION, EVALUATION, AND BIAS

Identification and evaluation are the first two steps in providing special education and related services to children who need them. In many ways, their importance and utility are self-evident: In order to deliver educational services to children, educators first must locate those who need such aid in order to design programs relevant to their individual needs and (this is the outstanding theme of P.L. 94-142) they must know what these needs are.

DANGERS OF OVER-IDENTIFYING OR UNDER-IDENTIFYING STUDENTS

The dangers involved are less obvious but still substantial. With identification, there are problems both of overidentifying (children may needlessly suffer debilitating, lifelong stigma, not to mention the possible unnecessary outlay of district resources) and of underidentifying (those who need services may not receive them).

The most controversial issue surrounding evaluations, certainly, has involved racial and cultural bias. In the 1970s, the courts responded to a rash of suits charging that culturally biased tests had led to the misclassification of large numbers of minority students. For example, judicial rulings included demands to dismantle certain programs for mentally retarded students in which cultural minority children were overrepresented and prohibitions on using IQ tests to place children in ability tracks or in classes for the mentally retarded if the tests bring about racial imbalance in those classes (Turnbull & Turnbull, 1982). P.L. 94-142 addresses the problems of cultural bias in three ways by requiring: (1) that all "testing and evaluation materials and procedures . . . must be selected and administered so as not to be racially or culturally discriminatory" (although these terms are not further defined); (2) that they be administered in the child's native language; and (3) that more than one evaluation be used.

PROBLEMS OF RACIAL AND CULTURAL BIAS

Even where nonminority children are concerned, there have been problems related to inaccurate evaluation. The requirement for multiple evaluative measures is geared toward eliminating inaccurate, incomplete, or irrelevant test results. Conclusions about a child can no longer be based on one standardized test; in fact, they should not be based on test-format evaluations alone but should include observation, diagnostic teaching, interviews, and/or other approaches. (The law requires that "no single procedure is used as the sole criterion. . . .")

LEGAL PROTECTIONS

The particular evaluations used will vary, of course, with the individual child and the preference of evaluators. They normally will include at least social/family, medical, educational, and psychological assessments. There are exceptions, certainly. For a child with a simple speech impediment, the full evaluation battery may not be necessary. The key is to assess all areas related to the disability and to determine what, if any, effects these have on educational progress.

TYPES OF TESTS REQUIRED

The law requires that each state develop a plan for locating all children in need of special education and related services and holds each local education agency responsible for those children within its jurisdiction. Also called "child find," "child search," and so on, the identification step includes public awareness programs such as media outreach, mailings to parents, and coordination with hospitals, clinics, and service agencies, as well as periodic and continuing screening and referral systems

CHILD FIND

Most schools give standardized tests to all students at certain grades; many have well-developed observation and screening procedures for preschool or kindergarten populations. Various kinds of automatic referral also fall under this heading. These include systems based on frequent and/or prolonged absences, danger of failure at midyear, or other criteria that trigger the institution's referral process.

Since all of these procedures are oriented toward general populations and not individual students, they fall under the identification rather than the evaluation sections of the law, so parental consent requirements do not apply. To quote P.L. 94-142:

EVALUATION IS INDIVIDUALIZED

> "Evaluation" means procedures used . . . to determine whether a child is handicapped and the nature and extent of the special education and related services that the child needs. The term means procedures used selectively with an individual child and does not include basic tests administered to or procedures used with all children in a school, grade, or class. Sec. 121a.500(c)

It is useful to think of evaluation as part of the law's general thrust toward individualizing handicapped education. Results of the evaluation will form the basis for development of the child's IEP and therefore ought to:

RELATION OF EVALUATION TO IEP

- be readily understood by both parents and professionals
- help pinpoint special education and related services needed
- suggest appropriate learning goals and short-term objectives
- suggest the extent to which the student can participate in regular education (see Chapter 5 on IEPs).

Since the role of school administrators in identification and evaluation is largely facilitative rather than technical, this chapter is short. It includes a discussion of some legal points that may need clarifying, then summaries of some successful approaches to streamlining student entry into legally governed special education programs.

LEGAL ISSUES

The most common disputes or problem areas related to identification and evaluation involve legal relationships between schools and parents. This section reviews the specific requirements for parental notice and consent and the legally defined means of resolving disagreements in these areas.

Prior Notice and Parental Consent

There is only one point in the identification and evaluation steps where parental consent is required. This is the initial or preplacement evaluation. (The law defines consent to mean that the parents have been fully informed in their native language,

PARENTAL CONSENT REQUIREMENTS

that they understand this explanation and agree in writing, and that they understand that their consent is voluntary and can be revoked at any time.) Reevaluation is required at least once every three years. It may happen more frequently "if conditions warrant" or if requested by the child's parent or teacher.

PARENT NOTICE REQUIREMENTS

On the other hand, prior notice to parents is required for all identification and evaluation activities, including screening and reevaluation. In addition to describing the activities to be performed and the reasons for them, this must notify parents of their rights and recourses if they object to those actions. Such notices must be written in language understandable to the general public and must be delivered to parents in their native language or other mode of communication. The schools are responsible for seeing that the notice is understood and for keeping written records of this and other contacts with parents.

When Consent Is Not Given

If parents refuse to consent to their child's preplacement evaluation, but the educators involved still feel strongly that the pupil ought to be considered for special education and related services, the following may happen:

STATE LAW AND PARENTAL CONSENT

- If the state has laws relating to parental consent (such as a requirement that the schools seek a court order, etc.) then state requirements must be followed.
- If there is no state law governing this situation, then the schools may initiate a due process hearing.
- If the impartial hearing officer agrees that the child should be evaluated, then evaluation may take place without parental consent (although parents have the right to appeal the decision).

The Right to an Independent Evaluation

If parents consent to the evaluation but are not satisfied with its results and can state specific reasons for disagreement, they have the right to obtain another, independent educational evaluation—one that is conducted by a qualified examiner who is not employed by the schools responsible for educating their child. In such cases, the schools must provide information about where an independent evaluation can be obtained and must pay its full cost or otherwise ensure that it is provided at no cost to the parents.

PARENT/SCHOOL RIGHTS AND RESPONSIBILITIES

However, if the schools feel strongly that the first evaluation was adequate and appropriate, they must contest the parents' request by calling for a due process hearing. Then, if the hearing officer decides in favor of the schools, parents themselves must pay the independent evaluation costs. (On the other hand, if a hearing officer requests an independent evaluation as part of the hearing, the schools must cover its costs.) The results of any independent evaluation—whether paid for by parents or by a public agency—must be considered in planning the child's educational program and may be offered as evidence at a hearing.

APPROACHES TO RESOLVING PROBLEMS

MINIMIZING INAPPROPRIATE REFERRALS

Once a child has been referred for a formal preplacement evaluation, a series of activities are initiated that are required by law and that generally result in substantial investments of time and resources. Realizing this, more and more districts are adopting policies and procedures that attempt to solve individual educational problems before the legal process is set in motion. These prereferral services generally entail informal interventions with students or teachers in the regular classroom.

Many schools now have some kind of prereferral team that meets regularly for a short time each week. The name of the team varies from district to district, as do its composition, specific activities, and structure. Team members often include special and regular education teachers, the school principal, counselor, and/or nurse, and possibly other specialists as well.

TEAMS HELP TEACHERS MEET STUDENT NEEDS IN REGULAR CLASS

Although, again, there are many variations, the procedure generally is this: teachers refer students directly to the team (rather than immediately identifying the student as a focus of concern and initiating the formal procedures). Team members then share information on these students gleaned from student files, interviews with the teacher, and observation of the child in the classroom. They discuss possible modifications in the curriculum, classroom environment or mode of instruction and make recommendations to the teacher. In some cases, committee members may offer direct assistance to students or classroom teachers. The goal of these teams is to help regular teachers meet the needs of as many students as possible in the regular classroom and to limit the number of inappropriate referrals for special education services.

DIAGNOSTIC/PRESCRIPTIVE TEACHER ROLE

In another approach, some schools have created a new full-time professional position with prereferral responsibilities. This position requires a teacher with special education training and expertise in diagnostic/prescriptive teaching. This staff person: (1) meets with teachers when requested to discuss individual students and offer suggestions for modifying the regular classroom to accommodate pupil needs; (2) mediates and coordinates relationships between regular and special education teachers; and (3) arranges preevaluation conferences. (A word of caution: It will be necessary to check funding requirements very carefully where staff members are not providing direct special education services.)

PREEVALUATION CONFERENCE

The preevaluation conference with parents is an important component of this particular organizational model and a useful tool in many situations. It is an opportunity for staff members and parents to share information on student performance and corrective measures being considered, in a setting somewhat less formal than that required by P.L. 94-142.

Some schools that make use of this model also use the preevaluation conference to inform parents of their rights and of the formal procedures available. At that point, parents can agree to the proposed program of informal interventions or they can request a formal evaluation and subsequent procedures. If permission for the informal program is received, then the diagnostic/prescriptive teacher can proceed to assist the classroom teacher by: providing materials; demonstrating materials and methods in class; providing direct, short-term instruction to the student in class; and/or observing student behavior in class (see Oliver, 1982, for more detailed descriptions). In each case, it is essential that all interventions be documented and recorded in student files.

PROBLEMS AND ADVANTAGES

There obviously have been difficulties in the implementation of such programs—e.g., teachers' resistance to paperwork, specialists, and changes in their classroom and methods. But in schools where the principal has taken a strong lead in encouraging and coordinating these new approaches, they have been highly successful in saving specialists' time and district resources and in raising the percentage of accuracy of referrals for formal special education.

REFERENCES

Oliver, T.E. (1982). Administrative systems for service delivery. In R.C. Talley & J. Burnette (Eds.), *Administrator's handbook on integrating America's mildly handicapped students*. Reston: VA: The Council for Exceptional Children.

Turnbull, H.R., & Turnbull, A. (1982). *Free appropriate education: Law and implementation*. Denver: Love Publishing Company.

Federal Register 42, 163, Part II, August 23, 1977.

Chapter 5

Individualized Education Programs (IEPs)

SUMMARY

Statement of the Problem

Challenges for administrators in the area of IEPs include devising efficient, appropriate implementation systems; improving communication and cooperation among the parties involved, and meeting student needs through efficient use of school resources.

Legal Issues

The law addresses two aspects: the IEP meeting and the program itself. The meeting must be:

- initiated by the public agency within 30 days after determining a child needs special education
- followed as soon as possible by implementation of the program agreed upon
- held at least annually to review and update each student's program
- attended by the parent(s) and teacher, a school district representative, the child if appropriate, and others at the discretion of parents or agency.

In addition, when a child is first identified, a member of the evaluation team or person familiar with the evaluation also must attend.

The IEP document itself must include:

- a statement of the child's present levels of educational performance
- annual goals and short-term objectives

- the specific special education and related services to be provided and the extent to which the child can participate in regular education programs (including physical education when it differs from that of regular students)
- projected dates and duration of services
- appropriate evaluation criteria and procedures.

As for accountability, the law is clear that no one may be held responsible if a student fails to meet the IEP's goals and objectives. However, the school district is legally bound to provide all services listed, and parents dissatisfied with their child's education always have the right to complain or call for a hearing.

Rationale

The requirement of an individualized educational program for each handicapped student is a response to (1) the reality that these pupils differ significantly from each other as well as from the norm, and (2) past abuses, in which handicapped students frequently suffered from inappropriate educational placements based on categorical labels alone. Furthermore, the practices of individualization, goal-oriented planning, and periodic evaluation embodied in the IEP process have proved educationally sound for all students.

Approaches

The best aid to efficient and successful IEP meetings is advance preparation and communication. While staff members should not arrive at the meeting with an IEP already prepared—real participation of parents and others is a necessary element of the program's success—they should be well prepared. They should be familiar with the student, the evaluation data, and the school system and should be ready to offer realistic proposals.

Parents should also be encouraged to prepare for and participate in the meeting. Previous communications with them can help build trust and understanding that, in turn, can make it easier for all parties to reach agreement.

Changes can and should be made in the IEP after implementation if needed, but there should be an effort to do the best possible planning the first time. Major changes (goals, placement) require another meeting; minor changes in objectives or methods do not.

THE IEP: KEY TO P.L. 94-142

KEY TO A NEW EDUCATIONAL PHILOSOPHY

The individualized education program, or IEP, is the key to the educational philosophy embodied in P.L. 94-142. Whereas in the past, educational placements (or denial of education) were based most often on generalized categorical labels such as "mentally retarded," the law now requires that each handicapped student be treated as an individual and educated according to the child's unique capabilities. In previous years, handicapped students were expected to adapt to the services available; now, schools are constrained to adapt themselves, to devise some means of providing the services that students require. The IEP represents a dramatic change in orientation from the general to the specific, from the convenience of the school district to the needs of the child.

Schools have come a long way in recent decades, from rigid homogeneity to much more flexibly arranged and fluid classrooms. The inclusion of handicapped students in that milieu can be seen as simply one step in an already established direction. Similarly, the process of writing and implementing IEPs can be seen as a training tool for educators in the continuing process of individualization of instruction for all students.

Writing an IEP for each student is time-consuming; scheduling problems may be substantial and disagreements common. However, a well-designed system can alleviate many problems, and an understanding of the educational value of the process builds tolerance. The IEP has five important purposes:

PURPOSES OF THE IEP

1. It is an extension of procedural protections guaranteed to parents and students.
2. It is a management tool to ensure provision of appropriate special education and related services.
3. It is a compliance monitoring device to determine whether a handicapped student is receiving a free appropriate public education.
4. It is a written commitment of resources.
5. It is a communication vehicle between/among all participating parties involved in the education of the handicapped student.

This chapter describes current official interpretations of legal points that may be confusing or ambiguous. It then presents a variety of information on "best practices," including sample IEP forms and systems, examples of IEP goals and objectives, suggestions for improving cooperation and communication, and other information related to the five points listed above.

LEGAL ISSUES

This section amplifies guidelines on the legal requirements for IEPs. Much of the information is taken from the Washington State government pamphlet (Division of Special Services, 1980) on individualized education programs.

When the IEP Is Required

The annual IEP meeting must be held within 30 days of determining that the student needs special education, and the IEP must be in place before the beginning of special education services. Additional meetings may be held as often as necessary.

YEARLY REVIEW REQUIRED

The statute requires that at least annually the IEP committee meet to review and to revise the student's educational program, if necessary. New annual goals must be determined, including objectives and whatever appropriate changes are necessary regarding related services or extent of participation in regular education. Thus, the implication of the law is that districts and parents, based on assessment/evaluation findings, review all of the components (service delivery and full continuum of placement options) to redetermine that both the placement and program are appropriate.

Participants in the IEP Meeting

The School District Representative

QUALIFIED SCHOOL DISTRICT PARTICIPANTS

The person who is designated in the written policy/procedure to represent the district at the IEP meeting must be "qualified to provide or supervise the provision of special education and related services" and must have the authority to commit agency resources. While this frequently is the school principal, it also may be a special education administrator or specialist and, in some cases, could be a contracted specialist, such as a speech therapist, as long as this person has been delegated authority to fill the role.

Clearly, the person acting in this capacity should have districtwide knowledge of resources and programs (e.g., transportation) in order to meet the intended role of district representative. It should be further understood that services agreed upon at the IEP meeting actually will be provided and not vetoed at a higher administrative level within the agency.

Either the agency representative or the teacher should be qualified in the area of the child's disability. The same person cannot serve as both teacher and district representative

The Teacher

Federal regulations suggest that:

WHICH TEACHER WILL ATTEND?

> In deciding which teacher will participate in meetings on a child's individualized education program, the agency may wish to consider the following possibilities:
>
> (a) For a handicapped child who is receiving special education, the "teacher" could be the child's special education teacher. If the child's handicap is a speech impairment, the "teacher" could be the speech/language pathologist.

(b) For a handicapped child who is being considered for placement in special education, the "teacher" could be the child's regular teacher, or a teacher qualified to provide education in the type of program in which the child may be placed, or both.
(c) If the child is not in school or has more than one teacher, the agency may designate which teacher will participate in the meeting (*42 Fed. Reg.* 163, Part II, p. 42490).

Attendance by too many teachers can make the meeting unwieldy. It is advisable to solicit opinions from the student's other teachers before the meeting without requiring more than one to attend. All teachers of that child should receive a copy of the IEP.

The Parent(s)

MEANINGFUL INVOLVEMENT OF PARENTS

A serious effort should be made to ensure that parents participate meaningfully. They generally should be notified of the meeting within 10 days after a decision is made that the child has a handicapping condition, thus allowing them time to prepare. The notice must inform parents of their right to bring other people to the meeting, and the agency must provide an interpreter if the parents require one.

All attempts to contact parents must be documented. If neither parent can or will attend the meeting, other methods such as individual or conference phone calls should be attempted. If they still refuse or are unable to participate, a meeting can be held without them, provided the efforts at contact have been recorded. A copy of the IEP must be made available to parents on request.

PARENT NOTICE AND CONSENT

Written parental consent is required prior to initial placement, which means before the implementation of a student's first IEP. Although not required by law, a parent's signature on the continuing IEP is generally the most efficient way to provide the required documentation of this participation. Signing the IEP does not prevent the parent, at some later date, from disagreeing with the student's program or initiating due process.

If School and Parents Disagree

The school and parents should attempt first to resolve differences through negotiation. If unable to do so, the district can provide parents with a written prior notice of the proposed action, along with a copy of parent rights. (This should be given even if there is no disagreement, as a matter of record.) At this point, the parents may initiate a due process hearing to challenge the appropriateness of proposed services. If the parents desire such a hearing, the school district must be notified in writing. If no hearing is initiated, the school district may go ahead and implement the proposed change in services.

DUE PROCESS HEARINGS

INTERIM AGREEMENTS

An interim agreement can be made and implemented while discussions continue. Otherwise, the previous program remains in effect until differences are resolved. It is also possible to implement all agreed-upon parts of the IEP while continuing to negotiate the others.

District Responsibility

An IEP must be fully completed for each student determined eligible for special education. This is true even if some parts of the IEP do not apply. (This can be indicated by writing N/A or NONE in appropriate spaces.)

If the student receives services under contract with another district or private agency, the district in which the child resides is still responsible for initiating and conducting the IEP meeting, covering costs, and seeing that the pupil's program complies with the law. (Once a child is placed in a private facility, the staff there, at the discretion of the school district, may initiate meetings to review and revise the IEP. The public agency still must ensure that one of its representatives and the child's parents attend those meetings and approve any program changes.)

PAYMENTS AND ACCOUNTABILITY

No agency, teacher, or other person can be held accountable if a student does not achieve the growth projected in the annual goals and objectives. However, this does not relieve agencies and staff from making good-faith efforts to assist the student in achieving these goals. Schools are required to provide all services listed in the IEP. Further, parents have the right to ask for IEP revisions or to invoke due process procedures if these efforts are not being made.

IEP Content

Child's Present Level of Performance

EVALUATION DATA IN THE IEP

This information should describe the effects of the child's handicap on any relevant educational area—academic, personal-social, living skills, or vocational. The statement should be accurate, in measurable terms as much as possible, and explained to all participants in language they can understand.

Statements should be based on the results of the assessment/evaluation of the student and should address all areas in which special education and related services are needed. There should be a direct, identifiable link between the present levels of educational performance and the goals and objectives and services provided.

Goals and Objectives

ANNUAL GOALS

Annual goals are written in response to the present levels of performance and are based on assessment results and parent input where it is provided. Annual goal statements should be specific and indicate (1) the direction of change (e.g., increase/decrease) and (2) desired or expected levels of change in specific skill areas. These goals should be the team's or the teacher's best estimate of what the student will be able to accomplish within one year. There generally should be one to three goals for each affected area.

THE DIFFERENCE BETWEEN GOALS AND OBJECTIVES

Short-term objectives describe the expected student behavior (what the student will do, under what conditions, with what level of accuracy, and in what time period) and are intermediate steps or benchmarks toward reaching the annual goals. These objectives should be broad enough to allow for flexibility in classroom teaching methods while also providing a means for evaluating student progress. They must be both appropriate for the student and useful to those carrying out the student's program, and they should be stated in terms of measurable behavior, making it easy to judge whether an objective has been met.

Short-term objectives should be reviewed for progress at regular intervals during the school year, most likely at the time of the regular district grading periods.

To assure individualization of objectives, an estimation of each student's progress per grading period should be considered when writing an IEP. The short-term objectives should include a description of the behavior a student is expected to demonstrate as well as the level of performance that would indicate achievement of the objective.

SAMPLE GOAL AND OBJECTIVES

Example:

Goal 1. To increase reading from the 3.5 grade level to the 4.0 grade level as measured by a standardized reading test.

Objectives:

1.1 Given a list of 10 words, the student will identify base words, suffixes, prefixes, and common endings with 90 percent accuracy by the end of the 1st grading period.

1.2 The student will correctly recognize 40 out of 50 given survival words by the end of the 2nd grading period.

1.3 The student will correctly answer comprehension questions at the end of each unit with 90 percent accuracy by the end of the grading period (Division of Special Services, 1980, pp. 26–27).

Specific Special Education and Related Services

SPECIAL SERVICES LISTED IN THE IEP

"Special education" is defined in the P.L. 94-142 as specially designed instruction to meet the unique needs of handicapped students (Sec. 4(2)(16)), and "related services" as those necessary to help the student benefit from special education (Sec. 4(2)(17)). The IEP must include all education services needed by the student, not just those readily available in the district. The document must say who will provide the services; no matter who provides them, they must be delivered at no cost to the student's family.

The extent and duration of services must also be stated, so that the resource commitment can be clear to parents and other IEP team members. Some general standard of time must be indicated that is (1) appropriate to the specific service to be provided and (2) clear to all participants.

Participation in Regular Education Programs

LEAST RESTRICTIVE ENVIRONMENT REQUIREMENTS

In line with the legal requirements that all students be educated in the "least restrictive" or most normal environment possible, the IEP must include a statement of the extent to which the student can participate in regular programs. Both academic and nonacademic activities should be included. Statements may be expressed in terms of percentages of time, particular classes, or as appropriate.

Modifications necessary in the regular program, such as special seating or equipment, should also be stated. The special services provided to the student should be indicated and accompanied by a brief justification of the placement in that setting. The related services and corresponding amount of time should be noted, as well as time in regular education and other categorical programs.

Evaluation Criteria

EVALUATION OF STUDENT PROGRESS

Such criteria might include percentage of correct responses, minimum or maximum number of behaviors in a time span, etc. They must not exceed the standards expected of regular students. Evaluation procedures might include teacher observation, frequency counts or other types of continuing data collection, graphs or charts, anecdotal records, student self-evaluation, and so on, as well as tests. The criteria need not be listed as a separate section but may be integrated into student objectives.

Format

The format and length of the IEP are not described or determined by the law. Generally, two to three pages should be sufficient. Some sample forms are included later in this chapter.

APPROACHES TO RESOLVING PROBLEMS

FUNCTIONS OF PRE-MEETING PLANNING

Good planning and clear communication are essential to the IEP development process. The law implies that staff members should not arrive at the meeting with the IEP already devised; participation of parents and others in the discussion should be genuine and meaningful. This is not to suggest that no planning or communication should take place before the meeting. On the contrary, it is advisable to solicit the opinions of any of the student's teachers not in attendance, and those of the people who might be providing special services.

The premeeting planning time offers opportunities to build relationships of trust and cooperation among the professionals involved and to develop a series of well-thought-out proposals based on the input of several individuals. It is equally important to establish communication with parents before the meeting and to encourage them to come prepared to participate. Exhibit 5–1 provides a format for documenting contact with parents.

Improving Communication

The following materials originally appeared in a publication (Shaffer, 1982) developed for the University of Washington teacher certification program.

> COMMUNICATING WITH PARENTS. A good line of communication with parents is an invaluable asset to the IEP process. By law, parents must be included in IEP meetings; by good sense, they should be.
>
> When a regular classroom teacher refers a student for assessment for possible placement into special education, parents must be contacted for

Exhibit 5–1 Sample Documentation of IEP Meeting Notification

Directions: This form is for the purpose of documenting efforts to notify parents of an IEP meeting. It is to be filled out for every IEP meeting, both initial and continuing. Such notification may include any or all of the various means of communication: telephone calls, correspondence, in person. Regardless of the mode, notification must include the purpose of the meeting, the time and location, and who will be in attendance.

Student ______________________ Birth Date ____________
School ______________________

Telephone Calls

Date *Time* *Staff member placing call*

____
____
____

Correspondence (Attach Copies)

Date *Correspondence signed by*

____
____
____

In Person

Date *Staff member meeting with parent*

____
____
____

I certify that the above is a true and correct record of the school's efforts to obtain parent participation in the specified IEP meeting.

Signature: ______________________
Position: ______________________

Source: Adapted from *Series on P.L. 94–142 and Related Washington Rules and Regulations: Individualized Education Programs*, Division of Special Services, Office of the Superintendent of Public Instruction, Olympia, Wash., 1980.

approval. Individual districts decide how and by whom this contact should be made—by telephone, letter, or by home visitation. Regardless of the method, the tone set during this initial contact can affect the parents' willingness to cooperate and participate with school personnel.

CONTACTING PARENTS

Parents must again be contacted to arrange a meeting at which the results are discussed and the IEP written, if appropriate. Communication must be especially good during the meeting itself. The following are guidelines for dealing with parents, guidelines that should facilitate the establishment of a working and trusting relationship between the home and the school.

TIPS ON PARENT COMMUNICATIONS

1. Use the names of the parents and child. Promote a personal atmosphere.
2. Do not refer to the student as a "kid;" this is too informal. Such terms as "child," "student," "pupil," indicate more professionalism.
3. Avoid terms likely to cause anxiety or misconceptions. Avoid, for example, words like dyslexia and hyperactivity.
4. Avoid jargon. Parents may feel excluded if they don't understand the language. If parents do not understand, they will have less reason to participate fully.
5. For the same reason, avoid acronyms, abbreviations, and initials. Terms should be stated and defined briefly and early on in the meeting if they are important to the discussion at hand.
6. Avoid labeling the child. Labels can cause anxiety, confusion, and stereotyping.
7. When discussing test information, explain any term necessary to the discussion briefly and clearly.
8. Use examples to illustrate subtests if they are not immediately obvious. Explain the procedures used in the tests.
9. Explain what the scores mean to the actual functioning of the student.
10. Augment testing information with observation, e.g., "Jim scored well on this test, but he grasped his pencil so tightly he seemed to be uncomfortable."
11. Discuss strengths as well as weaknesses. A positive outlook is more helpful than a negative one.
12. Be sure that all individuals present are introduced to the parents. Be sure the parents know the area of responsibility of each participant.
13. Treat the parents [as]: (a) equal participants in the IEP process; (b) individuals who know perhaps more about the student in some areas than anyone else; and (c) the child's concerned parents!

Some districts provide written guides for parents concerning special education services under P.L. 94–142. Teachers should be familiar with the contents of these guides to be able to discuss them knowledgeably with parents (pp. 15–16).

COMMUNICATING WITH PROFESSIONALS. The ability to deal with colleagues on a professional level is very important in the IEP process. Every participant in an IEP meeting must understand the level of responsibility and the role of each other team member. Each participant must understand exactly what kinds of information are expected from each member; in this way, important areas of information will not be lost or overlooked.

SHARING INFORMATION WITH COLLEAGUES

The ability to present one's own information clearly and concisely is a large part of effective, professional communication. [Specialists should] Be sure to define terms that might not be instantly recognized by colleagues with other areas of expertise, and to explain the importance of results in an informative but not insulting manner. The ability to concisely describe various tests and procedures as they relate to the student is also an important skill.

Just as important as the delivery of one's own information, however, is the ability to defer to someone else's greater knowledge or expertise. No one person is expected to know everything; for this reason, the IEP is developed, implemented, and revised by a team rather than by an individual.

TEACHER RESPONSIBILITIES

In the IEP meeting, the classroom teacher's responsibility is to relay information about materials and techniques planned as part of the student's educational program. After the IEP meeting, the regular teacher must keep in close contact with the special education teacher in particular, or with the other personnel responsible for providing special services to the child. These individuals together are responsible for maintaining and implementing the IEP after its development.

Many school districts have designated procedures for the referral and IEP processes. Many also provide opportunities for staff inservice training to help prepare teachers for compliance with P.L. 94-142. Familiarity with these procedures and guidelines is essential to provide the best education possible for all students (pp. 10–11).

EVALUATING THE IEP MEETING. By using a checklist, the IEP meeting leader and the other professional team members can ensure that the meeting fairly represents each participant's contributions and point of view. This evaluation will help strengthen future IEP meetings, too. Team members should review the questions before the IEP meeting, then assess how well the meeting adhered to the guidelines afterwards.

Exhibit 5–2 is a sample checklist form.

IEPs at the Secondary School Level

The IEP process, as Stewart (1982) notes, is "based upon an individual child orientation which typifies elementary school settings and the thinking of most special educators" (p. 65). Exhibit 5–3 provides a form for keeping a record of the IEP. The

Exhibit 5–2 IEP Meeting Evaluation Checklist

____ 1. Was information conveyed concisely but in enough detail so that all participants could understand the proceedings?
____ 2. Were all members of the committee allowed, even encouraged, to participate?
____ 3. Did all members conduct themselves with professionalism?
____ 4. Were all members prepared in their areas of responsibility?
____ 5. Were the goals and objectives appropriate for the needs of the individual student? Did they conform to standard form?
____ 6. Were all elements required in the IEP completed?
____ 7. Were jargon, initials, and abbreviations avoided?
____ 8. Were anxiety-producing words avoided?
____ 9. Were the child's strengths as well as weaknesses outlined?
____ 10. Did you feel that good communication was established with all participants?
____ 11. Comments:
____ 12. Suggestions for future IEP meetings:

Source: Adapted from *Developing Individualized Education Programs for Handicapped Pupils* by Chris Shaffer, the University of Washington Dean's Grant Project, Seattle, 1982.

secondary school setting poses a variety of unique challenges. Stewart addresses the following:

PARENT INVOLVEMENT ISSUES

- The IEP process is predicated upon the essential element of parent involvement; however, . . . many adolescents do not want their parents to be too involved with their schooling, and many parents respect this need for independence (p. 57).
- The number of handicapped students served by an individual classroom teacher is likely to increase significantly at the secondary level, which . . . coupled with complex, inflexible schedules, diminish a teacher's possibility for attending to students on an individual basis, either in planning or implementing educational programs. . . . The wide ability range found in a 50-minute class period increases the difficulty of individualized planning and teaching (p. 64).
- Most secondary level teachers are subject oriented and unaccustomed to sharing the responsibility for instructing their students and . . . most are not trained in special education nor did they ever want to be (p. 66).

SECONDARY TEACHERS' SPECIAL PROBLEMS

- The IEP must include vocational goals and vocational educators should play active roles in IEP team meetings (p. 68).
- The content of the IEP must [be consistent] with curriculum priorities at the secondary level, such as graduation requirements, competency

Exhibit 5–3 Individualized Education Program

IEP TEAM

Student ____________________
Parent(s) ____________________
Teacher(s) ____________________
____

Agency Representative ____________________
____
Other(s) ____________________

STUDENT INFORMATION

D.O.B. ____________ Age ____________ Grade ____________
Phone ____________ Address ____________
School ____________________

PROCEDURAL CHECKLIST—DATE
Written notice about program initiation/change
Consent for preplacement evaluation ____________
Consent for initial placement ____________

SPECIAL EDUCATION AND RELATED SERVICES TO BE PROVIDED	PERSONS RESPONSIBLE	DATE INITIATED	DURATION

EXTENT OF TIME IN REGULAR EDUCATION PROGRAM ____________________
____

EVALUATION DATA
____

Source: From ***Individualized Teaching: Writing Individualized Education Programs*** by Ann Stewart, American Association of Colleges for Teacher Education, 1982. Adapted by permission.

CURRICULUM AND GRADUATION REQUIREMENTS

> test objectives, grading standards set by individual schools or school districts, state-mandated curricula or systemwide objectives for courses that are so lengthy that individualized pacing is not feasible, and state-adopted texts that do not provide a variety of reading levels. IEPs must account for Carnegie Units, semester hours, or courses required in various disciplines for graduation from high school. Some states also require a passing grade on a competency test as a prerequisite for receiving a high school diploma. IEP goals should reflect the remediation needed to pass such a test (p. 69).

To facilitate the IEP process in secondary schools, principals should:

ADMINISTRATIVE SUPPORT FOR TEACHERS

- Involve regular class teachers from the very beginning of the IEP process, recognizing their contributions in providing classroom performance data and objectives and their need to have a sense of ownership of the final plan.
- Provide release time for teachers to attend IEP planning meetings and to consult with specialists.
- Provide support services to the teacher as well as the student.
- Assign one teacher (generally a special educator) responsibility for coordinating each student's program.
- Coordinate planning periods to facilitate cooperation among the professionals involved.
- Explore ways to involve parents in the planning process while at the same time encouraging students to take increasing responsibility for their education.
- Make use of some degree of ability grouping to narrow the spectrum of abilities found within classes and subject areas.

REFERENCES

Division of Special Services (1980). *Series on P.L. 94–142 and related Washington rules and regulations: Individualized education programs*. Olympia, WA: Office of the Superintendent of Public Instruction, pp. 10–11, 15–16, 26–27.

Federal Register 42 (163) Part II, August 23, 1977 (*Comment* on §1212.344, p. 42490).

Shaffer, C. (1982). *Developing individualized education programs for handicapped pupils*. Seattle: University of Washington Dean's Grant.

Stewart, A. (1982). *Individualized teaching: Writing individualized education programs*. Washington, D.C.: American Association of Colleges for Teacher Education, pp. 57, 64–66, 68.

Chapter 6

Placement

SUMMARY

Statement of the Problem

The placement decision is frequently the most important factor affecting the success of a handicapped student's education. It is inherently controversial, as it must balance the often conflicting demands and desires of a number of individuals and groups. While the law requires placement in a program appropriate to the student's needs and educational growth, the school's actual ability to do this often is limited by lack of funding, variety of program options, trained personnel, and support services.

Legal Issues

The placement decision, because it is so important, is protected by a variety of procedural safeguards, including the following:

- Parents (or their appointed surrogates) must receive written, prior notice (in their native language or other mode of communication) of each proposal to place or change the placement of their child.
- Parents must give written consent to the initial evaluation and placement of their child.
- Parental consent may be revoked at any time.
- The student will remain in current placement while any dispute is being resolved.

The law further requires that placement decisions be:

- reviewed at least annually
- based on the student's IEP
- as close as possible to the child's home
- in the most normal, or least restrictive, environment feasible and in contact as much as possible with nonhandicapped peers
- based on documented information from a variety of sources
- made by a group that includes persons familiar with the child, the evaluation data, and the placement options.

The school district is responsible for providing a continuum of alternative placements, including regular classes, special classes, special schools, or instruction in home, hospital, or institution. Whatever program and support services are prescribed in the IEP must be provided, according to P.L. 94-142, "at public expense, under public supervision and direction and without charge" (Sec. 4(a)(18), and the institution must meet the state's minimal standards and license requirements for public education.

Rationale

Given appropriate opportunities and support, all children can learn. A free public education is the right of all citizens in our democratic system. Handicapped children have so often been placed inappropriately, or denied public education altogether, that a strong public commitment has become necessary to correct this problem. Furthermore, both handicapped and nonhandicapped children benefit from an integrated educational environment.

Approaches

Placement decisions account for the vast majority of formal hearings called for by parents; it is unlikely that serious disputes in this area can be avoided entirely. The best preventive strategy lies in attending to the procedural requirements of the law and developing relationships of mutual trust and respect with all involved, including teachers, parents, community, and special education staff. Two key facts, frequently misunderstood, may help clarify communication: (1) The law does not require regular class placement for all students in all subjects. (2) The courts have ruled that "appropriate" placement does not necessarily mean best possible placement, but simply one in which the student makes reasonable progress.

THE PROBLEMS IN PLACEMENT

A 1980 survey of due process hearings in special education (Smith, 1981) showed that fully 89 percent involved placement disputes. The selection of and placement in an educational program is, quite simply, the most controversial point in the process of educating handicapped children. Even when there is agreement among all parties on the goals and services identified in the IEP, the means of carrying it out (which is essentially what placement means) may generate heated disputes.

A SUBJECT OF CONTRO-VERSY

And no wonder. A great deal hinges upon the decision. From the student's point of view, placement is often the main factor in determining whether the educational experience will be rewarding or frustrating, enjoyable or humiliating. Parents see the placement decision as key to the child's educational progress, behavioral and social as well as academic. They bring to the decision a host of other fears, doubts, and desires, ranging from concerns about past bad experiences in schools to hopes of placing a very difficult child in a residential program away from home. From the point of view of the school district, the chief question often is how to avoid overtaxing an already inadequate budget.

SCHOOL, PARENT, AND COMMUNITY ISSUES

Other voices in the community, particularly the parents of nonhandicapped children, may well complain that the exorbitant costs of special programs are draining the school's limited finances, just as they fear that mainstreamed students drain the resources of the regular classroom teacher. The complaints are especially frequent where school district funds are financing such apparently noneducational services as physical therapy and residential care. The fear, in each case, is that the result will be a lowered quality of education for all students.

Administrators, meanwhile, occupy a precarious position at the center of the storm, with their focus in four directions simultaneously: the consumers, the staff, the budget, and the law. And what about the law? Doesn't it offer guidelines large enough to stand behind? Don't the regulations point out clear resolutions to these controversies?

Not really. On the one hand, it is reassuring for administrators to know that the majority of impartial hearings are decided in favor of the schools. On the other hand, the laws and regulations governing placements are distressingly vague. They tend not quite to spell out but only to imply how the decisions must be made and evaluated.

THE AM-BIGUOUS NATURE OF THE LAW

While recognizing that there are no absolute answers, this chapter reviews the law and recent court cases and lays out some practical guidelines and approaches to placement decision making.

LEGAL ISSUES

As Shrybman (1982) points out in *Due Process in Special Education*, educational placement is the last in a series of steps described in the Education for All Handicapped Children Act. Beginning with the initial identification, each step influences (although it does not strictly determine) the next; and every later step relies on

THE LAST IN A SERIES OF REQUIRED STEPS

satisfactory completion of the previous one. Thus, the evaluation process helps determine the IEP, which in turn must form a basis for the placement decision.

The IEP sets the student's educational goals; placement is the means of carrying them out. There may be several very different educational settings in which this can occur, and the parties involved may have very different criteria for deciding which is the best. For example, parents may insist that the best placement for their hearing impaired child is an expensive residential program, while school officials argue for placement in a less expensive, district-run program in the child's community. The law offers leeway. It requires not the best setting, but an appropriate one.

WHAT IS AN "APPROPRIATE PLACEMENT"?

What then exactly does "appropriate" mean? Certainly it means a setting in which it is possible to meet the goals of the IEP, a setting in which the student can learn. It is a setting that meets the other requirements listed at the outset of this chapter, such as least restrictive environment, as close as possible to the child's home, and so on.

But the law is not entirely specific. It does not offer a closed and concise definition of "appropriate placement" such that one potential placement can be identified as clearly superior in each case. In fact, quite a large percentage of the court cases involving special education have, in the end, hinged on the judicial interpretation of this term.

A PROCEDURAL DEFINITION

What the law does offer is a procedural definition; that is, an educational placement is technically legal if all the required procedures have been carried out. If the identification and evaluation of the student, the development of an IEP, and selection of an educational program based on that IEP have all been completed in compliance with the law, the schools still may not be able to avoid controversy but at least will be on solid legal ground.

The key procedural requirements for the placement stage are listed in the chapter summary. Here are details on specific topics that may prove helpful.

Least Restrictive Environment

Under the least restrictive environment principle (defined in the regulations implementing P.L. 94-142 (Fed. Reg., 1977)) each public agency must ensure:

FEDERAL DEFINITION OF LEAST RESTRICTIVE ENVIRONMENT

> (1) That to the maximum extent appropriate, handicapped children, including children in public or private institutions or other care facilities, are educated with children who are not handicapped, and
>
> (2) That special classes, separate schooling or other removal of handicapped children from the regular educational environment occurs only when the nature or severity of the handicap is such that education in regular classes with the use of supplementary aids and services cannot be achieved satisfactorily (Sec. 121a.550(b)(1),(2)).

Turnbull, Leonard, and Turnbull (1982) offer a useful commentary on this definition:

Many educators erroneously interpret the least restrictive principle to mean that all handicapped children should be placed in regular classrooms. Rather, this principle requires that the regular classroom be chosen as the appropriate alternative for a child when, indeed, his needs can be met there. If the child's IEP cannot be successfully implemented in the regular classroom, then greater degrees of restrictiveness should be considered, such as the resource room, special class, or special school. According to law, factors to be considered in choosing among alternative placements include consistency with the IEP, proximity to the child's home (e.g., unless otherwise required by the IEP, the handicapped child should be educated in the school she would attend if not handicapped), and any potential harmful effect on a child regarding a particular placement. The determination of placement should be made on an annual basis. One required component of the IEP is the documentation of the extent of the child's participation in the regular educational program. Academic, as well as nonacademic and extracurricular, services and activities should be considerations in making this determination (p. 24).

FACTORS TO CONSIDER IN PLACEMENT DECISIONS

The following criteria by which to evaluate the least restrictive environment are suggested by Turnbull and Turnbull (1978) in *Free Appropriate Public Education: Law and Implementation.*

LEAST RESTRICTIVE ENVIRONMENT CRITERIA

1. The presence of nonhandicapped students in the same setting . . .
2. The extent to which the handicapped student has opportunities to interact with nonhandicapped students in the school environment . .
3. The extent to which nonhandicapped students in the educational setting are age peers of handicapped students . . .
4. The ratio of handicapped to nonhandicapped students . . .
5. The physical facilities of an educational placement (p. 147).

The federal regulations accompanying the Rehabilitation Act of 1973 make further clarifying statements, including·

FURTHER FEDERAL GUIDELINES

(1) The overriding rule in this section is that placement decisions must be made on an individual basis. (2) It should be stressed that where a handicapped child is so disruptive in a regular class that the education of other students is significantly impaired, the needs of the handicapped child cannot be met in that environment. Therefore regular placement would not be appropriate to his or her needs. (3) The parents' right to challenge the placement of their child extends not only to placement in special classes or separate schools, but also the placement in a distant school, particularly in a residential program. An equally appropriate educational placement may exist closer to home; and this issue may be raised by the parents under the due process provisions. (45 CFR Part 84—Appendix, Paragraph 24).

Accessibility

The following summaries of accessibility requirements relating to education are based on Section 504 and are quoted from Turnbull, Leonard, and Turnbull (1982):

> Subpart C of the HEW [now HHS] regulation prohibits recipients [of federal funds] from excluding handicapped people from their programs or denying them services because a recipient's facilities are unaccessible to or unusable by handicapped persons (Sec. 84.31). This means that architectural, communications, and environmental barriers must be dealt with and eliminated.

SECTION 504 REQUIREMENTS

> 1. *New construction.* New construction must be barrier free (Sec. 84.23(a), p. 81).
> 2. *Existing facilities.* Recipients shall operate each program or activity so that the program or activity, when viewed in its entirety, is readily accessible to handicapped persons (Sec. 84.22(a)). This requirement is referred to as *program accessibility*. It does not necessarily require that each existing facility or every part of a facility be made accessible to and usable by handicapped people. Rather, it requires that in many cases *at least* a part or percentage of each recipient's facilities must be accessible so that disabled people can participate in the program.
>
> Three things to remember in applying [the HHS] accessibility standard are:
>
> 1. There are *no prescribed numbers* or percentages set by [HHS] for buildings or floors of buildings which must be accessible.
> 2. Alternatives to structural changes are permitted if they are equally effective.
> 3. The decision whether to use alternate means must be made with handicapped people and their organizations.

ACCESSIBILITY REGULATIONS EXPLAINED

> *Special exception for small service providers.* A special exception to the program accessibility requirement is made in the regulations for small service providers which employ fewer than 15 people. In addition to the option of making home visits, if a small recipient cannot make its services available short of *significant alterations* in its existing facilities, it may, after consultation with the person seeking its services, refer the individual to another service provider whose facilities are accessible [Sec. 84.22(c)]. (This *outside* referral is a "last resort" measure.)
>
> *Effective communications for blind and deaf.* The duty to provide effective communication aids for blind or deaf people sometimes involves physical and structural modifications (e.g., telecommunication devices) and other times nonphysical or structural modifications like providing interpreters or

> making copies of printed material available in Braille, cassette, and large print.
>
> In addition, the [HHS] regulations impose a duty to publicize the accessibility and usability of programs by requiring that the recipient adopt and implement procedures to ensure that interested persons, including persons with impaired vision or hearing, can obtain information as to the existence and location of services, activities, and facilities that are accessible to and usable by handicapped persons. (Sec. 84.27(f)) (pp. 36–38).

Costs and Responsibilities

P.L. 94-142 requires that each handicapped child be provided an appropriate education "at public expense, under public supervision and direction and without charge. . . ." Specifically, the law says, this includes:

- nonmedical care in a residential program
- special education and related services called for in the IEP
- other nonmedical services that can be shown to be necessary in order for a student to benefit from the educational program.

SERVICES TO BE PROVIDED AND PAID FOR BY SCHOOLS

The related services identified in the law are: transportation, speech pathology and audiology, psychological services, physical and occupational therapy, recreation, early identification and assessment of disabilities in children, counseling services, medical services for diagnostic or evaluation purposes, school health services, social work services in schools, and parent counseling and training. However, the school is not responsible for "incidental fees which are normally charged to nonhandicapped students or their parents as part of the regular education program."

APPROACHES TO RESOLVING PROBLEMS

MINIMIZING PROBLEMS

As implied in the summary, the controversies surrounding placement can never be prevented entirely. A more realistic goal is to avoid unfavorable legal decisions by following the specifics of the law, minimizing disagreements by building a foundation of trust, and increasing the educational options available through openness to new possibilities.

A variety of information and suggestions are offered in later parts of this book on building better relationships among special and regular education students and staff members and among schools, parents, and the community at large. Since all of these are rooted in commitment to the concept of least restrictive environment, or mainstreaming, an analysis by Ponch (1981) is included to clarify the philosophical underpinnings of this approach.

Also in this section are descriptions of several widely used staffing models for mainstreamed schools. For additional information, consult the checklist on placement decisions developed by Shrybman (1982).

Philosophical Bases of Mainstreaming

The official definition of mainstreaming adopted by the Council for Exceptional Children reads:

DEFINITION OF MAINSTREAMING

> Mainstreaming is based on the conviction that each child should be educated in the least restrictive environment in which his educational and related needs can be satisfactorily provided. This concept recognizes that exceptional children have a wide range of special educational needs, varying greatly in intensity and duration; that there is a recognized continuum of educational settings which may, at a given time, be appropriate for an individual child's needs; that to the maximum extent appropriate, exceptional children should be educated with nonexceptional children; and that special classes, separate schooling, or other removal of an exceptional child from education with nonexceptional children should occur only when the intensity of the child's special education and related needs is such that they cannot be satisfied in an environment including nonexceptional children, even with the provision of supplementary aids and services. ("Official Action . . . ," 1976, p. 43).

Birch (1981) offers the following analysis and interpretation of that definition, detailing for educators the specific history, possibilities, and effects:

BROADER MEANING

> [Developments in mainstreaming] are part of a broader common theme: the greater inclusion of exceptional persons in the mainstream of all community life. Specifically in education they signify the reversal of the negative, rejection-oriented design that permitted the removal of some children from the mainstream of education and isolated them in "special" settings. They also signify the demise of what has been called the "two box" theory of education, that is, that there are two kinds of children—exceptional and normal—two kinds of school systems: one "special" for the exceptional children and one "regular" for the normal children. In sum, the developments encourage a unified school system in which exceptional children are part of the educational mainstream.

MORE THAN JUST PHYSICAL PROXIMITY

> Mainstreaming requires more than merely placing handicapped children in regular classrooms, however. Refusing to refer children to special education or simply dumping children back into community schools or into regular classes is a cruelty to everyone involved: pupils, teachers, and parents. Many children would be placed in environments where they would be poorly understood and poorly educated. . . .

Broadly speaking, mainstreaming is based on an inclusive attitude or general predisposition toward the education of children; that is, to provide education for as many children as possible in the regular class environment. But the regular teacher, alone or with help, will not always be the optimal instructor for all pupils; hence, a full continuum of instructional arrangements to meet the needs of individual children is integral to mainstreaming. However, each displacement from a regular teacher to a specialist in another setting, even in the same school, must first be justified and negotiated with the student and parents.

CONTINUUM OF PLACEMENT OPTIONS

Generally speaking, there are three forms of mainstreaming that may be identified. They are physical space mainstreaming, social interaction mainstreaming, and instructional mainstreaming. The first, *physical space mainstreaming*, is the most elemental and the simplest form. It means that

THREE LEVELS OF MAINSTREAMING

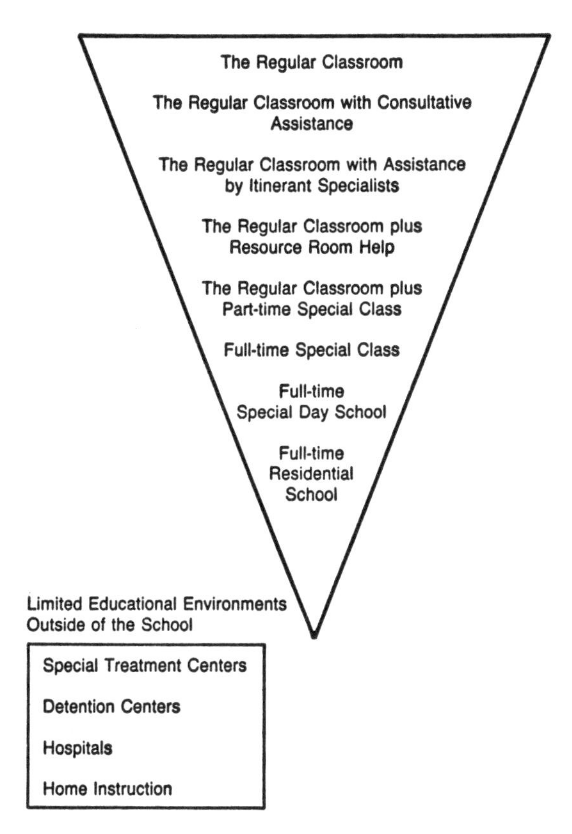

Source: From *Teaching Exceptional Children in All America's Schools* (p. 32) by M. Reynolds and J. Birch, 1979, Reston, Va.: The Council for Exceptional Children. Copyright 1979 by The Council for Exceptional Children. Adapted by permission.

exceptional children are physically present in the same school building as other children. In its plainest form, exceptional and other children attend the same school and use its facilities at the same time. That gives opportunities for all children to recognize that they are citizens of the same world—that their life spaces overlap—that they have much in common. Thus, being educated in the same physical plant is the most basic kind or degree of mainstreaming.

A step beyond simply being educated under the same roof is the next form, *social interaction mainstreaming*. That entails not only being in the same building, but it calls for deliberate, planned social interactions, arranged by the school's staff. It means mingling of exceptional and other children so they have many opportunities to get to know each other as persons and to engage in common social relationships of children and youth.

MANY CHILDREN CAN BE MAINSTREAMED

The most complex form is *academic and special subject instructional mainstreaming*. It includes [the first levels and] goes further. It includes exceptional and other children being taught skill, content, and related subjects, individualized to their needs, together by the same cadre of teachers.

Thus, it is feasible to talk of exceptional children being physically in the mainstream, while living and being instructed primarily in the company of other exceptional children. For some youngsters, that elemental level is the greatest degree of mainstreaming possible at a given time.

[In other cases] there can be meaningful social interactions with the other pupils in the school, if the interactions are deliberately planned, engineered to take place in ways that are mutually pleasing, and helpful to exceptional children and the other children.

The most complex level of mainstreaming, the instructional level, can be illustrated in many ways. Illuminating examples are found among totally deaf children and among totally blind children. Modern preschool preparation, technology, and support systems are so well worked out today that otherwise normal children who cannot hear at all, even with hearing aids, and children who cannot see at all, even with glasses, can enter kindergarten at the usual age and continue through school without ever leaving their regular classmates. Not all do, but that is only because the needed and available know-how, technical facilities, and special education support are not yet being brought to them while they attend regular classes. The main point, though, is that certain exceptional children, many more than once was supposed, can readily attain the highest level of mainstreaming. They can receive all of the combination of regular and special education they require while going to school full time in regular classes with other children from their own neighborhoods who are also receiving high quality education (pp. 34–38).

Staffing Models

Whereas in the past handicapped students were viewed as the exclusive responsibility of special educators, mainstreaming necessarily requires a cooperative effort on the part of a variety of professionals. Such cooperation, in turn, requires new staffing patterns and administrative structures, including closer involvement of principals. Several such staffing models have been developed and refined over the years since passage of P.L. 94-142. Following are descriptions of a few of the most common.

NEW STAFFING MODELS REQUIRED

Diagnostic-Prescriptive Teacher Model

This model makes use of a trained diagnostician-consultant to assist regular class teachers and has as its goal keeping the mildly handicapped student in the regular classroom. A typical collaborative process would involve some version of the following steps:

1. The regular class teacher initiates the process by filing a written referral on a student, with a brief description of the perceived academic or behavioral problem.
2. The diagnostic-prescriptive teacher (DPT) observes the student, consults with the teacher, and arranges to bring the student into the DPT classroom.
3. The DPT then forms and tests recommendations for individual teaching techniques and materials.
4. The DPT develops detailed teaching prescriptions and holds conferences with the regular class teacher to explain their use.
5. The DPT, as needed, enters the regular classroom to demonstrate methods and work alongside the regular teacher.
6. Followup and evaluation are carried out periodically. When both teachers are satisfied with the program, the case is considered closed.

DPT AIDS REGULAR CLASS TEACHER

Resource Room Model

In the resource room model, mild to moderately handicapped students spend part of the day in the regular classroom and part with specially trained staff in a separate room. The amount of time spent, subjects covered, and type of programming are determined on a highly individualized basis.

The resource room teacher should be trained in educational assessment and planning for students with a variety of disabilities and should have broad knowledge of strategies and materials for exceptional learners. In some schools, resource room duties are shared by more than one teacher; these may include professionals with particular expertise in hearing or visual impairments, behavioral disorders, or other fields.

THE RESOURCE ROOM TEACHER

The room itself should be set up for both small group and individual work and stocked with a wide selection of materials and equipment for meeting many different students' needs.

Although funding regulations must be checked carefully for this use, it is sometimes possible and beneficial to structure the resource room to serve all students in the school and, in some ways, not just the handicapped. This can help students with temporary difficulty in adjustment and also remove potential stigma from resource room assignment.

Itinerant Teacher Model

ITINERANT SERVICES

Rockoff (1980), in his chapter, "Delivery Systems to Implement Mainstreaming in Social Studies Classrooms," describes the itinerant teacher model as follows:

> The itinerant teacher, like the regular classroom teacher, works with students in their regular classroom environment, but the itinerant teacher is only responsible for the one or two identified students and not for the entire class. The itinerant teacher may provide a direct service to the handicapped student or may supplement the instruction of the regular teacher. If a teacher is looking for help with a particular student, a referral would be submitted through proper channels. The itinerant teacher model has been utilized extensively by students who are blind or visually impaired but remain in the regular classroom setting. The itinerant teacher aids the student in learning Braille, [makes] needed classroom materials in Braille, and provides any additional support services needed to help the handicapped student adjust to the regular classroom (pp. 19–20).

Consulting Teacher Model

CONSULTATION TO REGULAR TEACHERS

Another common mainstreamed special education model makes use of a consulting teacher. These specialists differ from those discussed previously in that they normally do not work directly with students but rather with the regular classroom teacher. Consulting teachers share their knowledge of handicapping conditions, special materials, instructional techniques, independent learning activities, diagnosis and evaluation techniques, class arrangements, and class management through processes such as this:

1. The regular class teacher initiates the process by making a request for assistance.
2. The consulting teacher helps the regular teacher pinpoint the problem and determine the goal of intervention.
3. A number of possible strategies are evaluated with the consulting teacher's help; one is selected, and specific techniques are developed.
4. The consulting teacher may provide additional support such as gathering special materials or demonstrating techniques.

5. The effects of the intervention are evaluated jointly and any necessary modifications are made.

Consulting teachers must have good professional communication skills and be able to adjust to classroom teachers' schedules, needs, and individual differences in teaching styles.

Practical Variations

COMBINING THE MODELS

In practice, the actual working responsibilities of special education teachers often include elements of more than one of these models. For example, the resource room teacher frequently serves as a consultant to regular class teachers in the school, and so on. Each school or district modifies or combines roles to meet the particular requirements of its students, staff, and community.

REFERENCES

Birch, J. (1981). *Variables in exceptionality: The meaning of exceptionality and the nature and scope of special education*. Washington, D.C.: American Association of Colleges for Teacher Education, pp. 32, 34–38.

Rockoff, E. (1980). Mainstreaming in social studies classrooms. In Herlihy, J.G., & Herlihy, M.T. (Eds.): *Mainstreaming in the social studies* (pp. 16–21). Washington, D.C.: National Council for the Social Studies.

Shrybman, J. (1982). *Due process in special education*. Rockville, MD: Aspen Publishers, Inc.

Smith, T.C. (1982). Status of due process hearings. *Exceptional Children, 48*(3), 232–236.

Turnbull, A., Leonard, J., & Turnbull, R. (1982). *Educating the handicapped child: Judicial and legal influences*. Washington, D.C.: American Association of Colleges for Teacher Education, p. 24.

Turnbull, H.R., & Turnbull, A. (1978). *Free appropriate public education: Law and Implementation.* Denver: Love Publishing Company, p. 147.

Chapter 7

Preschool Programs

SUMMARY

Statement of the Problem

Because federal legislation allows for, and some states mandate, educational programs for handicapped children under age 5, principals without special training for this age group frequently may become involved in preschool administration and/or programming.

Legal Issues

Several key federal laws and policies relate to the education of children ages birth to 5. These include:

- Head Start (1965), amended in 1974 to require that at least 10 percent of the opportunities for enrollment be available to handicapped children
- Handicapped Children's Early Education Act (1968) provided funds for the establishment of demonstration projects designed to test innovative models for early education of the handicapped
- Education of All Handicapped Children Act, 1975 (P.L. 94-142), gave states the option of providing education for handicapped children aged 3 to 5
- Amendments to P.L. 98-199, passed in 1983, allowed federal preschool funds to be used for programs serving the birth-to-3 population as well, although the amount of preschool funding allotted to a state is still based on the number of handicapped children aged 3 to 5.

Rationale

Research suggests that very early intervention increases handicapped children's likelihood of remaining in school, keeping up with nonhandicapped peers, and/or maximizing their educational potential.

Approaches

Preschool education for the handicapped encompasses a great variety of programs, including interventions provided in the child's home; classes at schools or centers; parent training; infant stimulation programs for hospitalized babies; traditional, nondirective preschool programs; highly structured curricula focusing on the development of preacademic skills, and other structured but child-directed curricula; programs for homogeneous (e.g., hearing impaired) and for highly heterogeneous populations (including, sometimes, both the handicapped and nonhandicapped), and so on.

All of these have proved beneficial when the programs:

- involved parents and were sensitive to their needs and preferences
- were well planned and administered and all staff members shared a commitment to the program's underlying philosophy
- used individualized educational planning for each child
- cooperated with related professionals in the community.

EMERGING PRESCHOOL PROGRAMS

FEW HANDICAPS ARE CLEAR AT BIRTH

Few children are identified as handicapped at birth. Mild handicaps in such categories as behavioral disturbance, mental retardation, and learning disabilities often do not emerge until the school years, and even rather severe cognitive or sensory impairments may not be identified correctly until the child is 2, 3, or 4 years of age or older. Yet some states begin educational programming for the handicapped from the first days of life. Who, exactly, are the children served by these programs, and what does the staff hope to accomplish?

PREVENTIVE AND COMPENSATORY GOALS

The answers to these questions can be summarized under the headings prevention and compensation. The latter, compensatory programming, is the oldest approach and the easiest to understand. A child who is blind, deaf, or paraplegic cannot be expected to make normal developmental progress with the same type of informal parental guidance that is adequate for most preschoolers. These children will need special training in speech, mobility, and other skills. They will need time, training, and special equipment to help them compensate for their disabilities. The advantages of beginning such training as early as possible include maximizing the children's ability to keep up with peers in later schooling and allowing them and their families more positive experiences in the early years.

The notion of prevention in this context is a relatively new one. It evolved from a complex of developments in the 1950s and 1960s, including animal research on the effects of early stimulation; the child development theories of Piaget, Erikson, and others; and mounting statistical evidence from actual program evaluations. Emerging themes such as the critical importance of early childhood development and the effect of the child's environment on intelligence were picked up and promoted by contemporary social movements. The result was widespread belief that gaps in educational achievement among different social groups could be prevented or mitigated through early intervention. The Head Start program was a response.

ROOTS OF EARLY CHILDHOOD SPECIAL EDUCATION

In the following decades, as new attitudes toward education of the handicapped developed, it was natural that the principle of preventive early intervention should be extended to the young disabled population. Early childhood education was advocated as a means of preventing or limiting the effects of handicaps on children's school experience. Head Start was amended to set aside 10 percent of enrollment opportunities for handicapped children, the federal government provided extra monies for demonstration projects, and a number of programs were established with the goal of:

> [intervening] during the critical developmental years from birth to age 6, in order to prevent or ameliorate the effects of a handicapping condition or problems that have a high probability of manifesting themselves as developmental or school-related difficulties in later childhood (Linder, 1983, p. 1).

Risk Factors

The relation of preschool intervention for the handicapped to earlier movements for social equality involved more than a simple, historical precedent. Research was

CHILDREN AT RISK FOR DEVELOPING HANDICAPS

showing that the great majority of children identified as mildly handicapped in the school years were from socially and/or economically disadvantaged families (including a disproportionate number of racial minorities). As the President's Committee on Mental Retardation (1976) reported:

> In perhaps 85-90 percent of cases, mild retardation not involving identifiable organic or physical causes is associated with conditions arising from the environment, poverty, racial and ethnic discrimination, and family disorders (p. 80).

From studies and statistics such as this arose the concept of infants and young children "at risk" for developing handicaps. Other at-risk groups have been identified since then, including children born prematurely, those of low birth weight or stressful births, and children of mothers exposed to toxic drugs or infections during pregnancy. In many cases, *at risk* is a more useful and more accurate term than handicapped when referring to very young children. Some childhood educators prefer it exclusively, fearing that the early application of labels such as mentally retarded may negatively affect adults' attitudes and expectations of a child and so cause permanent damage.

PROBLEM OF LABELS

Does It Work?

Although still a new and rapidly changing field (especially with the birth-to-3 population), early education has been around long enough to generate some follow-up data. What have been the results? Does early intervention work? The answer, it would seem, depends on the expectations, on the definitions of success.

QUALIFIED SUCCESSES

Early education does not seem to be preventive in the sense, say, that the Salk vaccine prevents polio. One or two years of special education—no matter how early—cannot be expected to counteract the effects of most risk factors or handicapping conditions. On the other hand, at-risk children who have had early intervention do fare better in measures of educational achievement than those who have not, and the gains can be sustained if students continue to receive special education services during the school years.

APPROACHES TO RESOLVING PROBLEMS

ELEMENTS OF SUCCESSFUL PROGRAMS

Preschool programs for the handicapped take many different forms, based on such factors as age, location, and handicapping conditions of the children; state law and funding levels; educational philosophy and professional competencies of the staff, and so on. Many authors (e.g., Lerner, Mardell-Czudnowski, and Goldenberg, 1981) suggest that the specific curriculum used is not as significant as requirements that: (1) the program is well planned and administered, (2) all staff members support the program's philosophical approach, and (3) the children's parents are involved. No one program model is appropriate for all communities; no one curriculum is appropriate for all children.

Location and Population

HOME AND CENTER BASED PROGRAMMING

The first major difference among preschool programs is whether they are center-based (the children go to a school or facility) or home-based (program staff members go to the children's homes), or a combination of the two. Center-based programming may be difficult or impractical in rural areas, as may programs directed toward a single type of handicap such as hearing impairment. Indeed, limited funds and other restrictions generally dictate that preschool programs be designed to accommodate children with a variety of handicaps and individual needs.

MAINSTREAMING AT THE PRESCHOOL LEVEL

At the preschool as well as school-age level, there is increasing interest in integrated handicapped/nonhandicapped settings. This can bring about certain staffing problems. For example, teachers may have general early childhood education backgrounds with little training in handicapping conditions; problems may arise among professionals from different disciplines regarding coordination, turf protection, and the sharing of skills and responsibilities.

Staffing models for the integrated preschool vary greatly. At one extreme is the "pullout" model, where a student is removed periodically from class for work with specialists who do not coordinate directly with the preschool classroom teacher. At the other extreme are fully cooperative models where all staff members are conceived as having joint responsibility for all the students, and there is extensive sharing of skills and expertise.

FAMILY SUPPORT SERVICES

Just as there will be a variety of needs and requirements among different communities and individual children, so also will there be differences among the children's parents. Providing support to families should be one of the chief goals of early education programs for the handicapped, and parent participation is perhaps the most important key to success.

For the families of young handicapped children, the needs may be great. There are tremendous emotional adjustments to be made, feelings of grief, guilt, or fear to be dealt with. There are new skills to be learned and new burdens on family time and finances. Siblings may need special support. (Some early childhood programs focus primarily on the parents; an example is parenting classes for mentally retarded mothers.) Program staff members must be sensitive to parental preferences, needs (including the need, sometimes, not to be involved), culture, and so on.

Curriculum and Instruction

PHILOSOPHICAL APPROACHES

In addition to variety in location of early childhood programs and in the population served, there are a number of alternatives in educational philosophy—each one giving rise to different approaches. A few of these are described next:

- Child Development Model: This traditional approach to preschool emphasizes age-appropriate skills and social-emotional development. Many activities are made available for the children to explore as they choose. The teacher's role is a relatively informal one.

- Montessori Model: Children are provided with a carefully sequenced and structured series of activities to explore at their own pace. The program emphasizes individual autonomy and the development of sensory, motor, and language skills.

DIFFERENT CURRICULA AND PROGRAM MODELS

- Cognitive Development Model: This approach is based on the theories of Piaget and others that conceive of development as the product of maturation through a sequence of distinctive stages and through interaction with the environment. There is emphasis on integrated cognitive development, and children are encouraged to invent, explore, play, question, observe, and experiment.
- Behavioral Model: This is the most controlled of the approaches and emphasizes the acquisition of defined, measurable skills. The skills are broken into their component parts (task analysis) and taught sequentially. As each skill is mastered, the next is introduced. Desired behavior is rewarded, and continuous data collection guides the child's program planning.
- Direct Instruction: A highly defined and specific method that includes essential behavioral elements, this approach was developed for use with children of low-income families, at risk for educational failure. It has six distinguishing elements: a movement from simplified to complex contexts, practice, prompting and then fading of cues, teacher feedback, a transition from overt to covert problem-solving strategies, and a shift from teacher to learner as a source of information (Carnine, 1979).
- Combinations: New curricula are being developed that combine cognitive developmental theories with measurable behavioral objectives and useful techniques from both approaches.

ALL MODELS HAVE YIELDED SIGNIFICANT GAINS

All approaches have yielded statistically significant improvements in children's tested achievement. Some are more appropriate for certain groups than others. (The behavior modification model has been particularly successful with severely handicapped populations, for example.) The greatest and most lasting achievements come from programs that last two to four years and are followed by appropriate special programming in elementary schools.

Relations with Public Schools

Where preschool programs are located in public school buildings, it is important that:

SUCCESSFUL PROGRAMS IN THE PUBLIC SCHOOLS

1. Preschool and regular school staff members have an opportunity to meet with each other before the school year begins.
2. Regular class teachers understand the preschool program and the rationale behind it

3. The building principal plays a committed leadership role and helps create channels for communication and input between the two systems.

REFERENCES

Carnine, D. (1979). Direct instruction: A successful system for educationally high-risk children. *Journal of Curriculum Studies, 11*(1), 29–45.

Lerner, J., Mardell-Czudnowski, C., and Goldenberg, D. (1981). *Special education for the early childhood years*. Englewood Cliffs, NJ: Prentice-Hall.

Linder, T.W. (1983). *Early childhood special education*. Baltimore: Paul H. Brookes Publishing Company.

President's Committee on Mental Retardation (1976). *Mental retardation: The known and the unknown*. Washington, D.C.: U.S. Government Printing Office.

Chapter 8

Secondary School Considerations

SUMMARY

Statement of the Problem

Special education programming at the secondary level must take into account a variety of factors, including diploma/graduation requirements, the coordination of class schedules, social and behavioral issues associated with adolescence, the cumulative effects of past schooling, vocational training, and preparation for adult life. Yet the great majority of special education models are elementary oriented; few regular secondary teachers have adequate preparation in special education issues; and many handicapped secondary students (especially the mildly handicapped) are inadequately served.

Legal Issues

In addition to P.L. 94-142 and Section 504 of P.L. 93-112, the main federal law affecting secondary education of the handicapped is the Carl D. Perkins Vocational Education Act of 1984 (P.L. 98-523). This law amends earlier vocational education funding acts with two outstanding goals: (1) to improve, expand, and modernize vocational education programs and (2) to make them more accessible, particularly to groups inadequately served in the past. The handicapped are one of six groups identified for special funding (10 percent of the basic state grant), and the Perkins Act requires that (1) handicapped students and their parents receive information about vocational education opportunities no later than the beginning of the ninth grade, and (2) all handicapped students in vocational education programs receive assessment, special services, counseling, and transition assistance.

Rationale

Appropriate educational programming greatly increases handicapped individuals' chances for success in finding and maintaining employment and leading independent adult lives. This benefits not only the individuals themselves but also society as a whole. It reduces the cost of social programs and relieves the fear and anxiety experienced by family members who are concerned about these students' future.

Approaches

School principals should:

- model acceptance and understanding of the students, acknowledge individual differences, and encourage flexibility in accommodating school schedules and programs to meet individual needs
- promote cooperation and regular communication among regular, special, and vocational educators, and see that teachers are provided with needed training and support
- guarantee that handicapped students have equal access to vocational training programs
- assign a faculty adviser to each student, one individual with responsibility for overall coordination and advocacy for that student; but also give all the student's teachers an opportunity to participate in program planning
- make use of community resources for transition services and vocational education.

The overall goal of secondary special education is maximizing students' potential for independent, productive, and satisfying life in the adult community. This should be reflected in the IEPs, which in turn should take precedence over standard graduation requirements as the guideline for programming. With many students, the focus of the curriculum in high school will shift from academics to practical skills including self-help and social skills and vocational education. Educators should plan ahead to prepare students with necessary prerequisite skills for each course and for transition from school to the postschool environment.

COPING WITH SECONDARY SCHOOL

Adolescence can be a rough time for almost everyone. The complex and mysterious process of transition from childhood dependence to adulthood is full of familiar perils, from acne to awkwardness, social and family pressures, and feelings that sometimes seem to race out of control. As every adult who works with adolescents knows, it is a time of testing authority (often of rebelliousness) as well as of optimism, as emerging identities are explored and plans for the future begin to be made.

PROBLEMS COMPOUNDED FOR HANDICAPPED

Young people with handicaps experience the same physical changes, the same quest for independence, the same feelings of hope and doubt, joy and disappointment that other adolescents must confront. But in addition to the challenges faced by all young people as they mature, these youths have the added challenge of learning to manage a handicap. It can make the difficult transitions of adolescence even more stressful when a young person is faced with the problems of:

- coping with a frustrating learning difficulty at a time when there is such a desire to feel competent and in control
- looking visibly different from one's peers when there is so much emphasis on achieving a common style, on "fitting in"
- managing behavior problems in a period of life when peers and personal stresses often encourage acting out.

If the teen years pose special challenges for handicapped young people, they also bring special problems for educators. The size, diversity, and complexity of the secondary curriculum make individualized instruction difficult to plan and carry out. The stress on Carnegie Units and graduation also contributes to the relative inflexibility of secondary, as opposed to elementary, programming. A secondary teacher who sees 130 to 150 students a day cannot be expected to assume the same level of responsibility for a pupil's educational program as can the elementary school teacher who has the same 25 to 30 students in class throughout the school day. Moreover, secondary teachers' training and orientation is generally more subject-centered than student-centered

The teachers in junior and senior high schools are not likely to have received the preservice coursework necessary to prepare them for the task of accommodating exceptional learners in the secondary classroom. Indeed, few teacher training institutions in the country offer programs of study in secondary special education and most states lack special certification for this population. The entire field of secondary special education is relatively undeveloped. Most special education instruction is still based on an elementary model, although clearly the approaches, strategies, and materials are often inappropriate for secondary students and unsuited to the secondary school environment.

Adequate educational programs for mildly handicapped adolescents are often unavailable. Researchers Miller, Sabatino, and Larsen (1980) found that there were

ADEQUATE PROGRAMMING LACKING

appropriate programs for only 54.8 percent of the learning disabled adolescents who needed them and only 44.1 percent of behaviorally disordered youths. They concluded that these two groups, together with mildly mentally retarded youths, make up "perhaps the most populous category of underserved—frequently unserved—handicapped" (p. 345).

The consequence of inappropriate services for many of these students is the repeated experience of humiliating and frustrating failure in school. This, in turn, is associated with both high dropout rates (D'Alonzo, 1983; Douglas, 1969; Smith & Payne, 1980) and delinquency (Berman, 1975; Murray, 1976). Virtually all mildly handicapped secondary students have behavior problems associated with their learning difficulties, and past school experiences are one reason for this.

D'Alonzo suggests that secondary level special education students belong to three groups: (1) those who have never received treatment, (2) those who have received it for a long time, and (3) those who have been inappropriately categorized or served. This notion challenges two myths, held by some, about special education for older students: (1) that all handicaps will have been identified by the time a pupil reaches secondary school, and (2) that youths who received special services in elementary schools will, by their teenage years, have ceased to need them.

SOME HANDICAPS NOT IDENTIFIED UNTIL ADOLESCENCE

In fact, some disabilities may not be serious enough to warrant special programming at a younger age (certain behavior disorders or health impairments, for example) but would identify a student for special education in secondary school. And while certain learning problems, such as some speech disorders, may be solved effectively through temporary interventions at an early age, many more will require lifetime accommodations. To be certain, the task of secondary special education is not only to provide the services that students need to profit from their high school education but also to look toward the future, to help the students build bridges between their school experience and their later life.

Legal Issues

All the legal protections of P.L. 94-142 for nondiscriminatory evaluation, individualized programming, least restrictive placement, due process, and so on apply to students in secondary level educational programs, whether academic or vocational. For example, handicapped youths should be placed into regular vocational programs (with appropriate support for student and teacher) when that is the least restrictive environment to meet the goals of the IEP. Any special vocational programming must be provided at no cost to the students or their families.

SERVICES FOR 18- TO 21-YEAR-OLDS

P.L. 94-142 requires states to provide special education and related services through the end of the school year in which these students turn 21, if they have not already graduated from high school. This gives students who need them extended opportunities for vocational training or other courses for which they may not previously have had the necessary prerequisites or maturity. It gives schools the opportunity to develop special programs in vocational training, work experience, and cooperative placements with business and industry. It is not intended as a time to recycle students through courses they have already completed.

Services for 18-to-21-year-olds need not be provided to all handicapped students but to those whose IEP calls for it. (Such an IEP would contain goals related to readiness for jobs, postsecondary programs, or related objectives.) Students who complete standard graduation requirements are not eligible for continued services. However, it is illegal for schools to award a diploma inappropriately or to force graduation as a means of getting a student out of the system. On the other hand, in consideration of social needs and self-esteem, students might be permitted to attend graduation ceremonies with their peers without actually earning or receiving a diploma until they have completed further years of study (Washington State Superintendent of Public Instruction, 1985).

The Perkins Act

FUNDING FOR VOCATIONAL PROGRAMS

The Carl D. Perkins Act of 1984, P.L. 98-523, is an appropriations law with emphasis on vocational needs. It awards program funds to states (and the states, in turn, distribute the monies to school districts and other institutions) that meet a series of specified requirements. In this respect, it is similar to P.L. 94-142. If states and local school districts are interested in receiving the financial assistance provided by the acts, they must comply with the requirements. The Perkins Act, however, provides a much smaller amount of money to public schools and demands much less in the way of detailed regulations and supporting paperwork.

The Perkins Act "has as its stated purpose the need to assure equal access to quality vocational programs and the need to provide the necessary special services to enhance the participation of special needs youth and adults" (Cobb & Mikulin, 1985, p. 1). The six special needs groups identified by the act are:

1. handicapped individuals
2. disadvantaged individuals
3. adults who are in need of training and retraining
4. individuals who are single parents or homemakers
5. individuals who participate in programs designed to eliminate sex bias and stereotyping in vocational education
6. criminal offenders who are serving in a correctional institute.

Regarding the handicapped, the law states:

> 1. equal access will be provided to handicapped and disadvantaged individuals in recruitment, enrollment, and placement activities.
> 2. equal access will be provided to handicapped and disadvantaged individuals to the full range of vocational programs available to nonhandicapped and nondisadvantaged individuals, including occupationally specific courses of study, cooperative education, and apprenticeship programs; and
> 3. (A) vocational education programs and activities for handicapped individuals will be provided in the least restrictive environment in

> accordance with . . . the Education for All Handicapped Children Act and will, whenever appropriate, be included as a component of the individualized education plan . . .
> (B) vocational education planning for handicapped individuals will be coordinated between appropriate representatives of vocational education and special education.
>
> Each local education agency shall . . . provide information to handicapped and disadvantaged students and parents of such students concerning the opportunities available in vocational education at least one year before students enter the grade level in which vocational education programs are first generally available in the state, but in no event later than the beginning of the ninth grade, together with the requirements for eligibility for enrollment in such vocational education programs (Sec. 204b).

SERVICES FOR THE HANDICAPPED

The law then specifies the following services for handicapped and disadvantaged students served under the act:

> 1. assessment of the interests, abilities, and special needs of such students with respect to completing successfully the vocational education program;
> 2. special services, including adaptation of curriculum, instruction, equipment, and facilities designed to meet the needs described . . .
> 3. guidance, counseling, and career development activities conducted by professionally trained counselors who are associated with the provision of such special services; and
> 4. counseling services designed to facilitate the transition from school to postschool employment and career opportunities (Sec. 204c).

In essence, these requirements are no more than should be carried out in any secondary school under P.L. 94-142, but they are notable in their explicit reminder that appropriate vocational programming for special needs students should include:

ELEMENTS OF VOCATIONAL SPECIAL NEEDS PROGRAMMING

- recruitment efforts
- access to all types of programs and least restrictive placement within them
- vocational goals in the IEP
- coordination between special and vocational educators
- vocational assessment
- career counseling
- transition services.

The Perkins Act sets aside 10 percent of its Title II funds for services to handicapped students in vocational education programs. These monies can be used by schools to cover half the costs of any special services required to educate exceptional students in a regular vocational program. In the case of special, self-contained vocational programming, Perkins funds can cover the excess costs involved (the difference between the cost of a regular and a special course) if the school can document those expenses. For example, Perkins could fund an aide to help a regular vocational instructor and thus allow handicapped students to be mainstreamed vocationally.

The Perkins Act reflects a new federal emphasis on increased school/community collaboration and interagency planning. It directly mentions, and is designed to coincide with, both P.L. 94-142 and P.L. 97-300, and the Job Training Partnership Act (JTPA) (1982).

THE ROLE OF THE JTPA

The JTPA is a federal law intended to bring about the identification, training, and job placement of youth and adults from chronically unemployed groups. It is administered by local government units in partnership with Private Industry Councils (PICs). The PIC is composed of representatives of private business (at least 51 percent), community organizations, and public agencies, including one representative of the public education system.

The principal JTPA program for high school age youth provides minimum wage salaries for a 250-hour job placement in the public sector and up to 200 additional hours of training in preemployment preparation, job seeking, and job market skills.

ELIGIBILITY FOR JTPA SERVICES

The JTPA is oriented primarily toward the economically disadvantaged, but most states have opened services to all handicapped youth by computing their incomes as though they were a family of one. The states differ, however, in defining handicapped eligibility. In some states, JTPA services are made available to any student with an IEP, and in others only to those with relatively severe handicaps. To get more information on programs in their area, principals can contact the educational representative to the PIC or the designated local youth employment service (frequently located in the state employment security office).

APPROACHES TO RESOLVING PROBLEMS

Although mainstreaming may be more difficult to implement at the secondary level, it is still important that handicapped adolescents and teenagers be educated as much as possible in the company of their nonhandicapped peers. For severely handicapped students, this may be limited to shared lunchtimes, assembly programs, and other nonacademic activities.

OPTIONS FOR INTEGRATING THE HANDICAPPED

Other options include: (1) a combination of self-contained and integrated classes, with integration in electives such as art, music, and physical education; (2) part-time placement in regular vocational or academic programs, with time scheduled in the resource room; and (3) regular class placement with either consultative assistance to the teacher or direct services, in class, to the student. (This last is a common model in vocational programs.) Such integration is essential for several reasons:

- Continued association with nonhandicapped peers provides needed role models and socialization experiences and helps prepare students to function in the world as adults.

- Placement in segregated settings, after successful integration experiences in elementary schools, would be traumatic and harmful to students' self-esteem.
- Education in the most normal possible environment is required by law.

Importance of the IEP

This is not to say that mildly handicapped teenagers should be "dumped" into regular classrooms without any special assistance for the students or their teachers. It does not mean they should be directed automatically through a standard curriculum that is not attentive to their special needs. As at every level, a handicapped student's placement must be determined individually, based on thorough and appropriate evaluations and the IEP. Generally speaking, the secondary program of special needs students will fall into one of four categories:

TYPES OF SECONDARY PROGRAMS

1. regular college preparatory programs, with support for student and teachers, such as consultation, deaf interpreter services, physical therapy, resource room tutoring, and so on
2. regular vocational programs that meet standard graduation requirements, with appropriate support services
3. special vocational/community living preparation programs that emphasize practical skills, with part-time placement in regular classes as appropriate
4. special programs for the more severely handicapped.

The importance of the IEP cannot be overemphasized. As is true at the elementary level, secondary students who qualify for special education and related services represent a full range of intelligence and abilities. Some will be able to complete a college preparatory curriculum and go on to postsecondary, even graduate study. For others, the focus of secondary programming will be on mastery of basic social, self-help, and vocational skills. It is as harmful to deprive an able student of the opportunity to achieve as it is to force another student through a standard high school curriculum at the expense of needed training in survival skills. Students who, with appropriate programming, can complete mandated Carnegie Units along with their peers should be assisted to do so.

However, it should be acknowledged that this will not be appropriate for all youths. Some simply will need too much of their limited class time to master practical skills. For a secondary student of low mental abilities, it may be much more critical to learn how to make change for a dollar than to struggle through algebra. It may be essential to learn how to vote, but not possible—within the time remaining after classes in vocational and daily living skills—to study more abstract social studies concepts such as the Constitution and the structure of U.S. democracy. Ideally, the school will be flexible enough to acknowledge this and to arrange, in some cases, for a student to attend a class such as Civics only when relevant lessons are being taught.

PROGRAMMING SHOULD BE BASED ON IEP

For these students, the overriding goal of secondary education is to maximize their potential for independent adult functioning and not necessarily to earn a diploma, although this should be attempted if possible. The focus should be on applied skills, in academic coursework and other areas. For all secondary special needs students, the IEP, and not standard graduation requirements, must be the ultimate guide to educational programming.

The Question of Diplomas

This approach does, of course, raise some difficult questions. Should a student who completes the IEP but not the required Carnegie Units be included in graduation ceremonies with classmates? Should a diploma be awarded? Should it be the same as that earned by other students or a special certificate instead? How does the nondiscriminatory requirement of Section 504 of the Vocational Rehabilitation Act fit in? (See Chapter 1 on Basic Mainstreaming.) What about the current push for competency tests for graduating seniors and for so-called "excellence in education"?

EXCELLENCE VS. PRACTICALITY

Advocates of the latter would add more academic courses to those required for graduation, making it difficult for even regular vocational students to complete both diploma requirements and important vocational training. The demand for pregraduation competency testing also would seem to jeopardize some handicapped students' ability to earn regular diplomas. The problem is controversial. On one side is the popular complaint that a high school diploma does not mean anything any more. If students cannot meet reasonable levels of competency in reading, other basic skills, and general knowledge, this argument goes, they should not receive a standard diploma; a certificate of attendance, perhaps, or some other alternative, but that is all. On the other side is the argument that exceptional students not be penalized or stigmatized by receiving an alternative certificate; some suggest that this would, in fact, be an illegal denial of equal benefits under the law.

The issues are complex, and solutions vary from state to state. It is important for school administrators to understand the nature of the dispute and the range of alternatives in place around the country. Some states do recommend awarding a standard diploma for completion of the IEP; others issue certificates of attendance instead. Some states administer competency tests but have special guidelines for handicapped groups; others simply stress the importance of reviewing a student's transcripts to determine what the diploma really means. In some cases, the policies apply statewide. Other states allow district discretion. Federal law does not explicitly address exit policy for high schools, although several statutes seem to apply. Legally, the issue of graduation and diplomas for handicapped students still is in the process of interpretation.

DIPLOMA ALTERNATIVES

Other IEP Issues

COORDINATION OF TEACHERS

In addition to graduation requirements, other factors not present at the elementary level affect the process of assessment, IEP development, and placement of secondary students. One is coordination of the many teachers involved. It usually is not feasible for all of a student's teachers to be present at IEP and placement meetings, but all should have a chance to have input into the process.

At a minimum, each teacher should contribute essential information about courses taught, including initial competencies required and expectations of students, so that a reasonable match between students and classes can be made. Students should not be placed in classes unless they have the skills and special assistance (for both student and teacher) necessary for reasonable success. All the student's teachers should be made aware of the IEP content, of course.

PLANNING FOR THE FUTURE

Another important consideration at the secondary level is the student's future. For many individuals with special needs, high school is the last opportunity for formal education before entering the adult world. The writers of an adolescent's IEP must ask themselves, "When that transition comes, will the student be ready for it? What skills must this student master before the end of schooling in order to achieve a maximum level of independent adult functioning? Which of these skills—or their prerequisites—should be taught this year to enable the student to meet those long-term goals?" Elementary educators enter the IEP conference with a focus on basic skills and the current school year. At the secondary level, the focus should be more on applied skills and long-term planning.

Brolin (1973) identifies the following 22 competencies as those that must be mastered for independent functioning in work and community life. They are a helpful guide to formulating many secondary students' IEPs and include:

COMPETENCIES FOR INDEPENDENT LIVING

1. managing family finances
2. selecting, managing, and maintaining a home
3. caring for personal needs
4. raising children, family living
5. buying and preparing food
6. buying and caring for clothing
7. engaging in civic activities
8. utilizing recreation and leisure
9. getting around the community (mobility)
10. achieving self-awareness
11. acquiring self-confidence
12. achieving socially responsible behavior
13. maintaining good interpersonal skills
14. achieving independence
15. achieving problem-solving skills
16. communicating adequately with others
17. knowing and exploring occupational possibilities
18. selecting and planning occupational choices
19. exhibiting appropriate work habits and behaviors
20. exhibiting sufficient physical-manual skills
21. obtaining a specific occupational skill
22. seeking, securing, and maintaining employment (Brolin & Kokaska, 1979, p. 108)

In some parts of the country, schools are writing "exit IEPs" for departing students—a plan for postschool services. The preparation of the exit IEP is a process that involves both school staff and service providers who know what resources are available. Although not required by law, it is highly recommended as an aid to successful transition to community life.

Transition

CROSSING THE BRIDGE BETWEEN SCHOOL AND WORK

Much attention has been paid to this transition in recent years. The federal Office of Special Education and Rehabilitation Services explains the term as follows:

> Transition is a period that includes high school, the point of graduation, additional postsecondary education or adult services, and the initial years of employment. Transition is a bridge between the security and structure offered by the school and the opportunities and risks of adult life. Any bridge requires both a solid span and a secure foundation at either end. The transition from school to work and adult life requires sound preparation in the secondary school, adequate support at the point of school leaving, and secure opportunities and services, if needed, in adult situations.
>
> Since the services and experiences that lead to employment vary widely across individuals and communities, the traditional view of transition as a special linking service between school and adult opportunities is insufficient. The present definition emphasizes the shared responsibility of all involved parties for transition success, and extends beyond traditional notions of service coordination to address the quality and appropriateness of each service area (Will, 1984, p. 2).

CAREER/VOCATIONAL EDUCATION IN THE IEP

STEPS IN THE CAREER EDUCATION PROCESS

An essential component of independent living is productive work. The Council for Exceptional Children (CEC) has stressed that "education for exceptional children must include the opportunity for every student to attain his/her highest level of career potential through career education experiences" (p. 5). Career/vocational objectives should be part of every secondary student's IEP. In fact, career education is a process that should be started in elementary school and included in all students' schooling, whether or not they qualify for special services.

The steps in this process include career awareness, orientation, selection, training and placement. Areas of personal/social, daily living skills, and occupational guidance and preparation, along with academics, should be covered at each step. (These are the areas covered in the previous list of 22 competencies.)

Secondary vocational education is more limited and specific. It focuses on specific preparation for gainful employment and is appropriate for some, but not all, high school students with handicaps.

Appropriate career/vocational goals, like all goals written into the IEP, should be based on accurate and appropriate assessments. Vocational assessments should address students' academic, perceptual, and social skills. They should include assessments of interests, attitudes, aptitudes, and achievement levels in areas related to work. They may include paper-and-pencil tests, apparatus tests, situational assessments, and job tryouts. (Smaller districts that cannot afford work sample tests should find they can work out an adequate combination of other types of assessments.)

VOCATIONAL ASSESSMENT

Three levels of vocational assessment may be carried out in the schools:

1. screening, including a limited number of tests, often general ones
2. partial vocational assessments, including only tests selected to answer specific questions
3. comprehensive vocational assessments, including a full range of tests of interests, aptitudes, and abilities.

Before completing a vocational assessment, an individual vocational evaluation plan should be developed that lists the questions to be answered by the assessment, gives background information on the student, and identifies the tests and situations to be used. This is essential; without such efforts to personalize the vocational evaluation, it will be too expensive.

At any level, the assessment process will yield a report that must be interpreted and used by the student's teachers. The information, therefore, must be clearly presented and easily understood. It is desirable for the vocational evaluator who prepares the report to sit in on the ensuing IEP meeting.

WRITING THE PROGRAM

When writing the program plan for a student in vocational education, the IEP team should (1) analyze both the student's abilities and the entry level requirements of the job or vocational course, (2) ascertain whether they are reasonably matched, and (3) determine the following:

- the appropriate setting for instruction
- support services needed
- staff person(s) responsible

A sample assessment form is presented in Exhibit 8–1. Similar forms should be completed for both the student and the course or job. On the student form, the evaluator should place a check in the first column for all skill/knowledge levels within the normal range and use the second column to describe specific achievement levels not within this range. On the course/job form, all factors that are important to the course of job (first column) should be checked, with the second column used to list the entry level skill required.

For special needs students in vocational education, there are four basic types of placement:

TYPES OF VOCATIONAL PLACEMENT

1. regular vocational program with minor adjustments and/or consultative assistance to the teacher

Exhibit 8–1 Sample Vocational Assessment Form

Perceptual skills	Normal range	Specific skill/ knowledge level
Physical Skills		
Mobility		
Strength		
Stamina		
Balance		
Use of lower limbs		
Use of upper limbs		
Manual dexterity		
Finger dexterity		
Eye-hand coordination		
Mathematical Skills		
Count		
Tell time		
Measure		
Add/subtract		
Multiply/divide		
Use common fractions		
Make change		
Estimate:		
size		
distance		
weight		
Verbal/Language Skills		
Communicate orally		
Communicate in writing		
Read		
Deal with technical vocabulary		

Exhibit 8–1 continued

Perceptual Skills	Normal range	Specific skill/ knowledge level
Spell accurately		
Maintain records		
Complete forms		
Use telephone		
Thinking Skills		
Remember:		
lists		
names		
locations		
sequences		
Follow instructions		
Plan		
Organize work		
Make decisions		
Solve problems		
Sustain concentration		
Maintain multiple operations simultaneously		
Change duties frequently		
React appropriately to:		
emergencies		
unusual situations		
Work independently		
Auditory Acuity		
use sound cues		
distinguish abnormal from normal sounds		
estimate distance		

Exhibit 8–1 continued

Perceptual Skills	Normal range	Specific skill/ knowledge level
Visual Acuity		
use color cues		
shade differences		
form perception		
space		
distance		
motion		
Touch		
determine size		
shape		
temperature		
texture		
moisture content		
motion		
Smell		
differentiate odors		
Taste		
Social Skills		
Accepts criticism		
Can meet public		
Appropriate behavior:		
language		
manner		
grooming		

Exhibit 8–1 continued

Perceptual Skills	Normal range	Specific skill/ knowledge level
Team cooperation		
Seeks/accepts help when needed		
Attentive to:		
directions		
details		
Pride in work		
Prompt		
Dependable		
Self-starting		
Independent follow-through		

Source: Adapted from *Vocational Education Curriculum Guide* (unpublished manuscript, 1985) by G.R. Weisenstein. Based on *Project VEIT Handbook* (unpublished manuscript) by M. Regan, 1979.

2. regular vocational program with more substantial direct assistance to the student
3. remediation first, then vocational program placement
4. specially designed vocational programs.

Although vocational educators' participation in the IEP meetings is not required, it can be beneficial. The instructors can contribute such important information as: expected course entry skills, physical and intellectual requirements of course activities, materials and equipment used and possible adaptations, supplemental materials and instruction required for attainment of vocational objectives, prerequisite courses, job opportunities and postsecondary training opportunities in the vocational area, work study and on-the-job training available, and courses available within each vocational area.

In turn, IEP participation can provide nonspecial education staff with information about:

- the student's learning style and achievement levels (in academic, personal/social, and daily living skills)
- special teaching techniques
- classroom accommodations
- assistance available from other staff members
- the most effective reinforcers for the student
- special education vocational options
- a system for monitoring student progress.

VOCATIONAL EDUCATORS AND IEP DEVELOPMENT

THE IMPORTANCE OF VOCATIONAL PREPARATION

Although state and federal laws prohibit job discrimination, the employment statistics for the nation's handicapped citizens are poor. The rate of unemployment among adults reporting a disability in the early 1980s was 50 percent to 80 percent, according to the U.S. Commission on Civil Rights and the U.S. Bureau of the Census. The social costs of this unemployment are high. "Approximately 8 percent of the Gross National Product is spent each year on disability programs, with most of this amount going to programs that support dependence" (Will, 1984, p. 1).

SOCIAL COST OF INADEQUATE TRAINING

Certainly there are many reasons for this situation, but it must be acknowledged that one of them is inadequate training. The record of public schools in vocational preparation of handicapped students definitely can be improved. In one state where a real effort is being made, for example, only 2.6 percent of the students in secondary and postsecondary vocational programs were handicapped (Vertrees & Quattrociocchi, 1984). In another state survey, both parents and teachers of secondary handicapped students identified vocational education as the area most in need of improvement in the school program. Cobb (1983), Hippolitus (1980), Miller, Sabatino, and Larsen (1980) are among many other researchers who have pointed to inadequacies in vocational education of the handicapped nationwide.

SUCCESS RATE OF VOCATIONAL EDUCATION

These findings are unfortunate because the success rate of vocational education programs is good. They have been shown to be related to higher rates of employment, higher annual incomes, lower dropout rates, and increased self-confidence for students (Vertrees & Quattrociocchi). For many mildly handicapped high school students, vocational education programs also appear to constitute the best and "least restrictive" educational placement. They can also be of great benefit to special needs students in developing socialization skills, positive self-concept, daily living experiences, and independence, as well as employability.

THE PRINCIPAL'S ROLE

There are several things that building principals can do to improve the enrollment of special education students in vocational programs. Vocational education instructors, like other regular education teachers, often lack training and experience in working with handicapped students and may have specific concerns about safety, behavior management, extra time required, ultimate employability of the student, and so on. Such concerns are understandable and deserve a serious hearing and response. As steps to winning instructors' support for mainstreaming vocational education courses, principals and program directors should:

STEPS TO TAKE

1. assign students appropriately, based on an honest and reasonable assessment of their abilities and of the requirements of the course (with reasonable adaptations and assistance)
2. provide adequate support to the instructor(s)
3. involve the vocational educator(s) in program planning and establish open lines of communication with special education staff
4. inform instructors about requirements of the law
5. counter stereotypes/misconceptions with the reality of disabled employees' record of job success
6. take advantage of community resources available (a sample list is presented as Exhibit 8–2 at the end of this chapter)
7. encourage flexibility in scheduling, to accommodate such possibilities as eight-hour job placements one or two days a week, attending classes for some units of study and not others, etc.
8. acquaint instructor with the handicapping condition and what can be expected from the student.

There also are many strategies for facilitating handicapped students' successful integration into vocational classes. A tryout period, in which the student is exposed to the class one semester before placement, is helpful. So is an orientation that is sensitive to the student's needs. (For example, a blind student should be introduced to the location of all desks, equipment, etc., and should have an opportunity to get accustomed to the room when no other students are present. A mentally handicapped student may simply need extra orientation to equipment use and safety strategies.) Before the course starts, the vocational instructor should try to meet the student and learn about the handicapping condition. In class, it is important that the instructor:

WHAT VOCATIONAL INSTRUCTORS CAN DO

- accept the student as an individual
- avoid overprotection
- encourage independence
- adapt the task and environment as necessary
- provide ample time for completion
- work ahead to avoid problems (e.g., introduce vocabulary before the lesson)
- use resource personnel within and outside the school
- be sensitive to the student's endurance/attention span

- provide simple, concise instructions
- change a strategy that does not work and try another

Other adaptations are discussed in Chapter 1 on Basic Mainstreaming.

SERVICES FOR STUDENTS 18 TO 21 YEARS OLD

VOCATIONAL OPPORTUNITIES

P.L. 94-142 gives states the option of providing educational services to handicapped students from age 18 through the end of the school year that they turn 21, if they have not already graduated from high school. This allows extended opportunities for vocational training or other programs for which they may not previously have had the necessary prerequisites or maturity. School districts can take advantage of this opportunity by developing special programs in vocational training, work experience, and cooperative work placements with business and industry. This should not be viewed as a time to recycle students through the same curriculum they have already completed. Planning for these years, as for others, should be appropriate and individualized.

Nonacademic Considerations

Secondary students have a variety of educational needs, not all of which are strictly vocational or academic. School personnel also should be sensitive to students' social needs, an area that has implications for classroom management as well as student growth.

PEERS: THEIR ROLE AND PRESSURES

All adolescents are affected by a strong student culture and a need to experience acceptance by their peers. Handicapped students, particularly those of low mental functioning, may be especially vulnerable to peer pressures that result in negative or socially unacceptable behaviors. When making placement decisions, it is important that school personnel safeguard against negative influences by assigning these students to classes where they will encounter positive, not detrimental, role models. The conscious development of social skills and self-esteem will contribute to positive in-school behaviors and preparation for adult life. Many excellent social/interpersonal curricula for exceptional students are now available.

EXTRA-CURRICULAR ACTIVITIES

Another means of promoting social development is through students' participation in extracurricular activities. Frequently, this does not occur without conscious effort by the school staff, from the principal on down. Exceptional students may be excluded formally or informally from clubs, organizations, and athletics through stereotyped negative attitudes, lack of recruitment efforts, lack of needed support, the pupils' low social status, and lack of a role to play that matches their abilities and needs. The result is to deprive these students of important opportunities to develop self-confidence, mix socially with their peers, and gain a sense of ownership and belonging to the school. (This sense of belonging, in turn, can be instrumental in improving students' attitudes toward school and in reducing the likelihood of their dropping out.)

Strategies for increasing exceptional students' participation in extracurricular activities include:

- actively recruiting the students (this can be done by teachers, special educators, club advisers, or other students)
- identifying or designing roles in the club/activity that the students can fulfill
- considering setting up a buddy system with a respected peer who is in that club or activity
- providing positive role models (faculty advisers should demonstrate acceptance of the exceptional students and respect for their contributions).

Competitive Athletics

Special problems arise in varsity athletics. Some special needs students have the potential to become outstanding athletes but are prevented from participation in varsity sports for a number of reasons:

PROBLEMS AND SOLUTIONS

- Some states have health and safety requirements that legally prevent such participation. This should be checked out in every case.
- The attitude that winning is the only goal often prohibits consideration of athletes with special needs. Some coaches and some schools are simply more open to the importance of other values: teaching cooperation and teamwork, developing self-confidence, rewarding excellence of effort, and so on.
- The lack of time can pose problems. Although clearly talented, exceptional students may require much more individual coaching and supervised practice to achieve their athletic potential.

Some possible strategies and solutions for the school include:

- encouraging students to try out and coaches to be openminded
- setting up extra coaching assistance provided by aides, adult volunteers, or other students
- making minor adaptations as needed; for example, a blind student could compete in varsity wrestling if competitors are required to be in physical contact at the beginning of the match.

OTHER SPORTS OPPORTUNITIES

Teachers should be aware that there are alternative sports opportunities for students with handicaps outside the school. Those with mental disabilities can participate in Special Olympics, which is relatively noncompetitive and emphasizes self-concept. For those with physical and sensory handicaps, other organizations provide highly competitive athletics such as wheelchair sports, athletics for the blind, and so on.

Students may be encouraged to participate in community leagues and recreational teams. However, these alternatives alone should not be considered sufficient for students who, with a little assistance, really are capable of varsity sports.

GENERAL CONSIDERATIONS

In addition to these specific topics, successful integration of exceptional students at the secondary school level can be enhanced in several general ways. One is to assign responsibility for each mainstreamed student to one staff member, much as college students each have a single faculty adviser. Professionals such as therapists, consultants, special educators, and willing regular class teachers can be assigned a limited number of special needs students for whom they will serve as advocates, advisers, and coordinators of overall educational plans.

ADVISERS AND COMMUNICATION

No matter how the responsibilities are divided, it is always essential in secondary school settings to keep lines of communication open among the various professionals involved in handicapped students' education. For example, if a resource room model is in use, the resource teacher might send a weekly or biweekly note to each instructor asking how the student is progressing and whether any particular assistance is needed. Such correspondence will help build beneficial relations of trust and cooperation.

Behavior is often a priority issue for teachers of mainstreamed secondary students. Chapter 2 on Discipline offers a variety of concrete suggestions to promote positive behavior within the rather complicated restrictions of special education law.

'PLAN AHEAD' FOR PROGRESS AND SUCCESS

The slogan "plan ahead" is useful for educators of secondary level handicapped students. The schooling time at this point in these adolescents' lives is limited, and attention must be paid to making the best possible use of it. This applies to preparing students adequately both for coursework, so that they get the most out of their formal schooling, and for productive employment and adult life.

Examples of the first might include giving students vocabulary lists or lesson plans at the beginning of the week, notifying the resource room teacher to work on prerequisite skills before they are needed in class, and so on. Taking full advantage of the public secondary schools' opportunities to prepare their handicapped students for adult independence includes keeping abreast of the services available in the community for secondary and postsecondary vocational training and adult assistance. A list of resources available in Washington State is presented in Exhibit 8–2. The names and availability may vary from one community to another, but national organizations usually can be contacted if local ones cannot be found. The array of services available statewide will be similar.

SECONDARY EDUCATORS' CHALLENGE

Secondary educators of the handicapped have greater challenges, in some respects, than those at the elementary level because of the unique problems of their students and their schools and because of the relative newness of the field. But the role they play is no less important to the students and to society as a whole. The continued evolution of secondary special education—and especially of assistance in the process of transition from school to adult life—undoubtedly will be a focus of educational research and development efforts over the next decade.

Exhibit 8–2 State (Washington) and Community Resources

Job Development/Employment Services

Washington State Division of Vocational Rehabilitation (DVR)
Washington State Employment Security: Job Service Center and Job Training Partnership Act (JTPA)
Transient labor centers
JOBS (National Alliance of Business Men)
Private Industry Councils (PICs)

Health and Counseling Services

County public health
County mental health
Community family counseling
Private/religious counseling offices
Planned Parenthood
Department of Social and Health Services (DSHS) local office, Children's Protective Services
Alcohol/drug abuse counseling services
County dental programs
University of Washington Dental School

Financial Support Services

Social Security local office
DSHS local office
Washington State Division of Developmental Disabilities
Society for Crippled Children
Easter Seal organization

Alternate/Auxillary Residential Resources

Group Homes
DSHS: foster care services, day care referrals
Local day care facilities

Support/Advocacy Services

Washington Association for Retarded Citizens
Washington Association for Children with Learning Disabilities
Troubleshooters
Community Action Councils

School District Resources

Building Personnel

1. Teacher
2. Counselor
3. Nurse
4. Principal
5. Teacher Aide
6. Work Study Coordinator

District Personnel

1. Special Ed Director
2. Program Manager
3. Psychologist
4. Specialist
   a. curriculum
   b. vocational/career
5. Communication Disorder Specialists
6. Visually Impaired Specialist
7. Itinerant or Consulting Teachers
8. Occupational or Physical Therapists

Exhibit 8–2 continued

Instructional Resources

School records
Staffings or conferences
Special or supportive services
Direct instructional services

Educational/Training Resources

Community Colleges
State or private colleges/universities
Vocational technical schools
Sheltered workshops, local/regional
Washington State Employment Security office: Job Training Partnership Act (JTPA)
Opportunity Industrialization Centers (OIC)
U.S. Department of Labor
Labor unions, local apprenticeship programs
Association for Retarded Citizens O-J-T
Washington State DVR

REFERENCES

Berman, A. (1975). *Incidence of learning disabilities in juvenile delinquents and nondelinquents: Implications for etiology and treatment.* Ann Arbor, MI: University of Michigan, ERIC Document Reproduction Service No. ED 112 620.

Brolin, D.E. (1973). Career education needs of secondary educable students. *Exceptional Children*, 39, 619–24.

Brolin, D.E., & Kokaska, C.J. (1979). *Career education for handicapped children and adults.* Columbus, OH: Charles E. Merrill, p. 108.

Carl D. Perkins Vocational Education Act of 1984, 20 U.S.C. 1013 et seq. (1984).

Cobb, R.B. (1983).

Cobb, R.B., & Mikulin, E. (1985). *Implementing the special needs provisions of the Carl D. Perkins Vocational Education Act of 1984*. Unpublished manuscript.

Council for Exceptional Children, The (1978). *Update, 10* (1), 5.

D'Alonzo, B.J. (1983). *Educating adolescents with learning and behavior problems.* Rockville, MD: Aspen Publishers, Inc.

Douglas, H.R. (1969). An effective junior high school program for reducing the number of dropouts. *Contemporary Education, 41*(8), 34–37.

Hippolitus, P. (1980). Mainstreaming: The true story. *Disabled USA, 3*(9), 58.

Miller, S.R., Sabatino, D.A., & Larsen, R. (1980). Issues in the professional preparation of secondary school special educators. *Exceptional Children, 45*(5), 344–350.

Murray, C.A. (1976). *The link between learning disabilities and juvenile delinquency.* Washington, DC: American Institute for Research.

Regan, M. (1979). *Project VEIT handbook.* Unpublished manuscript, University of Kansas.

Smith, J.E., & Payne, J.S. (1980). *Teaching exceptional adolescents.* Columbus, OH: Charles E. Merrill.

Vertrees, B.L., & Quattrociocchi, S.M. (1984). *Secondary vocational education: Preparation for a successful life*. Olympia, WA: Washington State Commission for Vocational Education.

Washington State Superintendent of Public Instruction (1985). *Diploma/graduation requirements for students in special education*. Olympia, WA: Author.

Weisenstein, G.R. (1985). *Vocational education curriculum guide*. Unpublished manuscript.

Will, M. (1984). *OSERS programming for the transition of youth with disabilities: Bridges from school to working life*. Washington, DC: Office of Special Education and Rehabilitation Services, pp. 1, 2.

Part II

Handicapping Conditions

Chapter 9

Behavior Disorders

SUMMARY

Federal Definition

"Seriously emotionally disturbed" is defined as follows: (i) The term means a condition exhibiting one or more of the following characteristics over a long period of time and to a marked degree, which adversely affects educational performance: (A) An inability to learn that cannot be explained by intellectual, sensory, or health factors; (B) An inability to build or maintain satisfactory interpersonal relationships with peers and teachers; (C) Inappropriate types of behavior or feelings under normal circumstances; (D) A general pervasive mood of unhappiness or depression, or (E) A tendency to develop physical symptoms or fears associated with personal or school problems.

The term includes children who are schizophrenic or autistic. The term does not include children who are socially maladjusted unless it is determined that they are seriously emotionally disturbed. (Federal terms and definitions for this disability are under study and may be changed.)

Common Characteristics

Emotionally disturbed students may exhibit one or more of the following: physical aggression, disobedience, or destructiveness; perfectionism; expressions of extreme fear, guilt, or self-doubt; strange movements or postures; cognitive disabilities, short attention span, or low tolerance for frustration. They may be impulsive or accident prone, have no time concept, be excessively dependent on the teacher, or unwilling to face reality. Not all of these characteristics will be present in any one child, and some may show up in both "normal" students and in those with other handicapping conditions. For a student to be served under this category, the evaluation team must eliminate other categories and assure that the legal definition is met.

Classroom Adaptations

Classroom Management: With students identified as behavior disordered or seriously emotionally disturbed, the most pressing issues for principals and teachers usually are in the areas of effective discipline and classroom management systems. (These and related topics are discussed in Chapter 2 on Discipline.) Key elements of good classroom management include: establishing a few clear and simple rules, making sure students understand the rules and the consequences if not followed, applying consequences consistently, and rewarding appropriate behavior.

Physical Environment: The teachers may divide the room to prevent too much freedom of movement, set specific work territories for students with problems, and allow no trespassing by other students into this area.

Social Environment: The teachers should observe the class at all times and intercede when other students begin to make remarks about those who have a history of behavior problems. It is also important to establish structures to encourage positive and constructive peer interactions.

Educational Strategies

Educators must:

- Build a positive relationship, with trust and appreciation for the students; emphasize strengths, and provide opportunities for successful learning experiences.
- Provide a high degree of structure, giving students a clear idea of what is expected of them, a sense of completion of one task before moving to another, and consistency in teacher response and class routine.
- Make it easy for students to tolerate frustration and to ask for help, reassuring them that they are not "stupid," that honest effort is important, and that mistakes can be helpful.
- Shorten assignments so students can see an end to work; if necessary, make assignments that are less difficult but provide appropriate practice of new skills.

PROBLEM BEHAVIOR: WHAT CAUSES IT?

HOW MANY CHILDREN HAVE BEHAVIOR DISORDERS?

Every teacher has had experience with "problem behavior"—far more experience than is represented by students actually identified for special education. Cullinan and Epstein (1982) estimate that in any given year, about "one third of all students show behavior problems that concern their teachers to some extent" (p. 212). They also note that research estimates have varied from less than 1 percent to more than 30 percent of the population. (Students served in this category under P.L. 94-142 amounted in 1983-1984 to 0.8 percent of the school age population, according to the U.S. Office of Special Education and Rehabilitative Services [U.S. Department of Education, 1984].)

PROBLEMS OF IDENTIFICATION

For no other category of handicap is there such great discrepancy in estimates, and actual case-by-case determinations, of students who qualify. With the possible exception of learning disabilities (and both of these are defined, in part, by ruling out other handicaps), no legally identified handicapping condition is so little understood or so difficult and subjective to define, let alone remediate. There are a host of theories but no widespread agreement or statistically satisfying proof of either the causes of behavior disorders or their cure, except in a very limited number of instances.

A number of significant factors contribute to this situation. First, the category of behavior disordered, or seriously emotionally disturbed, is by definition (even by federal definition) a conglomerate one, encompassing a variety of unusual, disruptive, and self-destructive types of conduct. Next is the fact that different adults have quite different standards of problem behavior; what one principal or teacher may consider intolerable, another teacher or parent or therapist may find, if not charming, then at least quite normal. In some cases accurate assessment is made more difficult by a child's lack of language and experience or by such behaviors as shyness, negativism, and hyperactivity, and complicated by the fact that children's behavior can change so rapidly. With or without therapy, a period of bizarre or disquieting behavior may disappear as part of the process of growth and development.

DIFFERING IDEAS ON CAUSES AND TREATMENT

Further, even when parents, principals, teachers, and specialists agree that a problem exists, they may have widely different ideas about what that problem is, the forces that caused it, and the best methods for effecting a change. All of these factors contribute to the ambiguity surrounding the identification of students who qualify for special education on behavioral grounds.

The difficulties in identifying these children are matched by the problems in finding effective treatments. Each theoretical framework for describing and analyzing behavior problems has its own associated educational strategies. The problem is that although all of these strategies have proved successful in a number of cases, they all have also been quite ineffective with other individuals, and many children have recovered from behavior problems with no treatment at all. Partisans of the various theories may argue their case passionately and convincingly; and highly skilled and gifted individuals may accomplish apparent miracles with children whom others called hopeless, but in the end, educators all must admit that they are dealing with very sparse and imperfect knowledge of a very complex subject (the human personality), and that despite their best efforts there remains an element of unpredictability.

This chapter offers brief summaries of several approaches to behavioral problems in integrated educational settings. As Meyen (1978) implies in his review of the theoretical history, professionals have much to learn from each approach, and more, perhaps, from the children themselves.

MUCH IS UNKNOWN

TYPES AND DEFINITIONS

Terms

PROBLEMS IN TERMINOLOGY

Just as this category seems hard to define, it also seems difficult to agree on terminology. The two most common general terms are "behavior disordered" and "seriously emotionally disturbed." (As this handbook went to press, there was continuing debate about changing the federal terminology to the former, just as there also was an effort to make autism a separate disability category.) A number of other terms have been used.

There also are several methods of classification and of separating and labeling different subtypes within the general category. The best known of these classification systems is probably the DSM—III (Diagnostic and Statistical Manual of Mental Disorders, third edition, by the American Psychiatric Association), which is widely used in clinical settings. It includes such headings as Conduct Disorders, Anxiety Disorders, Pervasive Developmental Disorders, Eating Disorders, and so on. Other systems focus on dominant characteristics, or syndromes, such as aggression, withdrawal, and immaturity. At both state and national levels, attention is being paid to developing more refined and accurate definitions and clearer eligibility criteria for special education.

Causes

While it seems clear that most behavior disorders are the result of multiple contributing factors, and while it usually is not possible to arrive at an exact analysis of them, many researchers identify two main types of causes: (1) the biological: these may be derived from heredity, brain damage or disorder, diet, or other physiological conditions, and are most evident in severe emotional problems; (2) the type variously identified as psychological, social, or environmental—the "nurture" side of the nature vs. nurture debate: these factors may include family dynamics, peer interaction, previous school experience, role models, cultural background, stress, socioeconomic status, and so on.

NATURE VS. NURTURE

The problems associated with any number of these may contribute to the child's troubled emotional state and may emerge as aggressive, withdrawing, immature, or bizarre behavior. It is important (though certainly not always easy) to remember that a child's inappropriate behaviors usually are "ways of avoiding circumstances associated with pain and failure and of coping with problems from within and without, problems for which they very much need assistance'' (Meyen, 1977, p. 345).

Identification

As the federal definitions suggest, students who qualify for special education do not all have behavior problems. Special education students with behavior problems are those:

CRITERIA FOR SPECIAL EDUCATION

- who exhibit the behaviors over a long period (particularly if they seem to grow worse over time)
- who have problems significantly more marked or serious than the average student
- whose behavior interferes with their own and/or other students' learning.

EDUCATIONAL STRATEGIES

DIFFERENT THEORIES YIELD DIFFERENT APPROACHES

There are a number of strategies for teaching behaviorally disordered children, each one derived from a different theoretical perspective. Specialists often borrow techniques from a variety of approaches, basing their choices on the individual needs and learning styles of the child.

Psychoeducational Strategies

PSYCHOEDUCATIONAL APPROACHES OFTEN THERAPY RELATED

Psychoeducational strategies are those intended to assist students in gaining control over their feelings and behavior through insights into the emotional and environmental forces behind them. The psychoeducational approaches are often related to different clinical strategies, such as psychoanalysis, client-centered therapy, play therapy, and so on. Barbara Coloroso's (1976) responsibility-oriented classroom is one that emphasizes student participation and responsibility. It includes the following components:

EXAMPLE: THE RESPONSIBILITY-ORIENTED CLASSROOM

- an attitude of acceptance, appreciation, and respect for the student, conveying a sense that the student is valued, capable, and important
- the selection of realistic and natural consequences geared to the individual child, both negative and positive
- establishment of a simple, clear structure in which the student understands the classroom rules, the terms of each assignment, and the consequences for completing or not completing it (rules and consequences can be developed as a joint effort of students and teacher; the resulting atmosphere is reasonable, fair, accepting, consistent, and firm)
- the practice of letting students know that it is all right to have feelings and that they can learn appropriate ways to express them; these steps are to (1) label the

feelings, (2) discuss appropriate ways of dealing with them and (3) actively encourage such appropriate expression

- inclusion of other elements such as group meetings (for academic planning, crisis resolution, and problem solving) and contracts (for short- or long-term goals, developed with the interest and participation of the student).

Applied Behavioral Analysis

USES OF REINFORCEMENT IN BEHAVIORAL APPROACH

Unlike the psychoeducational theories, behavioral strategies are based on the principle that behaviors are learned through modeling and reinforcement, not caused by emotional drives or distresses.

The behavioral approach offers very straightforward classroom techniques, involving the use of: (1) positive reinforcement for appropriate behavior (for example, a "token economy" in which students earn points or credits that can be exchanged later for food, privileges, favorite activities, etc.); (2) negative reinforcement (removal of an unpleasant stimulus as a reward); (3) timeout (preventing access to rewards for a period); and (4) various types of punishment, including response cost (withdrawing a specific amount of reward) and aversive consequences (such as additional tasks and assignments).

INDIVIDUALIZING REWARDS AND PUNISHMENTS

It is important that rewards and punishments be individualized. To one student, scolding may be reinforcing since it represents teacher attention; to a shy student, verbal praise may be aversive and embarrassing. (This approach is discussed in Chapter 2 on Discipline.)

The techniques of applied behavioral analysis are quite simple to master and have been used effectively with children with a variety of handicaps.

Medications

Stimulants, antidepressants, and other medications are prescribed by some doctors for a number of emotionally disturbed children, with a range of results. Medication may be necessary for some students whose problems have a physiological base.

When a student is receiving prescription drugs, it is essential that the educators involved with the pupil be aware of:

- the type of medication and its intended and potential effects
- the dosage to be given and, if given in the school, who is responsible
- safe storage in the classroom or office
- school liability
- any changes in treatment and possible relation to the student's behavior and/or academic performance.

Clarizio and McCoy (1983) and other authors caution that medications rarely are solutions in themselves. They should be combined with educational interventions and used only when clearly indicated. (The physician must distinguish between the wishes of anxious parents or teachers and true medical indications.) Most importantly, the prescription of educationally relevant drugs must be viewed as a cooperative effort involving not only the physician but also the principal, teachers, and other specialists responsible for the student's education. In particular, teachers must be informed of any changes in prescription to avoid confusing the effects of medication with the effects of educational interventions.

Some Common Elements

KEY ELEMENTS OF ALL PROGRAMS

Although there are striking differences in theory and strategy of educational programming for the behavior disordered, there are also some common elements. These include:

- creating experiences of success; behavior disordered children have often established a pattern of failure that must be reversed
- creating a consistent, predictable, structured environment; these children need a safe and controlled environment in which to try out new, socially acceptable behaviors; the imposition of clear rules and external controls can free them to learn greater self-control
- providing attitudes of acceptance, supportive firmness, and belief that the child can succeed.

Although behavior disordered students may be the most difficult for teachers to accept into integrated classrooms, there are important benefits for the affected children in being exposed to appropriate behavior models and having opportunities for success in the mainstream.

REFERENCES

American Psychiatric Association (1979). *Diagnostic and statistical manual of mental disorders* (3rd ed.). Washington, DC: Author.

Clarizio, H.F., & McCoy, G.F. (1983). *Behavior disorders in children.* New York: Harper & Row.

Coloroso, B. (1976). Strategies for working with troubled students. In B.R. Gearhart and M.W. Weishan (Eds.), *The handicapped child in the regular classroom.* St. Louis: C.V. Mosby Co.

Cullinan, D., & Epstein, M. (1982). Behavior disorders. In N. Haring (Ed.), *Exceptional children and youth.* Columbus, OH: Charles E. Merrill.

Meyen, E.L. (1979). *Exceptional children and youth: An introduction.* Denver: Love Publishing Co.

Federal Register, August 23, 1977, *42*, 1963.

U.S. Department of Education (1984). *Sixth annual report to Congress on the implementation of Public Law 94-142: The Education for all Handicapped Children Act.* Washington, DC: U.S. Department of Education.

Chapter 10

Hearing Impairments

SUMMARY

Federal Definitions

"Deaf" means a hearing impairment so severe that the child is impaired in processing linguistic information through hearing, with or without amplification, adversely affecting educational performance. "Hard of hearing" means a hearing impairment, whether permanent or fluctuating, that adversely affects a child's educational performance but is not included under the definition of "deaf."

Common Characteristics

In the classroom, students with a hearing impairment may: seem inattentive, especially to auditory activities; fail to respond to questions or make irrelevant comments; frequently ask to have words repeated; interrupt conversation; be unable to tell who is speaking in a group; incorrectly complete tasks for which verbal instructions are given; or become stressed by changes in class routine. Because they cannot clearly hear normal speech, their own speech may be characterized by unusual rhythm, timing, pitch, and articulation or loudness.

A number of behavior problems are associated with hearing impairments. These students may be naive, easily taken advantage of, or lacking self-confidence. They may be impulsive, egocentric, easily frustrated and "act out" frequently; or they may be perceived as snobbish or antisocial (for failure to respond because of poor hearing). Although their academic performance tends to be lower than their peers', hearing impaired children have a range of intelligence and abilities comparable with nonhandicapped students.

An undiagnosed hearing impairment sometimes can be identified through the student's physical behavior. An assessment may be called for with children who: often have earaches or colds, discharge from their ears, hold their heads in a peculiar position when spoken to, become tense during periods requiring listening, or frown or lean forward with intense concentration when addressed.

Classroom Adaptations

Physical Environment: It is important to seat these students away from distracting, external noises and where the teacher and other students can easily be seen as well as heard (usually at the front and window side of the room); allow switching of seats as necessary; avoid lecturing (1) with back to these students (2) in front of a bright light, or (3) while moving from place to place.

Special Materials and Equipment: The teacher should make extensive use of visual aids such as models, slides, captioned films (the resource teacher can help in locating supplementary materials); provide written material, when possible, to supplement oral presentations, including vocabulary lists, film scripts, outlines, study guides, carbon copy of another student's notes; become familiar with hearing aids and medical referral services; make use of specialists, aides, tutors, and interpreters when appropriate.

Presentation of Lessons: The teacher should avoid reliance on lectures and oral assignments; use models/demonstrations as much as possible; speak normally (not exaggerate lip movement); watch to be sure these students have understood; repeat or rephrase as necessary; allow for another type of response if oral communication is difficult; maintain consistent class routines and schedules; advise the students of the weekly plan in advance.

Social/Behavioral Factors: Educators should encourage students to ask questions when they do not understand the lesson, give them equal opportunity to speak and to demonstrate skills and abilities, set the same standards of responsibility as with other students, not accept either shouting or inaudible responses, model and encourage the support and understanding of other students.

THE ROLE OF HEARING—AND IMPAIRMENTS

THE IMPORTANCE OF HEARING

Most children acquire language so naturally and seemingly effortlessly that educators rarely think about the process, or about the consequences if it fails to take place. In the case of hearing impaired children, however, that process, and those consequences, are the overriding concern. Only in its absence do educators become aware of the vast importance of oral communication in a child's social, emotional, and cognitive development. It is through hearing the speech of others, primarily, that children learn to speak themselves; to express and satisfy their needs, desires, and curiosity about the world; to develop abstract thinking and rich relationships with other human beings. As the mother of one severely hearing impaired daughter said,

> . . . they always tend to think if a child has a hearing aid, well, that puts everything right. I don't think they understand about language and the use of language. I don't think people understand how important language is. They don't realize what a tremendous handicap it is in everything she does. (Gregory, 1976, pp. 197-198).

This chapter summarizes some of the variables in hearing impairments and the educational problems they cause, then describes some of the main educational approaches.

TYPES AND DEFINITIONS

DIFFERENT TYPES OF IMPAIRMENTS

"Hearing impairment" is a generic term that includes a variety of conditions, some quite mild and others profound. It represents a complex and multidimensioned continuum of physical handicaps and educational needs. Perhaps the most significant distinction is whether the child is able, with or without amplification, to process spoken language in some degree; this is the distinction made in the federal definitions of deaf and hard of hearing. But there are other important variables, a number of which are summarized next.

Site of the Impairment

Conductive Hearing Loss: Conductive losses include all problems in the outer or middle ear that block the mechanical transfer of sound from the visible outer ear through the auditory canal to the eardrum and then along the three tiny bones of the middle ear. The middle ear is connected to the throat by way of the Eustachian tube, and it is there that inflammation, the most common cause of conductive hearing loss, often occurs. Conductive loss usually can be improved through amplification, medication, or surgery, although chronic infections may cause permanent damage.

MECHANICAL VS. SENSORY IMPAIRMENTS

Sensorineural Hearing Loss: Most children receiving special education as hearing impaired have some type of sensorineural hearing loss. Unlike conductive losses, sensorineural impairments affect the inner ear and/or auditory nerve and are not medically reversible. They also cause distortions as well as reductions in perceived sound and thus may not be significantly improved by hearing aids.

Mixed Loss: When both conductive and sensorineural losses are present, the condition is known as a mixed loss.

Degree and Frequency

RANGES OF HEARING LOSS

Degree of Loss: The degree of loss is measured in decibels (dB), with zero representing the threshold of normal hearing and mild losses falling in the range of 20-55 dB. Sixty dB is the maximum conductive loss. Individuals with severe (sensorineural) ioss (70-90 dB) can understand only strongly amplified speech; more than 90 dB in the better ear constitutes profound loss, or deafness.

Frequencies, or Pitch, of Sound Perceived: There may be differences in the ability to perceive sound at different frequencies—an individual may suffer greater loss of hearing of high tones than low ones, for example. The most serious impairments are those that interfere with hearing the frequencies of normal speech.

Developmental Factors

POST-LINGUAL AND PRELINGUAL LOSSES

An audiological examination registers the amount of loss at key frequencies. However, measuring the extent of the physiological impairment does not present a full picture of a hearing impaired child's educational problems and needs. Several other factors have a critical impact.

Age of Loss: The most significant factor, aside from the type and extent of loss, is the age at which it occurred. Most importantly, was it prelingual or postlingual—before or after the child learned to speak?

Reynolds and Birch (1977) offer the following illustration. A child who became deaf at age 15 would have already mastered the following:

1. knowledge of the adolescent's own native language
2. clear oral speech
3. understanding of the oral speech of others
4. ability to read with speed and comprehension
5. understanding of abstract concepts.

A loss of hearing would result only in the loss of the third ability.

A child who is deaf from birth, on the other hand, would find it difficult or impossible to achieve any of these. This child would need special, intensive instruction not only to learn a spoken language but even to learn that such a thing as language exists. The more language a child has acquired before hearing loss, the greater will be the chances of maintaining that language and achieving a rate of cognitive development equivalent to that of hearing peers. There is, moreover, an optimal age for learning language, and the farther beyond that age special instruction is initiated, the more difficult learning will become.

A VARIETY OF DEVELOPMENTAL FACTORS

Other factors include intelligence, the presence or absence of any other handicapping conditions, and the amount of stimulation, reinforcement, and intervention received from very early infancy. All will affect hearing impaired students' educational performance. It also is true that children will have good days and bad days and that the level of language ability may fluctuate somewhat. As with other disabilities, it also is true that there are as many unique constellations of educational strengths and weaknesses as there are hearing impaired individuals.

EDUCATIONAL STRATEGIES

Philosophic Approaches

CONTROVERSIES IN EDUCATIONAL APPROACH

With probably no other disability is there such heated controversy about educational strategies as there is with the hearing impaired, particularly among those most severely involved. Within what is often known as the "deaf community" as well as without, there are profound disagreements about the value of mainstreaming, the emphasis to be placed on integration into the hearing world, the type of communication to teach, and how to teach it.

The dominant controversy is between the aural/oral approach, the manual (sign language), approach, and total communication (which combines oral and manual techniques).

THE ORAL APPROACH

The aural/oral philosophy is based on the conviction that hearing impaired individuals must learn speech in order to survive in the dominant, hearing world. It places clear emphasis on training in the development of oral language at the expense, and even outright prohibition, of manual methods. This approach begins with maximizing residual hearing through the use of hearing aids and systematic training in listening and speech. The oral method also teaches lip, or speech, reading and makes use of kinesthetic feedback—the sense of touch—as an aid to sound production.

The goal is to allow hearing impaired persons to be integrated as fully and normally as possible into the hearing world, thus minimizing the effects of discrimination in education, job opportunities, and social situations. Disadvantages of this method are that not all children seem to be able to master it, that even the most skilled speech readers can identify only perhaps 50 percent of speech through visual means, and that deaf persons' speech patterns may be viewed as a stigma or sign of mental retardation. The skills also are very difficult for many individuals to acquire, and some deaf people reject them as unnatural.

THE MANUAL APPROACH

This last group is among the advocates of a second approach, the manual one, which teaches sign language and finger spelling rather than oral methods. Manual communication has the disadvantages of being visibly different and inaccessible to the hearing majority, but the advantages for the hearing impaired are that it is more accurate and comfortable and that it can be used to introduce a means of communication at a very young age.

Among advocates of the manual approach, there are further controversies about which manual language to use. The chief conflict is between languages that approxi-

TYPES OF SIGN LANGUAGE

mate a literal translation of English vs. American Sign Language (ASL), which has a very different structural and syntactical base, with signs representing ideas rather than words. With ASL, some feel, the hearing impaired person is even farther removed from spoken communication and may have even greater difficulties learning to read and write.

TOTAL COMMUNICATION

A third and more recent approach—total communication—combines oral and manual techniques to maximize the communicative potential of these individuals. In a classroom, for example, a teacher using total communication might rely primarily on oral speech, with signs or finger spelling to clarify new or difficult points. Total communication comes under the same criticisms as other approaches: there are disagreements among educators as to how to teach and use it, and some children do not seem to be able to use it successfully. In any given location, the choice of which approach to use may be a matter of available staff experts as well as the preferences of the community.

THE QUESTION OF MAINSTREAMING

As this first controversy implies, there is another strong difference of opinion on the question of mainstreaming. There are mainstreaming advocates who propose full educational integration, with a move to progressively more segregated settings only if the child cannot benefit from the mainstreamed class. Some deaf adults feel strongly that the least restrictive environment is a segregated one. And there are those who feel that the hearing impaired should begin in segregated classrooms and be mainstreamed gradually, only as they develop adequate language, academic, and social skills.

Types of Programs

COMMON PROGRAM MODELS

There are seven common program models for educating the hearing impaired:

1. residential programs
2. special day schools
3. self-contained classes in the regular school
4. part-time special classes with children integrated into the mainstream on an individual, subject-by-subject basis
5. regular class assignment with part-time placement in a resource room
6. regular class placement with help from itinerant specialists
7. regular class placement with minimal consultative assistance.

ELEMENTS OF SUCCESSFUL PROGRAMS

Reynolds and Birch (1977) identify the following as elements of successful integrated programs for the hearing impaired:

1. Teachers are given options and are not forced into mainstreaming situations.
2. Staffing is appropriate for the setting.
3. Inservice training precedes program changes.
4. Needed facilities and materials are on hand.
5. Specific teaching plans are made.
6. Teaching responsibility is shared.

7. Separation from the regular class is minimal.
8. Each team meets on a regular basis.

They stress that participation in the hearing world is the goal toward which all available time should be directed; special education should be brought into the regular classroom; and the approach for each student should be individualized, planned, organized, and systematic. Special and regular education teachers should cooperate to create a preteach/teach/postteach approach in which the specialist prepares the hearing impaired student for, then follows up on, lessons taught to the whole class by the regular teacher. The whole approach depends, as well, on unified, consistent support on the part of all groups involved (parents, teacher organizations, staff, school board, principal, etc.).

REFERENCES

Federal Register, August 23, 1977, *42,* 1963.

Gregory, S. (1976). *The deaf child and his family.* New York: John Wiley & Sons.

Karchmer, M.A., & Trybus, R. (1977). *Who are the deaf children in 'mainstream' programs?* Washington, DC: Office of Demographic Studies (abstract).

Reynolds, M.C., & Birch, J.W. (1977). *Teaching exceptional children in all America's schools.* Reston, VA: The Council for Exceptional Children.

Chapter 11

Learning Disabilities

SUMMARY

Federal Definition

"Specific learning disability" means a disorder in one or more of the basic psychological processes involved in understanding or in using spoken or written language that may manifest itself in an imperfect ability to listen, think, speak, read, write, spell, or do mathematical calculations. The term includes such conditions as perceptual handicaps, brain injury, minimal brain disfunction, dyslexia, and developmental aphasia. The term does not include children who have learning problems that are primarily the result of visual, hearing, or motor handicaps; mental retardation; or of environmental, cultural, or economic disadvantages.

Common Characteristics

Students with learning disabilities have average or above-average intelligence but perform below tested intellectual ability levels. They may fail to master certain aspects of basic math and/or language skills—especially reading—and display irregular test performances. Learning disabilities are highly varied in their nature and effects. For example, a student may have normal hearing but be unable to perceive or discriminate between some sounds, follow oral directions, remember what is heard, or screen out nonmeaningful, distracting sounds; or the pupil may have normal vision but be unable to perceive or discriminate between some objects (e.g., may perceive letters in a written word in scrambled order).

Such difficulties, in turn, may lead to frustration and subsequent behavior problems such as poor self-image, task avoidance, excessive slowness or hyperactivity; poor self-management, lack of motivation, disruptive behavior; inability to categorize, classify, sequence, think abstractly, distinguish fact from fiction; and/or problems of attention, memory, or motor functions. No one student will exhibit all characteristics, and some of the characteristics may show up in pupils with other handicapping conditions.

Classroom Modifications

The teacher should reduce distracting stimuli as much as possible, have students work in the quietest possible area, and situate them near the teacher or the activity in which they are participating.

Teaching Strategies

Teachers should let the students know what is expected of them; explain and post class rules; be consistent; provide short-term schedules, lesson outlines, or other aids to prepare the pupils for class; discuss required information; and explain what is expected from them in terms of skill performance. If students do not learn with one mode or type of instruction, the teacher should try another; use demonstrations or multisensory materials as often as possible; provide alternatives to assignments in the student's weak sensory mode (e.g., an oral report instead of written); tape record and/ or make written copies of information delivered in other sensory modes.

Teachers must identify skill deficiencies and teach toward specific mastery, beginning at the lowest level not yet attained; structure tasks, breaking them into concrete, sequential steps; test periodically and chart progress; introduce new skills sequentially as previous ones are mastered. They also should highlight important information in texts, furnish study guides or chapter outlines, teach study skills, set realistic goals, give frequent feedback, deemphasize time limits, provide opportunities for success, and identify and use motivating rewards. Programming should be prioritized based on the students' long-term educational goals.

VARIED PROBLEMS, VARIED SOLUTIONS

The resource room teacher knows them well: There is one student who has above-average intelligence scores and performs well in arithmetic but who reads and spells at levels well below those of peers. Assessments reveal that although he can hear, he cannot discriminate well between sounds, cannot analyze words auditorially. Another student seems to comprehend at grade level but cannot communicate this. She frequently is unable to recall words for ideas she has just heard. She cannot follow oral instructions except very simple ones. Still another performs normally on written and oral language tasks but has failed to master basic arithmetic operations. He is highly distractable and disruptive in class, yet in the primary grades his teachers did not identify him as having a learning problem.

GREAT VARIATIONS IN LEARNING STYLES

What do all these children, with their highly idiosyncratic difficulties, have in common? They all have been identified to receive special education under the category "learning disabled." This category, perhaps more than any other, is a reminder that there are as many individual variations in the processes necessary for learning (thinking, listening, seeing, imitating, remembering, generalizing, and so on) as there are variations in physical features; children's learning styles are as distinctive as their appearance.

Those 2 to 3 percent who are identified as learning disabled are those whose styles (for reasons educators may or may not now be able to define) are so different that they are not served adequately by the methods and curriculum that reach the vast majority of their classmates. They are those who do not exhibit any of the other handicaps but who, quite noticeably and significantly, fail to progress educationally as expected.

CONTINUING DEBATES

The term learning disabilities in a sense is a provisional heading, still being debated, researched, and defined. That continuing debate touches many bases: Is "specific learning disabilities" the most appropriate term? Should the category exist at all? Are not many students needlessly stigmatized by being labeled as LD when the problem is really the school system's failure to deliver an appropriate education? What causes these learning problems? Are they remediable and, if so, how?

TYPES AND DEFINITIONS

HISTORY OF THE TERM

Specific learning disabilities is the newest of the categories served in special education. The term has been in use only since 1963, and there are still many unresolved disagreements about its accuracy, meaning, and application. There is fairly general agreement, however, that it is a better term than previous offerings. Those included such suggestions as brain injured, brain damaged, minimal brain dysfunction, or neurologically impaired, which parents objected to for their stigmatizing, permanent, and irremediable overtones and which educators found inadequate because neurological insult could not always be diagnosed.

Indeed, the origins of most learning disabilities remain complex and mysterious. Diet, developmental lag, brain dysfunction, perinatal stress, and inappropriate education have all been suggested as causes. In most cases, a number of different factors

POSSIBLE CAUSES

are probably interacting to create the condition. In all cases, it is more useful to come up with an accurate description of the condition than simply to apply a label—whether brain injured, learning disabled, hyperactive, dyslectic, perceptually disordered, or other. The more accurately students' particular disabilities can be identified, the more appropriate can be the educational plan.

Types of Learning Disabilities

MANY TYPES OF DISORDERS

The specific learning problems in this category include disorders of the following functions:

Perceptual: inability to perceive or discriminate correctly between visual and/or auditory stimuli

Memory: disorders of short- or long-term, visual, auditory, or tactile memory

Thinking: impaired ability to think abstractly or sequentially or to generalize

Attention: inattention, overattention

Orientation: poor spatial and/or directional orientation, also time orientation

Social-Emotional: impulsiveness, easily distracted, anxious, low tolerance for frustration, poor social perception

Motor Function: hyperactivity, hypoactivity, incoordination, perseveration.

EFFECTS OF LEARNING DISABILITIES

Any of these disorders, alone or in combination, can impair the ability to read, write, speak, spell, or do mathematical calculations. To give just a few examples: spelling problems might be associated with impaired visual perception, memory, or fine motor coordination; poor visual perception might hamper a child's arithmetic abilities (mixing up columns of numbers, misreading story problems); reading disabilities might be caused or compounded by auditory problems (incorrect discrimination between spoken words) or by confused directional orientation, as well as by impairments in visual memory or discrimination.

FEDERAL REGULATIONS

The common element in all children identified as learning disabled is discrepancy. This concept is defined in the federal regulations issued in December 1977:

DISCREPANCY IS KEY TO IDENTIFICATION

> A team may determine that a child has a specific learning disability if (1) The child does not achieve commensurate with his or her age and ability levels in one or more of the areas listed in [the federal definition] when provided with learning experiences appropriate for the child's age and ability levels; and (2) The team finds that a child has a severe discrepancy between achievement and intellectual ability in one or more of the following areas: Oral expression; listening comprehension; written expression; basic reading skill; reading comprehension; mathematics calculation; or mathematics reasoning. The team may not identify a child as having a specific learning disability if the severe discrepancy between ability and achievement is primarily the result of: A visual, hearing, or motor handi-

cap; mental retardation; emotional disturbance; or environmental, cultural or economic disadvantage (Sec. 121a.541).

Those regulations also spell out the following requirements for the evaluation of learning disabilities (in addition to the requirements for evaluating all handicapped children):

EVALUATING THE LEARNING DISABLED STUDENT

1. The evaluation team must include (a) the child's regular teacher or someone qualified to hold that position and (b) at least one person qualified to conduct individual diagnostic examinations of children, such as a school psychologist, speech-language pathologist, or remedial reading teacher.
2. At least one team member in addition to the classroom teacher must observe the child's academic performance in the class setting.
3. The evaluation team must prepare a written report, and each team member must either concur with it or present a statement of differing opinions. The report must include statements of: Whether the child has a specific learning disability; the basis for making the determination; the relationship of that behavior to the child's academic functioning; the educationally relevant medical findings, if any; whether there is a severe discrepancy between achievement and ability which is not correctable without special education and related services; and the determination of the team concerning the effects of environmental, cultural, or economic disadvantage (Secs. 121a.540 and 121a.543).

TEACHING STRATEGIES

Strategies for teaching the learning disabled vary greatly, for several reasons. First, of course, is the great diversity of the population. For example, highly visual methods that might work well for a student with auditory perception problems would be inappropriate for one with poor visual memory and discrimination. What these students have in common is that they have not learned successfully from methods previously used. For the greatest likelihood of success, then, new approaches must be tried that are individualized to fit each student's particular constellation of strengths and weaknesses.

NEW EDUCATIONAL APPROACHES REQUIRED

Another issue is the relative newness of the field. Research is scant, and consensus has not yet had time to evolve. There are several theories of educational programming for the learning disabled, with different classroom approaches corresponding to each. A key distinction has been between educators who advocate the teaching of processes (e.g., auditory discrimination) and those who concentrate on teaching skills (e.g., reading).

DIFFERENT THEORETICAL STRATEGIES

An example of the first is perceptual-motor training, in which students might be taught eye-hand coordination, gross and fine motor skills, body image, and so on. An example of the second model is direct instruction, in which students are assessed on their mastery of scope and sequence. Instruction begins at the lowest skill level not yet attained; students are tested periodically until that level is mastered, the next skill is introduced, and the process begins again.

Other approaches cited for this population include diagnostic-prescriptive and precision teaching, psycholinguistic approaches, and multisensory teaching. Generally, the skills-oriented models have proved more effective in raising educational achievement levels than have programs of process training.

COMMON TECHNIQUES

In addition to the steps summarized at the outset, other techniques recommended with the learning disabled include having teachers:

- teach students how to study and take tests
- orient lesson presentations as much as possible to reflect student interests
- involve adolescents in planning their own programs
- avoid calling attention to previous failures or the future importance of learning; avoid emotionally laden situations and methods that have failed earlier
- set objectives, make and use plans, monitor progress frequently.

REFERENCES

U.S. Federal Register, August 23, 1977, *42*, 1963.

U.S. Federal Register, December 29, 1977, *42*, 250.

Chapter 12

Mental Retardation

SUMMARY

Federal Definition

"Mentally retarded" means significantly subaverage general intellectual functioning existing concurrently with deficits in adaptive behavior and manifested during the developmental period, which adversely affects a child's educational performance.

Common Characteristics

Students served under the category mentally retarded frequently exhibit the following characteristics: limited ability to identify the important information in materials, slowness in relating the meaning of one word or idea with another, lack of originality or creativity, inability to analyze and solve problems, inability to learn without direct instruction on specific skills and when to use them, learning more slowly and forgetting more quickly than peers. They may demonstrate difficulty in following complex directions, poor short-term memory, short attention span, below-average language abilities, slower rate of physical growth and motor skills development, sensory and motor coordination problems, immature/inappropriate social behavior, low tolerance for frustration, outer-directed, dependent on others' guidance, or poor self-image. Generalized deficiencies in range and quality of mental abilities are present in highly varied degrees, depending on the severity of the handicap.

Classroom Adaptations

Teachers should break material into small, simple, sequential steps; assign only small segments of work at one time; provide continuous feedback and monitor progress frequently; explain mistakes and demonstrate correct procedures, allow for extra practice/repetition (overlearning). They should relate new concepts to familiar, concrete, and simple examples; demonstrate as well as explain; allow students to have firsthand experience. Scan materials for new words and check for appropriate reading level; rewrite or explain as necessary; use activities/materials of high interest to motivate and reinforce learning; design tasks that make success possible; structure activities and materials that are similar in appearance and content to those used by other students so as not to make the difference obvious; be sure to begin at the pupil's current level.

They should teach toward independent living, minimize irrelevant skills and materials, clearly define acceptable behavior and ways to accomplish it, call attention to positive role models, use positive reinforcement techniques, withhold reinforcement until a desired behavior is exhibited, praise appropriate behavior, emphasize strengths, help students develop alternate compensatory skills in problem areas, and be consistent.

THE MILDLY MENTALLY RETARDED

The term mental retardation covers individuals in a vast range of degree of mental handicap, from those who might be thought of as normal but slow learners to those who require lifelong custodial care. Programming for the more severely mentally retarded is discussed in Chapter 14, Severe and Multiple Handicaps. This chapter addresses primarily the mildly mentally retarded since they are the most likely members of this handicapped group to be served in integrated, public school classrooms.

OVERLAP WITH THE NORMAL POPULATION

In previous eras, when school attendance was not compulsory and literacy was rare, individuals of mildly "retarded" mental development did not necessarily stand out in the community. Nor are they necessarily visible in the adult community today. For some individuals, a diagnosis of mild mental retardation is relevant only during the school years. As adults, many of them are employed, self-sufficient, productive members of society, indistinguishable from "normal" adult peers.

DIVERSITY OF ABILITIES AND NEEDS

This is not to imply that these individuals do not need special educational services or that other, more severely involved individuals can lead fully independent lives, even with extensive training. It is, rather, a reminder that the label MR does not predict performance on an individual basis. As in other categories of disability, the individuals who fall within the heading of mentally retarded reflect a diversity of educational needs and capabilities. Some of these pupils may overlap in many areas of development—even in academic ones—with normal students. They may differ in their emotional, social, and physical development; in their abilities to live independently as adults or to exhibit behavior appropriate to their age level (and therefore in the degree to which they are perceived as different from the general population). They also may be similar to normal students in one or more of these areas.

Further, mental development may continue into the 20s or beyond, and (at least in part because of the difficulties and ambiguities of assessment) an individual's IQ may change over time. It may improve somewhat or, if appropriate stimulation is lacking, the tested IQ may actually decline.

INDIVIDUALIZATION IS THE KEY

As with all handicapped students, the challenge is to recognize that they are more like other students than they are different; to treat each as an individual; and to help them all achieve the greatest possible independence and personal, social, and academic development

TYPES AND DEFINITIONS

TERMS USED

Over the last century, a number of terms and definitions have been put forward to describe this category of handicap. Some of those now commonly in use include mentally retarded, retarded, developmentally or mentally disabled or handicapped, and low rate of cognitive development. Several other sets of terms indicate the degree of the handicap, including mild, moderate, severe, and profound; educable, trainable, and custodial; marginally dependent, semidependent, and dependent.

Statistically, the category includes those who score at least two standard deviations below the mean on standard intelligence tests.

Problems of Assessment

Table 12–1 is helpful in creating a general understanding of terms but is potentially misleading on two counts:

CULTURAL BIAS AND OTHER PROBLEMS

1. The divisions between degrees of handicap are not abrupt; for example, there may be little recognizable difference between students at the low end of the mild range and the high end of moderate.
2. There are important general problems with assessment methods that may call the meaning of these scores into question. Those problems include the changing definitions of mental retardation, the instability of test scores over time, and bias in the tests.

The cultural bias of IQ tests, of course, has been highly controversial in the past, and P.L. 94-142 sets several requirements aimed at minimizing this factor. For example, tests must be administered in the child's native language and placement decisions must be based on more than one test (see Chapter 4 on Identification and Evaluation of Students).

ADAPTIVE BEHAVIOR FACTOR

In the category of mental retardation, federal definitions require both "significantly subaverage" intelligence and "deficits in adaptive behavior." The latter behavior concerns an individual's ability to cope with the environment; it includes the skills needed to function independently and to maintain social relationships. Measuring it presents even more complications than measuring intelligence. There are several commonly used assessments of adaptive behavior, including the American Association on Mental Deficiency (AAMD) Adaptive Behavior Scales, the Vineland Social Maturity Scale (newly revised), the Adaptive Behavior Inventory for Children (ABIC), and others. But there is less consensus than with the standard intelligence tests on method, interpretation, and accuracy of results.

RELATION TO STANDARD INTELLIGENCE TEST SCORES

Table 12–1 Levels of Mental Retardation as Related to Standard Intelligence Test Scores

Level of retardation	*Weschler test scores*	*Stanford-Binet scores*
Mild	55-69	52-67
Moderate	40-54	36-51
Severe	25-39	20-35
Profound	less than 25	less than 20

Source: From *Manual on Terminology and Classification in Mental Retardation, 1977 revision*, by H. Grossman (Ed.), 1977, Washington, D.C.: American Association on Mental Deficiency. Copyright 1977 by American Association on Mental Deficiency. Adapted by permission.

Such problems and ambiguities in assessment have led, in the past especially, to mislabeling and misplacement of students—particularly minority students—with probable negative effects on their educational experience. This is yet another reason why care must be taken to respond to the person rather than the label and to maintain flexibility in response to the needs of individuals as they change over time. (Culturally different students may need some kinds of special programming, such as bilingual education, but they may not be diagnosed or placed in programs for the mentally retarded because of those differences.)

PROBLEMS OF OVER-IDENTIFICATION

A point worth mentioning regarding cultural bias and overidentification of minority students: many significant causes of mental retardation are associated with poverty, including malnutrition, unhealthy living environment, lack of adequate medical care, lack of stimulation in early childhood, and disrupted family life. Such conditions are involved with fully 85 percent of those identified as mentally retarded (Meyen, 1978) while organic or physical causes account for only 10 to 15 percent of this population (Reynolds & Birch, 1977).

RELATION TO POVERTY

Thus, while minority parents and their advocates have been proven justified in their complaint that the tests discriminated against their children, the underlying problem is a larger, social one: as long as minority adult populations are discriminated against on an economic level, as long as they are represented disproportionately among the nation's poor, then their children can be expected to be disproportionately represented among the identified mentally retarded. The need is to work toward elimination of racial and cultural bias in the schools while recognizing that bias in society, in the form of poverty, creates educational needs that must be dealt with.

Mainstreaming the Mildly Retarded

The vast majority of all students who qualify for special education as mentally retarded, and certainly of those served in integrated class settings, fall in the range of "mild" disability. Among their characteristics are that they can develop personal, social, and communication skills; they can live independently as adults; and (barring complications of additional handicapping conditions) they can be educated successfully in regular school settings. In physical and motor development and personal and social skills, they may approximate or even exceed the achievements of their peers. More often, though, their personal and social development is negatively affected by inappropriate behavior and resulting rejection by peers; their academic progress is inhibited by an expectancy of failure that leads them to perform at levels even lower than assessments would predict.

SOCIAL, EMOTIONAL, AND DEVELOPMENTAL VARIABILITY

EDUCATIONAL STRATEGIES

In the past, mild to moderate mentally retarded children were generally shunted into special schools and classes out of contact with the mainstream; more severely involved ones were removed even further, to institutions in which they might receive no education at all. Today, under the reigning principles of deinstitutionalization and

TREND TOWARD MAIN-STREAMING

normalization, these children increasingly are being reintegrated into their schools and communities. The mildly or "educable" retarded and even the moderate, "trainable" group are now likely to be in regular classes for at least part of their educational careers.

Mainstreaming Challenges

The great majority of these students are not visibly different from their peers, but they do pose a number of special challenges for principals and regular classroom teachers. Among the most common of these are the following:

NEW CHALLENGES CREATE NEED FOR TEACHER SUPPORT

- their need to be consciously taught a number of things that most students pick up incidentally (for example, how to generalize, to apply knowledge learned in one situation to another similar one)
- a rate and style of learning different from that of the majority of students in the class, and
- a sense of failure, developed early, that makes it difficult for these pupils to try new activities, have confidence in their thinking, or achieve even at their low tested ability levels.

These challenges can be met in an integrated school setting, but the responsibility cannot fall on the regular class teacher alone. Success requires teamwork—the cooperation, support, and commitment of administrators, of qualified specialists with clearly defined roles, and of parents and community members, too.

Program Content and Delivery Models

EDUCATIONAL GOALS

For retarded students, the most important educational goal is to maximize their ability to function independently as adults. This will take on different aspects depending on the abilities of each individual. For some students, it entails preparation for work in a special, sheltered setting, life in a supervised residence, and enough minimal reading skills to ensure safety and survival. For others, the goal may be full integration into the community, preparation for family life, economic independence, and satisfying leisure pursuits. For the most severely affected, training will be oriented toward basic self-care skills such as grooming and feeding. The educational needs of mentally retarded students often include gross and fine motor skills development, general learning readiness, communication, basic academic skills, self-care and independent living skills, prevocational and vocational skills, and recreation.

SECONDARY SCHOOL PROGRAMMING

As these students grow older, the individualized curriculum should reflect increasing emphasis on vocational and daily living skills. A career/vocational education approach is used most commonly with these students at the secondary level. Other approaches at this level include developing applied academic skills, tutoring in academic areas or building compensatory capabilities, teaching students how to learn, or emphasizing independent living skills.

Because they learn more slowly, forget more quickly, and require more repetition than normal students, educational time is at a premium. It is important to prioritize program content and not to waste precious time on irrelevant material. One caution, however: these students often are capable of more and higher levels of learning than is apparent at first; it may be equally easy to err on the side of too much repetition, of holding a student back by underestimating potential. The keys to good programming are individualization, adaptation, and flexibility.

TEACH TO INDIVIDUAL ABILITY LEVELS

Delivery Models

Common program models for educational delivery include:

- full-time regular placement with consultation, special materials, and other support for the teacher
- part-time regular placement with time in a resource room
- special classes in the regular school, with some integrated placement for non-academic subjects, field trips, assemblies, and so on
- special schools (students may be placed in community-based elementary schools and then in special regional schools for their secondary education)
- various residential settings.

PLACEMENT ALTERNATIVES

Where regular class placement is involved, the regular teacher must have support from a specially trained teacher who is available for team teaching, planning, consultation, or other kinds of assistance; input into program and placement decisions; and access to special materials. Both the regular and the special teacher need (1) inservice preparation for mainstreaming; (2) planning and preparation time; and (3) previously agreed-upon divisions of authority, responsibility, and accountability for the teachers and administrators involved (Reynolds & Birch, 1977).

TEACHERS' NEEDS

The Behavioral Approach

The work of behaviorists has contributed greatly to the educational programming for these students. Teachers have used techniques of operant conditioning to improve mentally retarded students' functioning in such areas as attending, task completion, language and arithmetic skills, self-help, vocational performance, and so on. The techniques are discussed in Chapter 9 on Behavior Disorders and Chapter 2 Discipline.

BEHAVIORAL TECHNIQUES HAVE PROVED SUCCESSFUL

Such techniques include continuous measurement of student behavior (for example, short skills tests to measure increasing mastery of basic arithmetic skills), observing and rewarding positive behavior, and consistent application of motivating rewards to increase the frequency of desired behavior. Many teachers use contingency contracts—agreements between student and teacher providing that completion of a specific task will result in an established reward (e.g., completion of all spelling lessons from Monday through Thursday will yield free time on Friday).

TASK ANALYSIS

Task analysis is an important and valuable part of programming for mentally retarded as well as other kinds of exceptional students. It involves breaking down learning tasks into their specific components, analyzing which parts the youngsters can or cannot do, and beginning at the lowest skill level the student has not yet mastered. From that beginning point the remaining skills and content should be presented in small, tightly sequenced steps with frequent repetition and review, plus frequent checks to be sure the students are attending and understanding. (Small, heterogeneous groups constitute an effective arrangement for teaching the mildly mentally retarded, but in such a setting, too, it is important to assess frequently whether the special students are mastering the material.)

Improving Self-Concept

CONTRADICTING FEELINGS OF FAILURE

The emotional/attitudinal problems that often accompany mentally retarded children's educational experience must be a focus of programming. Typically, the repeated inability to keep up with peers, master the material given, and make the "right" response results in feelings of failure, self-doubt, frustration, timidity, and dependency. To help contradict these feelings, teachers can:

- provide experiences of success by setting realistic goals, with rewards for specific behaviors
- recognize and praise persistence
- provide tasks at the students' ability level
- teach self-control, problem-solving, and appropriate social behaviors
- try to understand the causes of student frustration (observe and talk with the children, parents, and specialists) and create situations where these causes are minimized.

REFERENCES

Federal Register, August 23, 1977, *42*, 1963.

Meyen, E.L. (1982). *Exceptional children and youth: An introduction*. Denver: Love Publishing Co.

Reynolds, M.C., & Birch, J.W. (1977). *Teaching exceptional children in all America's schools*. Reston, VA: The Council for Exceptional Children.

Chapter 13

Physical Handicaps

SUMMARY

Federal Definitions

"Orthopedically impaired" means a severe orthopedic impairment that adversely affects a child's educational performance. The term includes impairments caused by congenital anomaly (e.g., clubfoot, absence or disformity of some member, etc.), impairments caused by disease (e.g., poliomyelitis, bone tuberculosis, etc.), and impairments from other causes (e.g., cerebral palsy, amputations, and fractures or burns that cause contractures).

"Other health impaired" means limited strength, vitality, or alertness because of chronic or acute health problems such as a heart condition, tuberculosis, rheumatic fever, nephritis, asthma, sickle cell anemia, hemophilia, epilepsy, lead poisoning, leukemia, or diabetes that adversely affect educational performance.

Common Characteristics

The characteristics of students with physical disabilities will depend on the particular handicap but can include limited mobility (walking slowly and with difficulty or relying on wheelchair, crutches, braces, other prosthetic device); full or partial loss of use of limb(s); poor coordination; low stamina; recurring health problems, frequent absences, easily injured; seizures; communication problems (may not be able to write or speak intelligibly); expressions of frustration at limitations; poor self-image. These students often have other handicapping conditions as well.

Classroom Adaptations

Physical Environment: Educators should arrange the classroom work areas at wheelchair level and in easily accessible locations; see that bathrooms, drinking fountains, play areas, etc., also are accessible; assign each such student a specific storage space near work areas to reduce the need for carrying materials; consult with specialists concerning the best seating position and posture and any special furniture needs.

Medical and Safety Needs: Educators must learn about the children's medical history, the disabling condition and its limitations, any medication taken regularly and its side effects, warning signals of seizures and what to do if a student has one, any other preventive health needs, and treatment preferences. They must tactfully alert other students to any special health considerations, and make arrangements for safety procedures in a building emergency.

Teaching Strategies: Teachers should not overprotect; instead, they should encourage these students to progress as far as possible in academics, responsibility, and initiative; encourage them to try new activities and help devise alternative ways of doing things (with help from specialists if necessary). They should make no assumptions about mental abilities based on the handicapping condition alone, but should base their teaching modifications on careful observation of students' abilities and stamina, on task analysis, and on their IEPs. They must allow time for students to try to complete a task independently, and devise easier, shorter, or alternative tasks as needed.

Special Materials and Equipment: Teachers should consult with the therapist/specialist to locate special furniture, tools, and materials; identify the students' best communication mode(s) and obtain typewriter, communication board, etc.; and learn about wheelchair, prosthetics, or other assistive devices used by the children and any necessary maintenance checks.

Social Environment: Educators should assess their own attitudes, model and encourage other students to create an accepting climate for the handicapped pupil, emphasize their strengths, and incorporate social learning activities.

COPING WITH PHYSICAL HANDICAPS

EDUCATION NOW MORE ACCESSIBLE

In years past, the majority of physically handicapped youngsters were educated in separate special classes, if they were educated at all. There were several reasons for this, some of them practical and financial, others philosophical or attitudinal. One of these reasons—the problem of physical access—has been diminished greatly as the result of legislation in recent years. The Rehabilitation Act of 1973 required that all new school construction be barrier free and that all programs, although not all buildings or all parts of all buildings, must also be accessible.

ATTITUDES GET IN THE WAY

A more difficult situation still exists in the attitudinal area. Unlike other handicapping conditions, orthopedic handicaps are almost always visible. Those visible differences provoke a variety of reactions in others: pity, embarrassment, ignoring, teasing, fear. The situation rarely is neutral; the nonhandicapped are seldom educated to be understanding, open, and comfortable. The physically handicapped experience constant reminders that they are different, excluded, misunderstood.

SPECIAL CHALLENGES FOR EDUCATORS

As a result, attitude becomes a primary challenge in the mainstreamed educational setting—the attitudes of educators, of other students, and of the handicapped themselves. Other, unique challenges are emotional such as the difficulties of working with children who are seriously ill or dying. All of these factors pose special problems for educators, particularly those such as principals, who usually have not been specially trained or prepared for work with the handicapped. With commitment to the potentials of mainstreaming, with openness to the challenge of examining and changing one's own views, with an effort to understand the handicapped child's experience, and with the help of qualified specialists, the program can succeed.

TYPES AND DEFINITIONS

MANY TYPES OF HANDICAPS

Conditions referred to under the more or less interchangeable headings of physical impairments, handicaps, disabilities, or "crippled and other health impaired" (COHI) are tremendously diverse. Some of these conditions are acquired as the result of illness and injury; some are present from birth and affect every hour and every aspect of the individual's life. Some such as epilepsy or asthma may affect the individual only occasionally. Some may cause the child to grow progressively worse (and in some cases to die within the school age years), some are unchanging, and others are debilitating for only a few months or years, after which there is full recovery.

And this is only the beginning of the diversity. Every individual is affected quite differently—physically, emotionally, and academically.

Cerebral palsy, the condition most often represented by children in this category, is an example. There are four major types (see following descriptions); each type may be mild to profound, may affect anywhere from just one to all extremities of the body, may or may not be accompanied by mental or sensory deficits, and may be handled in very different ways by different individuals.

IMPORTANCE OF INDIVIDUALIZATION

The key, or at least the necessary starting point, of educational programming for children with physical handicaps is individualization. Educators must begin by understanding the handicapping conditions but make no assumptions until they have carefully observed and understood the child.

Descriptions of some of the more frequently occurring physically handicapping conditions are given next. They are adapted from the project *Vocational Education Inservice Training (VEIT) handbook* (Regan, 1979).

SOME OF THE MOST COMMON PHYSICAL HANDICAPS

Cerebral Palsy: The term refers to a variety of physical disorders that result from damage to or improper development of the brain. There are four main types: athetoid, which is characterized by uncontrolled and irregular movement and muscle tone; spastic, in which muscles are overly tight and resistant; ataxic, lack of coordination related to balance; and mixed, or combination of these types.

Muscular Dystrophy: This usually is an inherited condition that causes a progressive weakening and deterioration of the skeletal and voluntary muscles. There are several types of muscular dystrophy, differing in degree of severity, age of onset, muscles affected, and rate of muscle degeneration. Affected persons usually need a wheelchair for mobility and require assistance in performing daily living activities. These individuals need initial training or retraining to hold jobs.

Spina Bifida: This occurs when the vertebrae fail to develop fully around the spinal cord, leaving an opening. The most severe type results in the protrusion of the spinal cord and spinal fluid into a sac outside the body. The damage to the spinal cord causes the person to suffer loss of nervous sensation from the opening down. This results in loss of leg usage, little or no bowel and bladder control, hydrocephalus and perceptual problems, urinary problems, physical limb deformities, and tendency to develop pressure sores on lower trunk and legs. The person is basically a paraplegic with normal intelligence and life expectancy.

Hemophilia: This is an inherited blood disorder that impedes coagulation, resulting in internal hemorrhages or in external bleeding or bruising from bumps, sudden twists, extreme pressure, even minor cuts, etc. Caution should be taken to avoid excessive body contact with such students that might rupture blood vessels.

Cystic Fibrosis: This is an inherited disorder that produces an abnormally thick, sticky, mucus secretion from the sweat, mucous or salivary glands. The result is blockage of the bronchial tubes and lungs and of the flow of digestive enzymes from the pancreas to the small intestine. Because of these respiratory and digestive system problems, the person may suffer extreme coughing, shortness of breath, low-grade fever, loss of appetite and weight, abnormal stools, and salt loss. The condition usually can be controlled with proper diet, medication, and inhalation therapy.

Sickle Cell Disease: An inherited blood condition that affects blacks. Abnormal sickle-shaped red blood cells form, resulting in damage to the spleen, bones, kidneys, lungs, gastrointestinal tract, brain and heart. This condition is manifested by periodic crises causing pallor, fever, severe pain in abdomen and legs, vomiting, and stiff neck. Between crises the person may appear anemic, barrel chested, and have a protruding abdomen. The crises tend to occur less frequently with age. Individuals grow to adulthood but may continue to be anemic and have infections.

Traumatic Conditions and Amputations: These conditions are the result of accidents or operations. Psychological adjustment considerations may overpower the physical disability. The use of prosthetic devices to replace missing limbs may require special equipment or training adaptations and extra efforts to cope with the mental trauma these persons can suffer.

Arthritis: This is an inflammation of the joints that may be progressive. Movement may be extremely painful and limited, with little or no relief possible from medication.

Multiple Sclerosis: This is a neurological disorder characterized by the formation of hardened scar tissue in place of disintegrated insulation tissue around the nerve fibers of the central nervous system. This process of disintegration and replacement takes place in patches throughout the central nervous system and eventually prevents nerve messages from being transmitted properly. The severity and extent of the condition varies with each person and the resulting disabilities are determined by the area of the central nervous system affected—spinal cord or brain. The person should avoid excessive fatigue and emotional stress. Schools should provide for makeup work when relapses occur and should modify physical facilities for crutches and wheelchairs.

Poliomyelitis: Infantile paralysis is a disease in which a virus damages the spinal cord, causing paralysis of limbs or respiratory functions. The Salk vaccine has greatly reduced its occurrence.

Epilepsy: This disease is not apparent except when a seizure occurs. However, 50 percent of all epileptics also have other handicapping conditions. There are three types of seizures:

1. Grand mal: Violent shaking of the entire body accompanied by temporary loss of consciousness, this usually lasts two to five minutes; may occur as often as one or more times a day or as infrequently as once a year.
2. Petit mal: A simple staring spell (often mistaken for daydreaming), this usually lasts less than one minute, often only several seconds but it may occur repeatedly in one hour.
3. Psychomotor: This produces inappropriate or purposeless behavior with subsequent amnesia regarding the episode; it usually lasts two to five minutes, and may occur one or more times weekly, monthly, or annually. This condition usually is controlled by medication.

Aphasia: This condition is characterized by a loss of language in some or all aspects of communication, speaking, writing, and/or gesturing or understanding written or verbal messages in persons who have had normal speech abilities before suffering brain damage. The brain damage may be caused by a stroke or a head injury accident. Sometimes secondary problems occur, such as severe headaches, physical disability, seizures, and emotional lability.

EDUCATIONAL STRATEGIES

EDUCATIONAL GOALS

The educational program for physically handicapped children has three main goals: (1) to prepare them for independent living, (2) to develop their self-image and social skills, and (3) to provide an academic education appropriate to their abilities. The first category involves a variety of subjects, depending on the nature of the disability, including: mobility training, self-help, daily living skills, vocational education, and recreational activities. The second is important because both the disability and others' reactions to it may cut children off from the full range of social interactions and experiences.

RANGES OF INTELLECTUAL ABILITY

As for the third (academic) goal, the most important point is that a physical handicap does not predict or reflect mental ability. Children identified as orthopedic or other health impaired represent the entire spectrum of intelligence and academic abilities. It may not be easy to assess those abilities, particularly if muscle and motor impairments render the youngsters incapable of speech. When there is doubt, specialists such as school psychologists and physical and occupational therapists should be able to help make accurate assessments and devise strategies to help the students progress as far as possible academically. A good rule of thumb is to treat the children normally, assuming average levels of comprehension unless assessments and careful observation suggest otherwise.

The Role of the Specialist

SPECIALISTS SUPPORT THE REGULAR CLASS TEACHER

A variety of specialists may provide support to the regular classroom teacher in meeting these general goals. Where the school employs an itinerant or resource teacher with special knowledge in physical handicaps, this professional generally will be responsible for:

- coordinating referrals, evaluations, placement
- coordinating efforts among parents, teachers, community service agencies, and so on
- interpreting therapy to the regular teacher (may assist in therapy sessions), observation, and follow-up
- observing the children in class and suggesting modifications in equipment, physical environment, materials, etc.
- arranging transportation
- keeping up to date on research and new technology
- tutoring, supporting the regular teacher as necessary, planning recreational activities, vocational education
- coordinating volunteers and aides.

In a smaller district, some specialists' services can be purchased on a contract basis and others can be assigned to the district's special education staff (see Chapter 17 on

Budgets and Funding). Principals can facilitate the delivery of services by assuring that there is adequate space and equipment available, clearly assigned responsibility, appropriate flexibility in scheduling, and open communication among staff members. Regular communication between therapists/specialists and the students' teachers is essential to ensure carryover and reinforcement of therapy and to help the teachers make adequate adaptations.

Task Analysis

TASK ANALYSIS FOR EXPERIENCES OF SUCCESS

With the specialists' help, the teacher's challenge is to learn exactly what the students can and cannot do and to provide opportunities for success and mastery within those abilities. The key to this process is task analysis—breaking down any given task into its component parts and determining which parts the students can or cannot complete successfully. Once difficulties have been identified, the teacher has three options:

1. to provide training to help the students master necessary skills
2. to devise alternative methods or equipment for completing the task
3. to substitute another task.

AVOID OVERPROTECTION

While it is important to avoid creating a sense of failure by burdening handicapped youngsters with tasks they cannot do, it is equally important to encourage them to try new activities and make discoveries about their potential for enjoyment and control. While it is important to follow guidelines for sound preventive medical care, it also is essential to avoid overprotection. With these children, the effort toward independence is of utmost importance. Principals and teachers must expect children to take risks and responsibility. In doing so, they help foster social/emotional as well as academic progress.

Adaptive Equipment

With appropriate adaptive equipment, physically handicapped students can accomplish many things they could not do on their own. Sometimes the equipment needed is simple and can be improvised by the teacher, for example, inserting a pencil into a rubber ball or lump of clay so that the student can get a better grip on it. Other equipment, of course, is highly specialized and expensive, including artificial limbs (prosthetics), braces, headwands, motorized and individualized wheelchairs, and a variety of computerized aids now being developed. In the near future, scientists are likely to perfect the technology to turn vocal commands into computerized actions and typed messages into speech. District specialists should be consulted for assistance and advice in improvising or purchasing adaptive devices for students. In smaller districts, specialized equipment for low-incidence handicaps can be purchased cooperatively with other schools in the state or region.

It is useful for school administrators and/or teachers (especially of young children) to have some knowledge of the use and maintenance of these devices. This can be acquired through meetings with parents or specialists and with the help of the students themselves. School staff members should not attempt to make substantial repairs or adjustments except in emergencies, because of possible liability if damage occurs. They should be familiar enough, however, to do minor checks for proper fittings and use, to know what to do when batteries run out, and so on.

Other Issues

FREQUENT ABSENCES

Classroom teachers must consider the fact that these students may have frequent or prolonged absences. It is important to learn the cause and develop independent work that can help such students keep up with the class. In more extreme situations, home tutors, telephone hookups, and other support services can help bridge the gap.

DEALING WITH EMOTIONAL ISSUES

Social and emotional issues must be addressed in the education of the physically handicapped. As Meyen (1982) stresses:

> Opportunities must be provided for learning to express feelings of happiness, sadness, anger, and other emotions without fear of repercussions. Disabled students need to know that to experience and to express a wide range of feelings is normal and acceptable. They need to learn to deal with constructive criticism to be able to meet frustration and disappointment without experiencing fatal blows to their egos. They also need to learn to evaluate each experience and use information from these self-evaluations for future planning. Thus it is the important role of the teacher to facilitate exploration of feelings, including those related to family life, sexuality, and death (p. 394).

To do this successfully, teachers must be willing to examine and convey their own feelings honestly and to respond flexibly to students' individual readiness to learn (rather than relying on a rigidly prescribed curriculum).

PHYSICAL EDUCATION

P.L. 94-142 requires that all handicapped children have a physical education program. If the program must be adapted/individualized, this should be noted in the IEP. "Adaptive" physical education may focus more on the performance of rudimentary physical skills than on athletic activities and may require special instructional techniques or apparatus. As is true in academics, students should be encouraged, and given the opportunity, to develop their athletic potential—whether through highly competitive wheelchair sports or simple recreational activities. The introduction to satisfying leisure activities should be an important part of these children's educational program.

WHEN TO MAINSTREAM

Since physically handicapped children are so divergent in their educational needs and abilities, there is no sound rationale for grouping all of them together in special classes. (In the past, this was done purely for the convenience of the school district.) Not all students, though, can benefit from a regular full-time class placement.

SUGGESTED CRITERIA FOR MAIN-STREAMING

Bigge and Sirvis (1982) suggest students be considered for integrated classroom placement on the basis of their mental ability, mobility (with assistive device), ability to interact with peers, their own and their parents' desires, independent living skills, emotional stability, and communication ability. In some cases, the appropriate placement will be part-time in regular classes and part-time in special ones.

Students probably should be placed in segregated special classes if parents and educators feel it is best; the pupils need extensive or intensive therapy; and/or they need a special protective environment.

REFERENCES

Bigge, J. & Servis, B. (1982). Physical and multiple handicaps. In N. Haring (Ed.), *Exceptional children and youth* (3rd Ed.). Columbus, OH: Charles E. Merrill.

Meyen, E.L. (1982). *Exceptional children and youth: An introduction*. Denver: Love Publishing Co.

Regan, M. (1979). *Project VEIT handbook*. Unpublished manuscript, University of Kansas.

Chapter 14

Severe and Multiple Handicaps

SUMMARY

Federal Definitions

"Multiply handicapped" means concomitant impairments (such as mentally retarded—blind, mentally retarded—orthopedically impaired, etc.), with the combination causing such severe educational problems that the students cannot be accommodated in special education programs solely for one of the impairments. The term does not include deaf-blind children.

"Deaf-blind" means concomitant hearing and visual impairments that in combination cause such severe communication and other developmental and educational problems that the students cannot be accommodated in special education programs solely for deaf or blind children.

Common Characteristics

The learning problems of students with severe or multiple handicaps will vary greatly, depending on the type and degree of handicaps involved but may include lack of self-help and daily living skills, limited communication skills, socially inappropriate and sometimes bizarre behavior, restricted mobility, seizures and/or other medical problems and other effects; and need for intensive individual attention in educational programming.

Classroom Adaptations

The great majority of these students will be educated outside the mainstream, at least part of the day, in special classes, special schools, or institutions. For those who can benefit from regular class placement, a number of adaptations probably will be called for to meet the requirements of each handicap in evidence (see related chapters in Part II). There is a growing effort to place these students in regular class settings for part of their education.

Teaching Strategies

Again, the teaching strategies vary greatly, depending on the individual. Generally, the emphasis is on functional skills, from self-help to vocational. The severely retarded require highly structured and systematic programs; behavioral approaches have proved most successful. Attention must be given to social and leisure skills and to the ability to maintain and generalize what is learned. Nearly all these students need some training in communication skills; with the deaf-blind and some others, this will be the first priority.

COPING WITH SEVERE AND MULTIPLE HANDICAPS

A SMALL BUT VARIED POPULATION

This chapter treats a very small but very diverse population, united not so much by similarity of handicap as by the fact that the great majority will be educated outside the mainstream. Most of these students require so much individual attention and/or have such limited communication skills that they will not benefit from integrated class placement, and thus will be educated instead in special classes, special schools, or institutions.

Regular school principals rarely have had responsibility for such programs although this is changing with the trend toward greater integration. Increasingly, special classes are located on the campus of regular schools, and multihandicapped students are assigned regular class placements—where appropriate—at least part of the time.

Examples include hearing impaired youngsters who also have learning disabilities, students with mild physical as well as behavioral disabilities, and so on. The trend toward normalization, toward greater inclusivity, makes it more likely that regular school principals will come into contact with multihandicapped students at some time in their careers.

LEGAL ISSUES

The key legal issue here, as far as regular school administrators are concerned, is the requirement that the handicapped be educated in the most normal or "least restrictive" environment feasible, specifically:

LEAST RESTRICTIVE ENVIRONMENT REQUIREMENT

> (1) That to the maximum extent possible, handicapped children . . . in public or private institutions . . . are educated with children who are not handicapped, and (Sec. 121a.550(b)(1)). . . . In providing or arranging for the provision of nonacademic and extracurricular services and activities, including meals, recess periods [and others, such as "counseling, athletics, transportation, health services, recreational activities, special interest groups or clubs sponsored by the public agency . . . (Sec. 121a.306(b))"] each public agency shall ensure that each handicapped child participates with nonhandicapped children . . . to the maximum extent possible . . . (Sec. 121a.553).

Thus, in a situation with special, separate classes on a regular school campus or close by, principals will be called upon to arrange appropriate contact in some classes and activities. Chapter 21 on Student Relationships offers suggestions on how to make such contact a positive experience for those involved.

Where students are in separate, private schools, federal laws and regulations govern the relationship of public and private agencies, as follows:

PUBLIC/ PRIVATE SCHOOL RELATIONS

1. The agency must pay if a child is assigned to a private school by the public agency (see Chapter 6 on Placement).
2. The public education agency still must provide special education and related services similar to those available to public school students if the placement is made by parents (equal expenditure levels and with the same procedural protections).
3. Public and private students may not be separated according to religion or school enrollment when joint classes are held at the same site.
4. Public funds may not be used in private schools to pay for existing instruction, new facility instruction, or other benefits to the private school.

TYPES AND DEFINITIONS

When speaking of individuals so profoundly handicapped as to require institutionalization or lifelong custodial care, this most often implies the presence of serious mental retardation, alone or in combination with other handicapping conditions. The degree of retardation generally is expressed with the terms mild, moderate, severe, and profound. (The same terms are used with other disabilities as well.) They correspond to the standardized intelligence test scores listed in Table 12–1 in Chapter 12 on Mental Retardation.

PROBLEMS OF ASSESSMENT

The categories in Table 12–1 appear more straightforward than they actually are, however, for several reasons. First, the tests do not yield highly accurate results in the lower ranges. Some new assessments have been developed for the severely/profoundly retarded population; structured observations of specific skills also are useful. The definition of mental retardation addresses adaptive behavior as well as intelligence. For this reason, too, the IQ score alone cannot give complete assessment information. It is important not to rely on tests that are inappropriate to the individual.

Further, the retarded or limited abilities of these individuals may not result from mental handicaps alone but may stem from emotional (e.g., autism), physical (e.g., epilepsy), or other causes as well. Professionals working with this group often speak of "functional retardation." As Snell and Renzaglia (1982) state, "For all practical purposes, parents and educators should focus on programming rather than on searching for a more precise definition of the causes involved" (p. 144).

EDUCATIONAL STRATEGIES

Students with so-called low-incidence handicaps—the deaf-blind, the multiply handicapped, the most severely disabled—represent a wide range of educational problems and needs. Some will be capable of high school graduation, postsecondary and professional education, and of productive and self-sufficient adult lives. Helen Keller is the best known of these individuals; there are many others with multiple handicaps of different kinds who have achieved success in conventional terms.

For a great many severely and multiply handicapped individuals, however, the educational goal is placement in supervised living and working situations. Others will not be able to attain even that level of self-sufficiency; they may require lifelong institutional care. But however different their needs, all of these young people can learn. All can benefit from an educational program structured to their individual needs, whether the focus is on self-feeding, toileting, and grooming; communication and preacademic skills; appropriate social behavior; or advanced mathematics. Brief notes on the strategies appropriate to selected low-incidence groups follow.

ALL CAN BENEFIT FROM INDIVIDUALIZED INSTRUCTION

Multihandicapped Students in the Regular Classroom

The procedures in P.L. 94–142 contain guarantees to ensure that these students are adequately assessed, placed, and served. The key, in each step, usually is the involvement and coordination of specialists from the various disciplines. Each step and relevant requirements are summarized next.

SPECIAL EVALUATION REQUIREMENTS

- Evaluation: Multiple disabilities should be assessed accurately by the legally defined evaluation process (see Part I), which includes the requirements that: (1) Assessments must be designed to give accurate results despite a child's physical, sensory, or speaking skills, and (2) The child must be assessed in all areas related to the suspected disability, including, where appropriate, health, vision, hearing, social and emotional status, general intelligence, academic performance, communicative status, and motor abilities.
- IEP and Placement: Professionals familiar with educational programming for each of the handicapping conditions assessed should be involved in interpreting evaluation data, developing the IEP, and making placement decisions.
- Program: The delivery of appropriate education and related services to a multi-handicapped child will require multiple adaptations and additional coordination (e.g., scheduling of more than one type of therapy/special training; coordination of lessons between the regular class teacher and special educators). The strategies suggested in these chapters for each of the handicapping conditions (as modified by the requirements of other conditions) generally will apply.

MULTIPLE ADAPTATIONS

Deaf-Blind

Deaf-blind students vary in their level of intelligence. Their first educational need is a system of communication. The method taught to these students is manual signing. The "listener" holds the speaker's hands as information is being signed and reads the signs by touch, rather than by sight, as the hearing impaired would do. One-to-one interpretation is required.

Severely/Profoundly Retarded

Educational programming for the seriously functionally retarded focuses on functional activities—self-help and daily living skills, communication, basic social skills, and vocational education—and seeks to help students achieve the maximum degree of

PROGRAM CONSIDERATIONS FOR THE SEVERELY RETARDED

independence of which they are capable. (This is called habilitation.) These students require a highly systematic, structured program geared to their level of availability. A behavioral approach has proved successful most often.

Extensive preparation and task analysis are key elements of programming, as are selection of individually appropriate reinforcers, verification that the student is able to use the skill in "real life" (generalization from one context to another is very limited with this population), and additional evaluation/training to ensure that the skills are maintained over time. (Twelve-month, year-round programming often is necessary for such maintenance.) The behavioral approach also is used to extinguish socially unacceptable behaviors, to teach basic social and leisure skills, and to train those more able for employment.

REFERENCES

Federal Register. August 23, 1977, *42*, 1963.

Snell, M.E., & Renzaglia, A.M. (1982). Moderate, severe, and profound handicaps. In N. Haring (Ed.), *Exceptional children and youth*. Columbus, OH: Charles E. Merrill.

Chapter 15

Speech and Language Impairments

SUMMARY

Federal Definition

"Speech impairment" means a communication disorder such as stuttering, impaired articulation, a language impairment, or a voice impairment that adversely affects a child's educational performance.

Common Characteristics

Students served under this category demonstrate one or more of the following: speech that deviates significantly from the norm in flow, quality, pitch, intensity, breathiness, nasality, etc. This can include omissions, distortions, and/or substitutions in the production of sounds; physical impairments such as cerebral palsy, cleft palate, etc. (that affect speech); or failure to develop receptive and/or expressive language commensurate with age level.

Classroom Adaptations

Educators should provide a good speech model and assist language development with all students; create an accepting environment; model patience and tolerance; not embarrass or stress pupils by calling attention to speech problem or reprimanding or singling them out for corrective drills in class; not fill in words for those who stutter; discourage teasing; encourage speech when the students are doing well and cut short situations that add stress. Teachers also should arrange class schedules so that pupils receiving speech therapy miss less the essential parts of overall classwork; assist the speech pathologist by referrals and monitoring of student progress; and consult with specialists about normal speech and language development before becoming concerned about any individuals.

ROLE OF SPEECH AND LANGUAGE DISORDERS

SPEECH-IMPAIRED STUDENTS IN THE REGULAR CLASSROOM

Mainstreaming (educating in the regular classroom) is a fairly recent development for many individuals with handicaps. However, those with speech disorders have long been accepted into regular schools and integrated into the adult community. Defects of speech and of language development generally are considered less debilitating than other handicaps, but they can have profound effects on such individuals' social, emotional, and vocational, as well as academic, experiences.

TYPES AND DEFINITIONS

SPEECH AND LANGUAGE ARE SEPARATE SYSTEMS

P.L. 94-142 uses the single term "speech impaired" to include both speech and language disorders, but the two systems, although related, develop separately. Language is cognitive, while speech is motoric, or mechanical. Language impairments affect children's ability to understand and use the symbols, patterns, and structure of language. Speech impairments, narrowly defined, affect the organs and processes involved in producing the sounds of speech. One term used to include both of these is communication disorders.

Causes and Degree

Although the causes of many communication disorders remain open to debate, the majority seem to have developmental, rather than physiological, roots, and in only a small number of cases (generally related to strokes or head injuries) are speech and language abilities acquired and later lost.

POSSIBLE CAUSES

Some physiological causes can be fully or partially corrected by medical treatments, including surgery. Cleft lip and some allergies are examples. Other causes, generally more difficult to pinpoint and remediate, include neurological damage, maturational lags, environmental toxins, parent example and early encouragement, school experiences, misuse of the vocal system, and psychological problems.

Often, there will be more than one contributing factor and the exact nature of those factors will not be known. With stuttering, for example, there is continuing debate as to whether the origins are biological (caused by inherent, possibly genetic, factors), psychological (signs of neurosis), or environmental (the product of negative responses to early speech attempts).

Many children, even adults, have speech and language patterns that differ from the norm. By what criteria do they become disorders, requiring treatment? In addition to differing significantly from normal social expectations for each individual's age and culture, these communication problems must be severe enough to:

CRITERIA FOR SPECIAL EDUCATION

- affect educational performance negatively
- interfere with communication
- cause negative reactions from listeners
- be upsetting to the speaker.

Disorders may be assessed as mild to severe, depending on the extent of deviation from the norm and the degree of impact on the individual and the family. Language differences that are culturally based (e.g., the English of nonnative speakers) or within the normal range of variation for each age level do not qualify for special education services.

Types

Some terms used in describing children's communication disorders include:

SPEECH DISORDERS

- Fluency Disorder: disorder of speech flow, stuttering, problems with repetition, hesitation, prolongation
- Voice Disorders: abnormalities of pitch, quality, flexibility, etc. (usually too hoarse, breathy, or nasal)
- Articulation Disorders: problems of omissions, distortions, additions, substitutions in oral speech
- Orofacial Disorders: physical deformity of the jaw, mouth, or other speech-related organ(s)
- Developmental Phonological Disorders: delay in acquiring speech

LANGUAGE DISORDERS

- Developmental Language Disorder: failure to acquire language in early childhood (a severe disorder)
- Language Learning Disorder: delay in the acquisition of oral or written, expressive or receptive language (a milder disorder assessed in school age children of average or above-average intelligence)
- Aphasia: loss of acquired language, a result of brain injury.
- Hearing Impairment: see Chapter 10 on this handicap for definitions and discussion.

EDUCATIONAL STRATEGIES

THE ROLE OF SPECIALISTS

The most common model of service delivery for children with speech and language disorders is the itinerant speech pathologist who sees pupils individually or in small groups at various schools for about 30 minutes twice a week. These specialists, also called speech/language pathologists, communications disorder specialists (CDSs), or speech clinicians, also may be called upon to provide audiological services, work with hearing impaired and learning disabled students, and play a role in prevention and speech development for all students.

The three types of therapy generally provided are speech improvement, remedial speech correction, and speech and language development (this last, and to a lesser extent the first, overlaps with the regular language arts curriculum). The stages of therapy include:

ELEMENTS OF THERAPY

- reducing or eliminating known causes
- teaching the child to recognize the speech error
- helping the child learn to produce the correct sound (establishment) and practice it in a structured, clinical setting
- teaching the child to incorporate the correctly learned sounds into daily speech (transfer)
- helping the child maintain the skill, including the use of periodic monitoring.

The principal should assure that the specialist and the regular class teacher cooperate for referrals, assessment scheduling, monitoring, and, most importantly, creating an accepting, nonpressured environment in which students can work out their communication problems with a minimum of stress, embarrassment, and social pressure.

Chapter 16

Visual Impairments

SUMMARY

Federal Definitions

"Visually handicapped" means a visual impairment that, even with correction, adversely affects a child's educational performance. The term includes both partially seeing and blind children.

Common Characteristics

Visual impairments include several basic factors:

- The Self in the Environment: Students with visual impairments often have poorly developed concepts of space and objects (size, shape, relation to each other); poorly developed sense of self in the environment; difficulty in moving from place to place.
- Communication: Reading standard print materials and making use of other visual aids is difficult to impossible for students with severe impairments. Less severe visual handicaps may cause the student to read slowly or show a lack of interest in reading. Blind students lack communication through facial and body gestures.
- Behavior: Students with severe visual impairments may exhibit inappropriate mannerisms, such as rocking, eye poking, looking away from speaker, etc., or inappropriate behavior because of a lack of visual behavior models. They also

may appear slow, confused or disoriented. (Such behavior may be mistaken for mental or emotional problems but probably is not.)

- Physical signs: Students with visual handicaps may stumble or trip over things, blink often and be overly sensitive to light, rub their eyes excessively, shut or cover one eye, tilt their head or squint while looking, hold books very close, and be unable to see distant things. They may have eyes that are crossed, red, swollen, or watery or that itch or burn; recurring styes; poor sight, blurred or double vision; or dizziness, headaches, or nausea following close work.

Teaching Strategies

Principles should ensure that teachers deal effectively with the following factors:

- Physical Environment: Teachers should provide students with orientation to the physical arrangement of the classroom before school starts and each time the room is rearranged; select a willing peer to act as guide for the first few weeks and in emergencies such as fire drills; help students to make maximum use of residual vision by allowing them to sit close to the blackboard, demonstration, etc.; use adequate, nonglaring lighting; not do demonstrations with a bright light directly behind the speaker; install floor and ceiling materials that reduce glare.
- Special Materials and Equipment: Communication aids that visually impaired students can use include tape recorders, Braille writers, Braille slates and stylus; large type, tape-recorded, or Braille books; hand magnifiers; special electronic reading aids; abacus, tactile maps, speech-plus calculators; walking canes; and electronic mobility aids. They should rely on the visual impairments specialist for help in getting special materials from local libraries, community and school services, etc.
- Classroom Modifications: Educators should expect and encourage visually impaired students to participate and take responsibility as fully as others, encourage leadership, expect the same standard of behavior and responsibility for themselves and their belongings; expect the students to move around room and building; encourage them to ask questions when concepts or explanations are not understood clearly; use logical, sequenced instructional procedures; help the pupils compensate for lack of experience with objects and spatial concepts by defining terms and explaining ideas before the lesson, providing models or materials for the students to feel, avoiding abstract terms such as "over there" or "right here;" and start with concrete and specific examples before moving to the abstract.

It is important that teachers allow adequate time for completing assignments, especially reading; that they work ahead, preparing students for upcoming tasks; encourage pupils to use adaptive aids and provide a space for storing them; and given written tests, study sheets, etc., to the vision resource teacher to encode in Braille or make arrangements for an oral test. If students can type, they should be required to type written assignments. Teachers should use visuals with heavy, dark print; when using the chalkboard or showing filmstrips, they should read the titles aloud. A sighted student can relate or describe what is happening during a film or filmstrip to the visually impaired pupils.

THE IMPORTANCE OF SIGHT

People rely heavily on sight in their daily lives for communication and mobility, for enjoyment, and for meeting their most basic needs; it is through vision more than any other sense that they experience and make use of the world around them. The loss of that sense is a handicap with immediately obvious implications: without vision, people are greatly restricted in mobility and in the range of both actual and vicarious experiences that they can have. These restrictions, in turn, limit their abstract understanding and also the sense of control over themselves and their environment.

Since the losses are so obvious, the blind were one of the first handicapped groups to be served by special programs and today are accorded a wide range of special benefits by various levels of government.

SERVICES FOR THE BLIND

The term visually impaired encompasses many more individuals than those who are totally blind. Among them are many who can see shapes and even read print; thus the educational needs of these students will vary. All of those identified for special education and related services under this category will require assistance in many areas from trained specialists, but experience has shown that a great many of them can be integrated successfully into regular community school classrooms.

TYPES AND DEFINITIONS

LEGAL DEFINITIONS OF BLINDNESS

The legal definition of blindness includes those who can see at 20 feet what a normal person can see at 200 (20/200 vision) and those who have a restricted visual field of no more than 20 degrees. (The classification applies to the better eye with corrective lenses.) All individuals who meet these criteria are viewed as blind in terms of Social Security, tax, and other government benefits. However, children with corrected visual between 20/200 and 20/70 also may require special education services, and a significant number of the legally blind have in fact learned to use their residual vision to read large and/or regular print.

VISUAL READING ABILITY IS KEY DISTINCTION

It is this distinction—whether students can read visual materials of some kind—that makes the greatest difference in educational settings. For educational purposes, then, a different set of definitions is needed. The following are suggested in the *Project VEIT Handbook* (Regan, 1979):

- Totally Blind: Those who have no functional vision to see print or objects in their environment.
- Visually Impaired: Those who have low vision and can see print or objects with optical aids.
- Nearsightedness (Myopia): A common condition which causes blurred vision when the eyes try to focus on distant objects. A myopic person can see better when the object is brought close to the eye. The condition can be corrected by lenses.
- Farsightedness (Hyperopia): A common condition which causes the eye constantly to adjust in order to get a clear image of close work. Excessive

adjusting may cause symptoms such as eye fatigue, blurring, and headaches. This condition can also be corrected by lenses.

- Astigmatism: A condition which prevents rays of light from coming to a single point of focus on the retina of the eye and consequently produces an image that is distorted. Special lenses can correct most cases.
- Muscle Disorders: These conditions which may be either constant or intermittent are frequently associated with other visual defects. They include: crossed eyes, wall eyes, rapid involuntary eye movement (p. 157).

TYPES OF VISUAL IMPAIRMENTS

EARLY IDENTIFICATION IS IMPORTANT

Most seriously visually impaired children will have been identified before reaching school age, but it still is important to be aware of symptoms and conditions and to refer students for examination where visual impairment is suspected. Early identification of muscle disorders and other minor impairments can prevent further complications.

EDUCATIONAL STRATEGIES

A significant proportion (one half, according to Reynolds and Birch [1977]) of visually impaired special education students have other handicapping conditions as well. The seriously multihandicapped are likely to be served in residential or self-contained, rather than integrated, programs.

INTEGRATED VS. SELF-CONTAINED PROGRAMS

In the past, residential programs for blind children were the norm; today, most visually impaired students without further serious complicating conditions are educated in integrated classrooms. Special, self-contained classes in the regular school are rare. Much more common are instances in which students are assigned to regular, integrated classes with support from itinerant specialists or with time in a resource room.

Since serious visual impairments are quite rare, using the resource room model may be feasible only in large urban school systems. The most practical alternative generally involves special educators who make regular visits to visually impaired children in a number of schools and who are responsible for direct services, such as those described in the next section, and for supportive services to parents and teachers, including parent counseling, location and preparation of special materials, inservice training, and coordination of outside related services.

Special Education Needs

After being examined and fitted with corrective lenses to maximize any residual vision, the kinds of special education that visually impaired children will need include:

Educational Readiness: This involves home- and preschool-based training in gross and fine motor skills, social skills, self-concept and self-help.

COMMON PROGRAM ELEMENTS

Sensory Skills: These involve training in the use of residual vision (to help students make the most use of what vision they have) and in compensatory use of listening and other senses.

Reading and Writing: For visual readers, this may include additional reading and writing instruction (since visual impairments make reading slow and difficult) as well as instruction in using a conventional typewriter. The specialist is responsible for locating appropriate special materials such as large print or Braille books, magnifying lenses, and so on. New developments in computer technology are making available a wide range of electronic reading aids, including devices that greatly magnify writing, convert written words to Braille or to speech, and vice versa. Tactile readers will need training to read Braille and to use the Braille typewriter, or Braillewriter, and the Braille slate and stylus, a portable device that can be used with special paper for taking notes. Students also need to learn a written signature for daily use. With either tactile or visual methods, visually impaired students will require more time for reading than will regular students.

Orientation and Mobility: Specially trained instructors give formal training in various methods of moving through different environments safely without sight. Early training includes following a guide, using the forearm as a bumper, and trailing the fingers along a wall. Adolescents and teenagers may receive instruction in the use of a walking cane, and qualified young adults may choose the special training and commitment necessary to use a Seeing Eye dog. Electronic orientation devices also are being researched and developed.

Social and Daily Living Skills: Since they are unable to observe and imitate others, severely visually impaired children must be consciously taught many skills that seeing children acquire informally. Examples range from eating and bathing through using telephones and money. Similarly, the students may need instruction in posture, in turning the face toward the person to whom they are speaking, and in mastering a variety of standard social behaviors and in eliminating those that are socially unacceptable.

ASPECTS OF SUCCESSFUL PROGRAMMING

Reynolds and Birch (1977) suggest that every successful integrated program for educating the visually impaired should include: early education, parent education, individualized educational plans, well-oriented staff, quality leadership by visual impairment specialists, appropriate special materials, good counseling, coordination of school and health services, and statewide coordination of programs.

REFERENCES

Regan, M. (1979). *Project VEIT handbook.* Unpublished manuscript, University of Kansas.

Reynolds, M.C., & Birch, J.W. (1977). *Teaching exceptional children in all America's schools.* Reston, VA: The Council for Exceptional Children.

Part III

Administrative Issues

Chapter 17

Budgets and Funding

SUMMARY

Statement of the Problem

Special education, by definition, is more expensive than regular education and accounts for a significant portion of school budgets. Many services are mandated by law, but government financial support to pay for them is not always there.

Legal Issues

State and federal laws, primarily P.L. 94-142, require that special education services be provided to eligible students—whether or not the government has supplied adequate funding. Most federal monies are cycled through state governments that devise their own formulas for distributing them. (Administrators need to become familiar with the financial policies of their particular states because there is much variation among them.)

Funding is available from a variety of sources at the federal, state, and local levels. Each source has specific restrictions and regulations that must be checked before funds are applied for or spent. Among the practices that universally are illegal are: using federal funds in place of basic state allocations to all students ("supplanting") and charging more than one source for the same service ("double dipping").

Rationale

The federal role in education is primarily to protect the civil rights of individuals and the interests of the nation. State and local agencies, in turn, are responsible for providing the equitable public education services that the laws (and the Constitution) demand. Although state and district level administrators have ultimate responsibility for acquiring and budgeting the funds to do this, building principals with a solid understanding of special education financing often can locate additional resources, use existing ones more efficiently, do better planning, and provide higher quality services to students.

Approaches

Principals should become familiar with funding sources and their state's funding formula; after checking with district administrators they should take the initiative to locate and apply for new sources, such as private charity funds, state and federal vocational education programs, etc.; explore potential sources both within and outside the departments of education; be aware that special education students may qualify for some services not explicitly intended for handicapped populations because they meet other program requirements, such as low income, etc.; analyze a new funding source to be sure it is appropriate by asking:

- What types of funds are available?
- Who is eligible to receive them?
- How is application made?
- Are there any restrictions on the use of these funds?
- What are they?
- How are funds transferred from the funding source (delayed payment schedule, etc.)?

It is necessary to become familiar with the five steps in budget preparation: (1) identification of educational needs, (2) analysis of service delivery options, (3) exploration of funding sources, (4) matching appropriate source to cost items, and (5) preparation and submission of budget requests.

COPING WITH BUDGETS AND FUNDING

It is a commonly recognized fact that the cost of educating handicapped students is higher than that of nonhandicapped students. Indeed, the intent of special education is to provide instructional, and instructionally related, services not available in the regular program. Therefore, the total expense of educating a handicapped student will consist of the cost of the regular program plus the special educational needs created by the handicapping (or disabling) condition. These special programming expenditures beyond the basic student allocation in any district are referred to as excess cost and may range from a few hundred dollars to more than $25,000 per pupil per year. They represent a substantial portion of a school district's instructional budget.

DEFINITION OF EXCESS COST

Special education costs and finance policy can strongly influence delivery options. Administrators who are responsible for programs or schools having special education students must be aware of the costs of those options and services. Administrators also must be knowledgeable about the sources of funding for special education programs, how dollars earmarked for handicapped students are distributed, alternative sources of support for their services, and the ethical and legal responsibilities in managing such finances. This information is needed for a variety of purposes:

- to aid in planning and evaluating education programs for individual students
- to improve systemwide planning and evaluation
- to determine the levels of financing required to provide an appropriate education for all handicapped children
- to avoid inappropriate student classification and placement that may result from a misunderstanding of special education financing.

While district directors of special education are ultimately accountable for such financing, school administrators are assuming increasing responsibility for all programs in their building, including special education.

Armed with an understanding of special education finance, principals can:

WHAT SCHOOL ADMINISTRATORS SHOULD KNOW

- monitor effectively the special education portion of their building's programs
- participate as partners with special education administrators in planning for these services
- obtain access to funds for innovation, program development, special projects, teacher inservice training, or other activities to improve the education of students with handicaps.

This chapter is designed to assist administrators in gaining the fiscal information needed for effective programming in this field.

LEGAL ISSUES

Requirements for the education of handicapped students have been derived from court cases (e.g., *Mills v. D.C. Board of Education*, 348 F. Supp. 866 (D.D.C. 1972) and *Maryland Ass'n for Retarded Children v. Maryland,* Equity No. 100/182/77676 (Cir. Ct., Baltimore Cty., April 9, 1974) from legislation requiring services but providing no supportive funding (e.g., P.L. 93-112) and from laws that provide both directives for service and supporting funding (e.g., P.L. 94-142).

LACK OF FUNDS IS NOT A LEGAL EXCUSE

In the first two sources of requirements noted above, the public school system, even without funding, is expected to support required services and procedures. Lack of funding is not an acceptable excuse for failing to provide required services, nor should it be the major factor in determining service options. The individualized education plan for each student is to be established without regard to cost or present availability of services in the school district. Obviously, the consequence of having requirements without funding is that state and local educational agencies must provide resources from existing, or new, dollars to meet their legal obligations.

Federal Level

Some of those resources are available from state and federal programs and legislation. The most significant federal act is P.L. 94-142. This law is designed to provide monetary incentives for developing nonmandatory programs (e.g., early childhood education, extended public school programs serving handicapped youth ages 18 to 21) as well as monetary penalties for failure to provide required services.

FEDERAL SHARE: A LOT OR TOO LITTLE?

The federal share of the total costs of special education (primarily P.L. 94-142 funding) varies somewhat from state to state. According to Hartman (1980), local educational agencies often see the federal government as being in the position of dictating many rules of special education under the authority of legislative action but paying only a minor portion of the costs. From the federal perspective, acts such as P.L. 94-142 can be regarded as civil rights legislation for the handicapped that reinforces the state's own statutes and that needs to be carried out regardless of the level of U.S. funding. No matter what the perspective, it is clear that federal support for special and vocational education and rehabilitation is extremely important to school districts. (Each major source of federal support is discussed later in this chapter.)

State Level

State educational agencies are responsible for the distribution of state (and most federal) dollars to local school districts for special education programming. This state support includes two parts: (1) the handicapped allocations (excess program costs) and (2) basic program allocations. The latter is made up of basic educational support for all students equally, including the handicapped. It is illegal to substitute dollars provided directly or indirectly by federal allocations. For example, if state funds provide $1,000 per student in basic allocations, a federally supported allotment of $200 for special education and related services could not be used to reduce the state commitment to $800. This practice is known as "supplanting" and is strictly prohibited.

VARIATIONS AMONG STATES

Each state, through its legislative authority, has established funding formulas to be used in distributing the handicapped allocations to local educational agencies. These formulas often are complex in their consideration of staffing ratios, program costs, etc., and vary considerably from state to state. Local efforts also vary widely among and within states, and with some providing close to 100 percent funding of excess costs for special education, others much smaller shares (Department of Health, Education, and Welfare, 1979). (Because of the importance of state funding formulas, the subject also is discussed later in this chapter.)

Regional/Local Level

LOCAL TAX REVENUES

The greatest portion of the special education dollar comes from the federal and state levels. Smaller portions can be generated at the regional or local levels through some taxing scheme. Some states permit regional education units to levy taxes specifically for special education. Local school districts also may use special levies. (These sources, too, are explained in detail later.)

RELATIONSHIP BETWEEN SERVICES AND COSTS

The cost of special education is determined by the programming options selected for each handicapped student. Programs appropriate for mildly handicapped students obviously are less expensive than those for pupils with severe handicaps. However, they may vary considerably from student to student, depending on the complexity and intensity of services selected to meet unique needs. These costs also may vary within a school district from year to year, again depending upon the individuals in this population.

Another factor is the extent to which the district provides its own services or contracts with other districts or cooperatives. Smaller districts commonly purchase or contract out services they cannot themselves supply feasibly. For example:

EXAMPLES OF CONTRACTED SERVICES

- Comprehensive vocational assessments may be purchased for high school students from a regional vocational assessment center. Because of the expensive equipment and highly trained staff this service requires, the per-student costs of supplying such assessments in a small district could be three or more times the expense of purchasing the service. Contracted assessments also may produce a higher quality of service.
- A residential placement may be needed for a student with unique needs, such as a deaf/blind pupil. Only very large school districts would be expected to have comprehensive services for students with such low-incidence handicaps. While it always is preferable to keep students in their home community, those with multiple handicaps may be served best (although not always) in a residential center. When this option is chosen, the sending district must pay for both residential care and educational services. These may exceed $25,000 a year.

- A physical or occupational therapist may be obtained by a local school district on a part-time basis from the intermediate school district to serve a limited number of handicapped students. In such a case, the local district would have determined in advance that because of the few students needing such therapy, it would be most economical to contract for itinerant specialists. The alternative would be to hire these specialists through the local district. Contracts can run a year or longer, depending on need.

Hartman (1980) analyzes the relationship between special education programs and their costs, suggesting that a better understanding of the basis for the costs can lead to more realistic, effective, and efficient program selections and funding decisions. He cites the following reasons for excess costs (beyond regular education costs) of these special programs:

REASONS FOR EXCESS COSTS

- Additional and Related Special Education Services: Most handicapped students receive programs and services in addition to enrollment in regular education from itinerant specialists, consulting teachers, resource rooms, and other program formats described in this handbook.
- Special Classes: Self-contained classes for the moderately handicapped typically have much smaller student/teacher ratios, and the additional classroom costs (teacher salaries and benefits, operation and maintenance expenses) greatly increase the per-student expenditures.
- Multiple Special Education Services: Some students require a combination of services—for example, special classrooms plus physical therapy.
- Residential Programs: Public or private residential settings are the costliest placements because they involve such additional expenses as housing, feeding, etc.
- Identification, Assessment, and Educational Planning: The process of individualized assessment and planning required for each handicapped student creates additional expenses, primarily in staff time.
- Additional Staff Support and Training: Support and training also are needed for teachers, principals, administrators, parents, nonhandicapped students, and others to make the least restrictive placement approach effective. This involves the services of trainers, consultants, school psychologists, counselors, social workers, etc.
- Greater Age Span: P.L. 94-142 encourages education for handicapped students under age 5 and from 18 to 21. These are an additional financial burden for schools, especially since they may require large concentrations of resources for few students.

A TAXONOMY OF SPECIAL EDUCATION FINANCE

To enhance understanding of a complex system, Crowner (1985) has developed a taxonomy of special education finance. The taxonomy appears to have advantages over other sources of finance information that lack consistent terminology and fail to cover all of the relevant elements. It is used as a basis for the following discussion of special education funding.

The taxonomy classifies financial terms into four categories:

1. base, the element(s) upon which revenues are figured
2. formula, the method used to compute revenues generated by the base elements
3. source, the agency from which revenues flow
4. type, restrictions placed on the possible use of revenue by the source (p. 504).

Bases for Computing Revenue

Different states compute the amount of funding allotted to districts according to different bases. Crowner lists five of these upon which special education funding may be determined.

DIFFERENT WAYS OF COMPUTING FUNDING

1. *Pupil Base:* Funding is generated on the basis of numbers of students served. This base figure includes all students from the district eligible for special services under the guidelines of the funding source, including those in residential placement or those receiving purchased services from another agency.
2. *Resource Base:* Funding is generated on the basis of the specific resources needed to meet student needs. The resource most typically identified is personnel, but others may include facilities, equipment, supplies, etc.
3. *Service Base:* Funding is generated on the basis of the type of service supplied—an itinerant program such as speech therapy, or placement in a resource room or a self-contained special classroom.
4. *Cost Base:* Funding is generated on the basis of the actual cost of operating a special education program. Cost guidelines often are established for various services so that expenses claimed by districts do not exceed a percentage of the cost to be covered or level of cost per service that the funding source has established as reasonable.
5. *Unit Base:* Funding is generated on the basis of a combination of possible funding bases. For example, a unit may include a teacher, an aide, and a fixed number of students, with moneys provided for the resources necessary to operate it. A school district would be reimbursed for each such unit claimed. Funding sources usually allow reimbursement for partial units (e.g., one-half a unit) since enrollment rarely matches the fixed number of students in a given unit. A special case of unit-based funding arises when reimbursed costs are limited to all or a portion of the salaries of persons who work with handicapped students.

Formulas for Computing Revenue

As Hartman (1980) suggests, funding formulas for special education are simply vehicles for transferring dollars earmarked for educating handicapped students from

FUNDING FORMULAS PROVIDE INCENTIVES

one governmental level to another (e.g., state department of education to local school district). He adds that, "given the same assumptions for a special education program, the funding levels would be identical under any formula" (p. 6). Therefore, the choice of formula at any level becomes important for the incentives and disincentives it creates for the school districts in providing services for handicapped students, not necessarily for the amount of money it will generate.

Crowner (1985) lists five different (although not necessarily mutually exclusive) types of formulas in his taxonomy of special education finance:

> *Excess cost formula.* This formula (A) takes the cost of a basic education program, (B) compares that figure to the cost of a given special education program, and then (C) applies funding to make up some or all of any discrepancy associated with excess costs of special education. Typically, this formula is applied to the pupil base where the per-pupil cost of a basic education is compared to the per pupil cost of special education.
>
> *Percent of cost formula.* This formula limits the revenue generated by a base to some fractional percentage of the real cost associated with that base. For example, in Wisconsin, it is applied to the cost base by reimbursing a limit of about 70 percent of allowable costs.
>
> *Straight sum formula.* This formula applies a fixed reimbursement for each base element reported; for example, $2,000 per pupil or $10,000 per teacher.
>
> *Weighted formula.* This formula applies differential weights to base elements (Rossmiller, Hale, & Frohreich, 1970). These weights may be based on indices of actual cost or on a perceived relative need. For example, a severely handicapped pupil's educational program can be assumed to be more costly than an educational program for a mildly handicapped pupil, or a resource service may be considered less costly than a self-contained class.
>
> *Mixed Formula.* This formula may consist of any combination of the other four formulas. Many combinations are possible. For example, percent of cost could be applied with the weighted formula, resulting in reimbursement of some percentage of the relative higher and lower cost figures associated with different services. That is, the state could determine that a student in a resource room should be weighted 1.5 times a regular student, in the basic education program, but choose to reimburse on 75 percent of the resulted figure (p. 505).

Type of Revenue

Certain restrictions always are placed on funds supplied by the various sources. These constraints may set limits to the length of the fiscal support or the population to which it is directed, or they may require a percentage of support from the recipient school district. Such controls are an attempt to ensure that the funded program reflects the goals of the financial source. For example, funding intended to stimulate program development in school districts would not be available on a continuing basis; rather, it would be provided for a fixed time to support start-up costs. Once a program is established, the school district would be expected to find other sources of support.

In his taxonomy, Crowner (1985) identifies seven types of revenue and their restrictions:

TYPES OF REVENUE

1. *Continuing Fund*. This type can continue for several years, although the level of funding may fluctuate according to yearly appropriation levels or other factors. Continuing funds usually are stable and can be relied upon to support long-term services. State funding for basic education can be considered a form of continuing funds.
2. *Noncontinuing Funds*. These are provided for a fixed period and usually are intended to remedy a short-term need (e.g., teacher inservice course), stimulate a district-supported program (e.g., establishment of an assessment center), or address other district problems of a short-term nature. Competitive grant awards offered by state or federal agencies are examples. While they have a definite termination date, and rarely extend beyond three years, they can be excellent sources of support for program enhancement or development. However, administrators and principals must keep in mind the time limitations of this funding and not become dependent on it for essential services such as classroom teachers or aides.
3. *Targeted Funds*. This type of revenue is earmarked for specific items: program types (e.g., vocational education), classifications of students (e.g., secondary special education), or categories such as personnel and equipment. Dollars not spent on targeted items are considered misused and must be returned to the funding source. Examples of targeted funds are those set aside in the Carl D. Perkins Vocational Education Act (P.L. 98-523) for exclusive use with handicapped populations; they may not be used for any other purpose.
4. *Discretionary Funds*. These may be used to support whatever activities are considered relevant to the objectives of a funding source. Certain moneys coming to the states from the federal government fall in this category.
5. *Inside Formula Funds*. These are received from one funding source and must be deducted in part (or entirely) from a request for reimbursement from another source. This is simply a mechanism used internally by a school district or other agency to distribute financial support from different sources to various special education program areas.
6. *Outside Formula Funds*. This type of revenue, when received by a school district or agency, is not deducted from other primary sources of funding. However, administrators should be warned that under no circumstances may they use two sources of funding to pay for the same item. This sometimes is referred to as double dipping and is strictly illegal. An example would be requesting reimbursement from a granting source for a cost item that has been

paid for by state basic education funding. While the terms "inside" and "outside" funding are not used commonly, they do illustrate an important concept in sorting out the many different sources of fiscal support for special education.

FUNDS AWARDED IN DIFFERENT WAYS

7. *Matching Funds*. The restriction on this type of revenue is that the receiving agency must provide a preestablished portion of the cost of a funded program. In the true sense of the word, "matched" cost would be equal contributions from the receiving agency and the funding source. In practice, the portion contributed by each will vary depending on the funding source's guidelines. Further restrictions may exist on the source of the matching dollars contributed by, say, the school district. It often is illegal to match one batch of federal dollars with other federal dollars. This is reasonable in light of the fact that a major purpose of the matching requirement is to show commitment by the agency receiving the funding. When it is necessary to match a funding source 50-50, or at any other percentage, the matched portion may not need to be in actual dollars; "in-kind" contributions often are permissible—services, facilities, and/or equipment provided by the agency. Of course, these contributions must be real and must represent necessary program items.
8. *Mixed Funds*. These represent any combination of two or more of the types of funding above.

SOURCES OF REVENUE

School districts may draw upon many sources of revenue to support the excess cost of special education services. Prudent administrative practice suggests that a district utilize its funding resources to the maximum extent possible. This requires knowledge of the funding possibilities, ability to match a funding source with a district need, skill in obtaining and managing funds, and supportive school district administration that recognizes the benefits of a broad base of financial backing.

Knowledge of funding possibilities extends beyond simple awareness of the existence of a source of funds. An administrator who is effective in this area must find answers to questions such as the following:

FUND-FINDING SKILLS

- What are the types of items supported by the funding source?
- Who is eligible to receive funding?
- How is the application for funding made?
- What are the restrictions on the use of funds?
- What are the conditions for transferring dollars from the funding source to the recipient agency?

Governmental funding sources are obligated to make information available through rules and regulations that answer these and other pertinent questions. While not required to do so, private funding sources also usually make information available to potential grantees as a means of stimulating a large pool of qualified applicants. It is preferable to request information from a funding source by means of a formal letter so that it is documented, as opposed to telephone calls that can be forgotten in the midst of a busy schedule.

Once aware of various funding possibilities, the administrator needs to determine whether a potential source can be a good match with a particular program need. Considerations in making this decision include:

MATCHING FUNDING SOURCE WITH PROGRAM

- whether the intent and budgetary needs of the program to be funded are understood
- whether any restriction on the funding would jeopardize program outcomes (e.g., necessary equipment cannot be charged to the funding source)
- whether restrictions, either programmatic or fiscal, would be unacceptable to the school district (e.g., cost reimbursed on a delayed schedule).

Skill in obtaining and managing funds is necessary for any school district administrators, but it is especially important for those involved with special education programs. While the same financial opportunities are available to all districts, those whose administrators have fund-seeking skills almost always will have more dollars available for special education than will their counterparts. The process of writing a grant proposal, for example, is not nearly as difficult as it may seem, but some administrators have trouble mastering it. Numerous resource materials are available to aid those seeking out-of-district funding in support of a worthwhile project.

FUND-SEEKING SHOULD BE ENCOURAGED

It should be made clear that the district director of special education is the person responsible for obtaining and managing continuing funding for this field. However, other district personnel should be encouraged to seek out special funding opportunities, too; as long as appropriate channels are followed, communication is maintained and turf infringements are avoided.

Supportive district administrators are an essential ingredient in establishing a broad base of funding for special education. Because of special accounting procedures, required reporting, or other procedural requirements that often follow such funding, a school district's central office can be reluctant to approve requests for such moneys. The advantages and disadvantages of a source such as a federal grant award should be weighed carefully. Obviously, such consideration involves questions: (1) How badly needed is the program to be supported? (2) If it is badly needed, are other funding opportunities available?

Crowner's (1985) taxonomy lists five major sources of funding, discussed next.

Federal Sources

FEDERAL ROLE

The role of the federal government, as noted earlier, is to protect the constitutional rights of children for equal access to educational programs and to provide the physical resources necessary to maintain programs of national interest. Most federal money reaches school districts indirectly by flowing through state departments of education or intermediate school districts. Methods of dispersing federal dollars may be classified as full support, partial assistance grants, grants based on formula, and set-aside moneys (Marinelli, 1976). A few of the many federal sources are described next.

The Education for All Handicapped Children Act of 1975 (P.L. 94-142)

94-142: A FORMULA GRANT SYSTEM

This act is an example of a formula grant system to distribute resources and provide basic support to state-operated or state-aided schools in providing adequate services to handicapped students as defined by the law. Allocation of funding is based on a percentage of the average annual per-student expenditure (in the state or the nation, whichever is higher) multiplied by the number of eligible handicapped students in average daily attendance in these schools. Student eligibility criteria are specified in the implementing regulations and may be refined through state formulas for the distribution of funds. These formulas vary considerably from state to state. Administrators should consult their state departments of education for specific details.

Title VI-B of P.L. 93-380 provides grants to states to stimulate programs and services for handicapped students. Local school districts usually are required to make competitive application to the state department of education for these funds. Exhibit 17-1 indicates how funds from this source have been used in Washington State. Partial program assistance is provided through Title VI-D moneys to institutions of higher education, as well as other agencies, to stimulate the training of professionals in special education. These funds can be used for training program development or for fellowship grants to students pursuing careers in special education.

Supplemental Education Services for the Handicapped in State Facilities (P.L. 89-313)

This 1965 act provides full or partial support of four schools for the deaf, regional model centers for specific disability or age groups, and media-related services for the blind.

Carl D. Perkins Vocational Education Act of 1984 (P.L. 98-523)

SET-ASIDE FUNDS FOR VOCATIONAL EDUCATION

This act is an excellent example of setting dollars aside in an appropriation to be used for a special purpose or a special group. This method of funding, known as "set-aside," is designed to ensure that the money appropriated under a part of an act will be used exclusively for a specific purpose and not commingled with dollars intended for other purposes. Part A represents 57 percent of the moneys available under the Perkins Act and provides vocational education services and activities to only six targeted groups: handicapped (10 percent), disadvantaged (22 percent), single working parents and homemakers (8.5 percent), adult training and retraining (12 percent), those in programs to eliminate sex bias and sex role stereotyping (3.5 percent), and criminal offenders (1 percent). Funds set aside for the handicapped are allocated based on the number of such students served in the previous year (in relation to the total within the population of the state). Additional stipulations: (1) federal funds under this act used to pay administrative cost must be matched 50 percent at both the state and local levels; (2) funds for disadvantaged and handicapped students can pay

Exhibit 17–1 Use of Title VI-B Funds in Washington State

1. *Discretionary Competitive Funds*: These involve an annual competition for support of projects proposed by local and intermediate school districts and universities. Priorities for funding are established each year based on a state needs assessment. Priorities for the 1983-84 school year, for example, were rural-remote service delivery, services for behaviorally disordered students, regular education/special education interface, transition models, and career and vocational education.
2. *Adoptions:* These involve an annual competition for support of local education agency proposals for adoption of nationally validated projects/programs. Some 60 of these programs are available, including: (a) Learn cycle-responsive teaching, (b) MAcomb 0-3 regional project: a rural child/parent service, (c) Oklahoma child services demonstration center for secondary LD students, (d) PEOPLE—Physical Education Opportunity Program for Exceptional Learners, Rutland Center: a developmental therapy model for treating emotionally disturbed.
3. *Regional B Funds:* These involve applications by local school districts to intermediate education agencies (ESDs) for funding of inservice training or supplemental costs associated with continuing direct services to handicapped students. These funds are made available by a committee of special education directors from the region served.
4. *Products/Practice Dissemination Grants:* The State Department of Education in 1983-1984 asked ESDs to nominate exemplary projects in their region, then invited these projects to submit proposals for state funding support.
5. *Training Grants (from Title VI-B and Title VI-D):* These provide funds for training projects related to personnel needs identified through the statewide needs assessment. Examples include grants for parent training and to institutions of higher education for training teachers and administrators.
6. *Vocational Education Minigrants:* These grants give priority to training for vocational and special education teachers of handicapped students. Training must include both groups, and both the local district vocational education director and the special education director must sign the proposal.
7. *Preschool Incentive Grants (annual competition):* These are designed to assess local education agencies (LEAs) in their efforts to expand the scope of services available and to upgrade the quality of existing preschool programs. Priority content areas considered for the 1983-1984 fiscal year were: cooperative screening and assessment, parent involvement/training, interagency transition efforts, and mainstreaming.
8. *Preschool Incentive Grants (RFA):* These moneys were made available during the 1983-1984 fiscal year (one-time-only application process) for the start-up costs associated with providing special education services for 3- and 4-year-old students.

Source: Adapted from Office of the Superintendent of Public Instruction (1985). *Sources of Funds Available for Special Education*, Olympia, WA: author.

for 50 percent of the cost of supplemental services if the pupils are mainstreamed, or 50 percent of the excess cost of those supplemental services if the youngsters are in separate programs.

Job Training Partnership Act (P.L. 97-300)

Some sources of federal funding for schools come from outside the Department of Education. Among these is the 1982 Job Training Partnership Act (JTPA), which is under the Department of Labor. It replaced the 1973 Comprehensive Training and Employment Act (CETA), which also had helped fund some programs for the handicapped. The JTPA is intended to

> . . . establish programs to prepare youth and unskilled adults for entry into the labor force and to afford job training to those economically disadvantaged individuals, and other individuals facing serious barriers to employment, who are in special need of such training to obtain productive employment (sec. 2).

JTPA MAY PROVIDE EXTRA VOCATIONAL FUNDS

Educational agencies may apply for funds under certain sections of the act (e.g., Title II-A and Title II-B). However, regulations governing JTPA are somewhat complicated and require a thorough understanding of the various parts of the act before an application is developed. Administrators must take the initiative in seeking out JTPA funds because school districts may not be notified of their eligibility to participate in this program.

Although handicapped individuals are not mentioned specifically as a target population, they are eligible for services under parts of the law. Restrictions on some JTPA moneys, such as those concerning performance expectations, may prove cumbersome in working with handicapped populations. Other parts of the act (Title II-B) are more flexible and offer special opportunities for handicapped students (e.g., summer youth programs). Information about JTPA is available through the local Private Industry Council or through the governor's office. JTPA is only one example of many programs operating through the Department of Labor and other federal agencies that supply dollars that can be tapped to support services for handicapped students.

Other Federal Funding

HANDICAPPED STUDENTS MAY MEET OTHER CRITERIA

While it is not within the scope of this chapter to review all possible sources of federal funding, school administrators should be aware of major sources of continuing categorical aid, including vocational education, education of children from low-income families, compensation to schools for federal tax-exempt property, school food services, and educational research and development. Although these aid programs may be intended to serve different populations, handicapped students often qualify as a result of meeting criteria other than disability (e.g., low income).

State Sources

While the role of the federal government in the education of the handicapped has been to encourage innovation and stimulate program development, it is the responsibility of the states to provide the actual education. Sources of state financing for special education consist of:

- regular state funds for each student, including special education students
- state aid for special services distributed on a formula basis
- local tax levies.

EFFECTS OF STATE FORMULAS

The dollar amounts and formulas used to distribute special education funds to local school districts vary considerably across states. Some states cover close to 100 percent of the excess costs for special education while others provide much smaller amounts. As discussed earlier, the state formula appears to have greater impact on the percentage of children served in any given category of handicapping condition than on the total dollar amount distributed. States using a weighted approach to funding special education report slightly higher percentages of the school age population served as handicapped (McGuire, 1982).

Education Funding

Because of the differences between states in the selection of funding formulas, and the frequency with which these formulas are revised, it is not possible to discuss this area in specifics. Administrators should obtain, and become familiar with, a copy of their state's regulations concerning the disbursement of such funds.

EXAMPLE OF ONE STATE

Under the Washington State formula, for example, resources (teachers, classified staff, assessment personnel, administrators, instructional materials, and equipment) are allocated to each of 14 handicapping categories according to assumed need. Students with more severe handicaps have greater resources than those with less severe dysfunctions. State guidelines assist in the reasonably objective identification of handicapping conditions; the actual program and resource provisions for each student are left for district determination. The funding-distribution formula is complex in its consideration of local district staffing considerations and ratios; however, it can be viewed as simply a weighted student allocation that gives consideration to existing salary levels and staffing characteristics in each of the districts (Johnson & Reff, 1983).

Funding Outside the State Education Department

OTHER STATE FUNDS

As is the case with the federal government, states also provide support for school-age children from sources outside of the department of education. These may offer local school districts dollars for special projects, equipment or supplies, resource personnel, or entire programs. For example, a state department of vocational rehabilitation (DVR)—operating under federal guidelines and receiving partial federal support—often works closely with public school systems. It can enter into agreements with local districts to provide employment-related training and services to eligible secondary school students.

In some states, the DVR is extremely active in the public schools, offering a variety of services to handicapped students of 16 or older; in other states, it has taken a somewhat hands-off position toward involvement with potential clients who are still being served in public schools.

Administrators must become knowledgeable about their state's interpretation of eligibility criteria, services provided, and methods of distributing funds.

Other Sources

Intermediate Education Agencies

ROLE OF INTER-MEDIATE DISTRICTS

These entities play an important role in the distribution of funds and services to local districts within their jurisdiction. In some states, they may generate revenue through special regional taxing schemes. In Michigan, for example, intermediate units have authority to levy taxes for special education. However, the role of intermediate agencies usually is limited to distributing special education funds from state and federal sources for such activities as special projects, teacher inservice training, research, etc., or providing those services directly to local districts. They also may offer special programming options or equipment (e.g., vocational assessment, equipment for the blind) on a cooperative basis to districts. Intermediate educational agencies can be excellent sources of information about state and federal funding possibilities.

Local Sources

Local revenues for special education include funds generated by taxing mechanisms such as property or other taxes. At the discretion of local school districts, special levies may be placed on the ballot and, if approved by voters, can support educational programs for all students, including the handicapped. Occasionally, a levy to support only special education services will be on the ballot. Local districts also may request bond issues to support facilities for general education, special education, or both.

Private Sources

PRIVATE FUNDING: A LARGELY UNTAPPED SOURCE

Revenue may be given by, or solicited from, individuals, charities, or private businesses. This is the least-used source of funds for public school special education, in part because the procedures used in obtaining private funds, as well as the specific sources, are not well understood by school personnel. In the past, public school education has been perceived as a public obligation rather than a cause for charitable donations. However, in recent years, school administrators are recognizing the advantage of private funding to assist with special programs, to purchase equipment and supplies, to conduct research, and to improve education in other ways.

Private funding normally is obtained through some sort of application process, depending on the source and often on the level of request. Applications may range from simple to quite complex—from a simple letter requesting funds to a detailed document. Schools seeking funding for a worthwhile cause that have exhausted governmental sources should explore private funding. Local libraries should have lists, journals, and books on funding sources.

PREPARING BUDGETS

There are five essential steps in the preparation of budgets for educational programs:

STEPS IN BUDGET PREPARATION

1. identification of educational needs to be addressed
2. analysis of services needed and cost variations between service delivery options
3. exploration of funding sources, including restrictions and methods of disbursement of revenue
4. matching of sources of funding to cost items or service units
5. preparation and submission of program budget requests, along with program justifications.

The regular administrators' role in budget preparation will vary, depending on the distribution of responsibilities between themselves and the special education administrators. At the very least, the former should provide input into the first two steps above. In smaller districts, or those with strong tendencies toward building level control, the regular program administrator (e.g., principal) could become involved in all five steps. Preparation and submission of a competitive grant proposal also would involve the administrator at all five steps. Therefore, four of the five are discussed next; Step 1, identification of educational needs, is addressed in other chapters.

Step 2: Analysis of Services

The cost structure of special services for handicapped students involves the type of delivery system options available (e.g., self-contained classrooms, resource rooms), type of the students' handicapping condition(s) and their severity, and the relationship between special and regular education costs (excess costs). The costs of each special program, including its activities, organizational units, or individual cost items can be analyzed.

Marinelli (1976) suggests that "any of several techniques can be employed for determining special education costs. An excess cost approach may be employed which is based on (a) the current best practice of programs within the jurisdiction of a local educational agency, (b) a step-by-step documentation of need for each potentially employable type of delivery system, or (c) an accounting model" (p. 188).

Step 3: Exploration of Funding Sources

This begins by looking at the continuing funds already available to the district. Funding such as state formula grants for excess costs may wholly or partially support the program under consideration. If current district funding is not sufficient, or cannot be matched appropriately to program activities, the search must continue. The district's grants specialist, if there is one, should be consulted. The person in this position frequently has a broad base of information about federal, state, local, and even private funding possibilities. If there is no such individual, the intermediate educational agency and/or the state department of education should be contacted.

Step 4: Matching of Sources of Funding

Once possible sources of funding have been identified, regulations governing the use of the moneys should be reviewed thoroughly. Special attention should be given to restrictions on the use of the funds. Among the questions that should be asked:

PAY ATTENTION TO FUNDING RESTRICTIONS

- Can the funds be used appropriately to support the desired activities?
- Can the funds be obtained quickly enough?
- Is there a matching requirement?
- Will the funding continue for as long as it is needed?
- Can the district really compete if the funds are distributed on a competitive basis?
- Does the funding agency have any expectations of the administrator or the district that are not acceptable (e.g., reporting requirements)?

If the answers to these questions are acceptable, then a probable funding source has been found.

Step 5: Preparation and Submission of Program Budget

The annual budget request for special education is prepared, along with a program justification, and submitted with those from other organizational units to be reviewed by the district. These budget requests then are submitted to the school board for review and are accepted or revised.

BUDGET LINE ITEMS

Traditionally, in the preparation of the budget, figures are grouped by "line items" or "objects of expenditures" such as personnel, fringe benefits, supplies, equipment, travel, and so forth. These line items are called direct costs of program operation since they are related directly to the delivery of services. Expenses of supporting activities are referred to as indirect (or overhead) costs and include administrative expenses, accounting, and other costs associated with housing the program. In budget planning for grants and contracts, these indirect charges may be fixed at a predetermined level, say 8 percent of the direct costs.

In addition to projecting the line item costs, it is necessary to figure those of certain components of special and regular education. These components allow budget planners to determine excess costs of special education services and to plug necessary figures into state formulas. Components to be figured include:

- regular program costs
- regular program costs per pupil (regular program cost divided by the number of full-time pupils in regular education)

- special program costs by category of exceptionality, unit, or other element upon which revenues are based
- special program costs per pupil, unit, or other base element (cost of special education divided by the number of full-time pupils in special education, units, or other base elements)
- the cost differential or excess costs per pupil, unit, or other base element (component 4 minus component 2)
- the cost index of special to regular programs (component 4 divided by component 2).

Once this information has been obtained, it can be applied in the state special education funding formula, and to other sources of funding, in determining the district and nondistrict share of special education financing.

A principal or administrator who has mastered these basic aspects of budget preparation and special education funding may find that the school has more resources available more easily than previously seemed possible.

REFERENCES

Carl D. Perkins Vocational Education Act, P.L. 98-523, 98 Stat. 2433 (1984).

Crowner, T. (1985). A taxonomy of special education finance. *Exceptional Children, 51*, 503–508.

Education for All Handicapped Children Act of 1975, P.L. 94–142.

Educational Amendments of 1974, P.L. 93–380, 88 Stat. 484 (1974).

Hartman, W.T. (1980). *Policy effects of special education funding formulas*. Palo Alto, CA: Stanford University.

Job Training Partnership Act, P.L. 97–300, 96 Stat. 1322 (1980).

Johnson, J. & Reff, D. (1983). Funding for special students. *Olympia Schoolwatch*, Citizen Education Center Northwest.

Kerr Center Parents Association v. Charles, 572 F. Supp. 448 (D. Ore. 1983), 581 F. Supp. 166 (D. Ore. 1983).

McGuire, C.K. *State and federal programs for special education finance: A guide for state policy makers*. Princeton, NJ: Educational Testing Service, Educational Policy Research Institute.

Marinelli, J. (1976). Financing the education of exceptional children. In F.J. Weintraub, A. Abeson, J. Ballard, & M.T. LaVar (Eds.), *Public policy and the education of exceptional children*. Reston, VA: The Council for Exceptional Children.

National School Boards Association (1979). *A Survey of Special Education Costs in Local School Districts*, Office of Federal Relations, June.

Rossmiller, R., Hale, J., & Frohreich, L. (1970). *Educational programs for exceptional children: Resource configurations and costs*. Madison, WI: University of Wisconsin, Madison.

Supplemental Education Services for the Handicapped in State Facilities, P.L. 89–313, 79 Stat. 1158 (1965).

U.S. Department of Health, Education, and Welfare (1979). *State financing of special education* (Technical Analysis Paper 6). Washington, DC: Author.

Chapter 18

Community Relations

SUMMARY

Statement of the Problem

The integration of handicapped students into the regular schools often affects school/community relations by generating both new areas of controversy and new demands for community resources to meet student needs.

Legal Issues

Ordinarily, when educators think of legal relations between school and community, it is, correctly, in terms of local or perhaps state government (which are not covered in this handbook). However, federal laws do call for community involvement in requiring that both state and local education agencies make public their applications for federal handicapped education funding, that they provide for public participation in formulating them, and that the state hold public hearings on the plans.

Rationale

Like other public agencies, the schools are funded by and intended to serve the citizens; they must be able to convince the community that they are indeed serving well. This is quite complicated in today's extremely heterogeneous communities. In fact, it has become impossible to please everyone, so it is even more important to consciously promote positive public attitudes toward the schools whenever possible. It also has become important to cultivate good community relations as schools become more dependent on nonschool local resources in their attempts to meet growing demands on increasingly limited budgets.

Approaches

Good community relations begin with good programs, good staff, sound educational policy, and so on. It also is helpful and important to give prompt and courteous response to community concerns, inform local news media of school/student/staff achievements and special projects, and actively seek positive publicity; invite the public to become familiar with the school and its programs; make facilities available as a community service; make use of volunteer programs and cooperative arrangements with local business, community, and service organizations; encourage school staff members to become involved in such organizations; provide adequate support to school advisory boards; and treat parents as equal partners in their children's education.

THE NEED FOR COMMUNITY RELATIONS

SCHOOL/ COMMUNITY INTERCON-NECTIONS

Public schools, as their administrators know all too well, do not exist in a vacuum. They are part of a larger community that they both affect and are affected by. Politics, funding, racial tensions, educational trends and styles—these are a few of the many strands that make up the web of school-community interconnections. The system is a complex and sensitive one; each part affects many others.

The demand that exceptional students be integrated into neighborhood schools creates extra community relations pressures on those schools. As a controversial and expensive educational policy, mainstreaming often has become a focus for negative attitudes toward the schools. These may come from parents of the nonhandicapped, who may feel their children's education will suffer because of the increased demands on limited educational resources or from nonparents who see special education as just one more unjustified public expense. While there also are supportive partisans who recognize the social and economic benefits of mainstreaming, they have a tendency to appear less vocal than the critics.

MAIN-STREAMING CREATES NEW PRESSURES AND NEEDS

At the same time, it is true that since handicapped students need extra help from the schools, their schools need extra help from the community: higher levels of funding, increased cooperation from local businesses, service agencies, civic organizations, and so on.

School administrators find themselves in the vortex where all these pressures converge. They are responsible for making the best possible use of community resources, minimizing negative attitudes and incidents, presenting school policies in a positive light and winning over support for them. Fulfillment of those tasks must begin with substantive achievements—good teachers, sound educational programming, and so on—but it also requires that principals have knowledge of the community, public relations skills, and a measure of creative problem solving.

THE FIRST STEP: GOOD PROGRAM-MING

This chapter discusses two important topics in the area of school/community relations: (1) setting up volunteer programs and (2) gaining good publicity. (For related topics, see Chapter 19 on Interagency Cooperation.)

VOLUNTEERS

About six million volunteers, from school age to senior citizens, donated their time to American schools in 1978 alone (Cuninggim, 1980). They are perhaps the most valuable resource that communities can offer. Volunteers cannot solve the problems of increased demands and shrinking budgets that face schools today, but they can offer much-needed assistance. Depending on the size and nature of the school district, they may become involved in special education programming through tutoring, providing enrichment activities, helping parents and families of the handicapped, reading or Brailling books for the blind, building special toys and equipment, raising additional funds, and in many other ways.

ROLES OF VOLUNTEERS

The following tips and guidelines about setting up a volunteer program and making it effective are drawn from several authors writing for an audience of special educators (Cuninggim, 1980; Greer, 1978; Shellem, 1982).

Administration

MAKING SCHOOL POLICIES ON VOLUNTEERS

In most districts, volunteer policies are set by the school board. (It is important that these policies not be so complex as to discourage participation.) For a smoothly functioning program, it is strongly advised to have a paid coordinator on staff at the district level. Most districts' volunteer programs also make use of an advisory committee that includes teachers, community representatives, parents, and volunteers.

A typical start-up scenario is this: In its first year, a volunteer program is planned to produce measurable evaluation data such as number of students served. Those data then can be used to back up requests for districtwide funding, with a paid coordinator as the first priority.

CRITERIA FOR SUCCESS

Volunteer programs have proved most successful when teachers really want them (the teachers should share in planning and placement decisions) and when teachers "respect the volunteers as individuals and make them a vital part of the educational team by making use of a volunteer's creativity, critical thinking ability, experiences, and unique skills" (Cuninggim, p. 110).

Recruitment

The first steps in volunteer programming are recruitment and screening. Senior citizen organizations or institutions can be fruitful places to advertise for volunteers.

SOURCES OF VOLUNTEERS

Seniors often have a special attraction to volunteer programs in the schools both because they have more free time than younger, employed adults, and because many of them have their own needs that participation in these activities can help fulfill—needs to feel useful, to be active, to be with other people. They may have a special empathy for handicapped children since they too belong to a social group that often is isolated and neglected.

Volunteer recruitment can be carried out through church, civic, and business organizations, military organizations, sororities, and fraternities. It also is worthwhile to publicize programs through the local media (see following section on publicity). Other students may serve successfully as volunteer tutors as well; information on peer and cross-age tutoring is provided in Chapter 21 on Student Relationships.

SCREENING PROCESS

Once the administration has located people who are interested, there should be some kind of screening process to identify those who are really appropriate for the program. Ideally, this will be a self-screening method, such as a written application procedure that allows these individuals to realistically assess their commitment (including available time), needs, attitudes, and abilities. All volunteers should receive a job description that outlines their responsibility and the work expected of them.

Along with a standard application form, each volunteer should have a personal interview to ascertain more about their education and experience, interests, special skills, time available, and so on. References are imperative, particularly for legal reasons.

Training

Training is essential for effective use of volunteers. Greer (1978) suggests a training program of

RECOMMENDED TRAINING PROGRAM

> five hours of preservice orientation, 20 hours of instruction specific to the task, and on-the-job training under the classroom teacher, volunteer coordinator, or designated administrator. Instruction specific to the task might include subject area orientation, training in the use of instructional supplies and equipment, human relations, and child growth and development (p. 6).

It also will be important for the principal or teacher to provide information on class rules and classroom management techniques.

Training sessions should include only brief lectures, should make use of audiovisual materials, and should be sensitive to volunteers' needs. For example, it is not advisable to produce volunteer materials on a ditto machine since many seniors have poor eyesight and require dark, high-contrast printing in order to read.

Role of the Teacher

The classroom teacher, according to Cuninggim, is responsible for the following:

RESPONSIBILITIES OF THE CLASSROOM TEACHER

- Requesting the volunteer; stating the duties, days, and hours desired, keeping in mind realistic expectations of the commitments a volunteer will be willing to make. Typically, availability will be about 1/2 school day per week, though some volunteers may commit up to 10 to 15 hours weekly.
- Orienting the volunteer to classroom policies and procedures, including school and class rules, discipline, emergency procedures (e.g., fire drills), legal issues such as confidentiality of student records, the teacher's philosophy of education, divisions of duties (the teacher's, the volunteer's, those that are shared), what to do if the volunteer is unable to come on a scheduled day, the school calendar, and holidays.
- Leaving instructions for the volunteer with the substitute teacher if the regular teacher will not be in class.
- Setting up a communication system (e.g., file folder of activities, phone call in the evening before, lunch together, brief talk before the volunteer leaves) that is effective but does not waste valuable class time.
- Expecting volunteers to be prompt, committed, and reliable (this includes explaining to students why the volunteers are leaving if they do so in midyear).
- Letting volunteers know that their contributions are important, such as by sharing with them indications of student progress, inviting them into the teachers' lounge or lunchroom, and considering some kind of formal recognition at the end of the school year. (This task actually should be the responsibility of the principal.)

- Including volunteers in the evaluation process.

Sample Programs

Around the country, schools have developed ideas for using volunteers in both traditional and highly innovative ways. Here are a few examples:

SAMPLE PROGRAMS: KINDER-GARTEN SCREENING

In Houston, more than 1,500 volunteers help screen all the city's kindergarten children. While trained specialists are responsible for the actual diagnoses, volunteers greatly extend valuable staff time by administering the initial, general screening procedures.

MOTOR SKILLS, EMOTIONAL PROBLEMS

In Oakland, volunteers provide children who need it with an extra hour per week in motor skills development, using gymnastic equipment and programmed exercises.

In Rochester, N.Y., adult volunteers establish listener relationships with emotionally troubled youngsters. The opportunity to share their problems and experiences with a nonauthoritarian adult meets important emotional needs and helps the students to cope with stress.

One town in Massachusetts worked out an in-school suspension alternative with the help of volunteers and local police. Now students with behavior problems receive individual tutoring instead of being dismissed from the school campus (and frequently getting into trouble in the town).

In another town, with the cooperation of the school librarian, volunteers put together a special education-oriented lending library for home use.

OTHER VOLUNTEER PROGRAMS

The Foster Grandparent program of the federal action agency paid low-income seniors a small stipend to give two hours of one-on-one attention and care to children, most of them handicapped and many institutionalized.

Volunteers are being used to tape record or Braille books for the visually impaired, to tutor students in reading and math who are significantly below their age level in basic skills, to help run swim programs, design parent application forms, and evaluate school programs. There is room in every school district to design volunteer programs consistent with the needs and resources of the community, and principals would do well to tap this resource.

PUBLICITY

THE VALUE OF POSITIVE PUBLICITY

Community relations are not a matter of image alone; the route to community support begins with high-quality educational programming. On the other hand, if the programs are good, why keep them a secret? The press will not be shy about covering a story the principal considers negative, such as a rise in vandalism or a decline in test scores. Modesty should not prevent educators from seeking equal publicity about the positive aspects and achievements of their school, staff, and students. Such publicity can have many benefits. For example, it can:

- help obtain proschool votes in local elections
- promote understanding and support for current educational policies

- promote acceptance of the handicapped by other students, their families, and the larger community
- increase staff morale
- generate community interest and willingness to share resources with the school
- counterbalance or minimize the (inevitable) negative attitudes, events, and publicity that can arise.

What to Publicize

For the media to be interested in covering a story, it must be "newsworthy;" that is, new or novel, of direct importance to many people, of human interest, involving a famous person, funny, tragic, or involving conflict, money, or intrigue.

NEWS-WORTHY SCHOOL EVENTS

When administration's goal is promoting support for special education programs in the public schools, possible stories might include: an increase in test scores, a moving story of individual achievement, a student or teacher who receives a special award, a well-known visiting lecturer or researcher, an interesting project undertaken by a class, a school event such as a student play, science fair, Special Olympics, and so on. (These events may call for several types of press announcements over the course of the event: stories about preparation/training, notice to members of the public who might want to attend, reports of the actual event, etc.)

How to Publicize

To play an active, initiating role, the principal will need to learn the school district's policies on publicity and:

GETTING GOOD PRESS COVERAGE: USEFUL HINTS

- Pay attention to which of the media normally cover the types of stories at hand. They will be the ones to contact.
- Get to know at least the names of the reporters and editors assigned to school issues—and to know them personally, if possible. Be aware of whom to notify of what. Depending on the type of story, this might be the assignment editor, city desk, entertainment editor, education editor or writer, sports editor, etc. (Make, keep, and update a list.)
- Use the standard form of notification—the press release—effectively (Exhibit 18-1). Be sure to send it far enough in advance to (1) meet media deadlines, (2) give adequate notice of public events. Telephone calls can be used in conjunction with written releases, for inquiries, or for more immediate stories. However, be careful not to pressure, nag, or harass. Be courteous and discriminating in contacts.
- Be sensitive to reporters' time schedules. It's a good idea to make contact, interviews, etc., early or in the middle of the day, not in late afternoon when they are hurrying to meet deadlines.

Exhibit 18–1 Format for a Press Release

Name and address of organization
Name and phone number of contact person

Release date (Usually this will read: FOR IMMEDIATE RELEASE)

TITLE (HEADLINE)

The first paragraph (as much as possible the first sentence) should answer the questions: Who? What? When? Where? How? Why?

Additional information, in short paragraphs, is included in descending order of importance. (If the story needs to be shortened or edited, editors usually cut from the bottom up.)

Text must be double or, preferably, triple spaced.

- Prepare for any interviews and make sure other staff members do so; be sure to be as well informed as possible on the topic. Be truthful; if the answer to a question is not known, admit it, and forward the information as soon as possible.
- Obtain more information and ideas from books on publicity or public relations in the library (there are quite a few) and learn from the media themselves by reading, listening, and watching critically, by calling to verify their policies on deadlines, free public service announcements, whether they accept prepared stories, and so on.

REFERENCES

Cuninggim, W. (1980). Citizen volunteers: A growing resource for teachers and students. *Teaching Exceptional Children, 12*(3), 108–112.

Greer, J.V. (1978). Utilizing paraprofessionals and volunteers in special education. *Focus on Exceptional Children, 10*(6), 1–16.

Shellem, G.W. (1982). Community involvement. In R.C. Talley and J. Burnette (Eds.), *Administrator's handbook on integrating America's mildly handicapped students*. Reston, VA: The Council for Exceptional Students.

Chapter 19

Interagency Cooperation

SUMMARY

Statement of the Problem

Cooperative agreements with public and private agencies outside the school district can provide highly efficient and productive means of meeting handicapped students' educational needs. However, there often are many barriers to such arrangements, including legal constraints, funding problems, philosophical differences, and feelings of distrust or competition.

Legal Issues

The public schools retain responsibility for handicapped students within their service area, even if they are placed by the schools in other public or private programs. The local education agency, by law, must assure that students in private school placements have an IEP and receive prescribed special education and related services, that these are provided at no cost to the family, that they are comparable to benefits received by similar students in the public schools, that the programs meet state educational standards, and that students and their families have all the rights guaranteed by the law.

When a free appropriate public education is available but parents choose to place the child in a private or parochial school, the local education agency must make it possible for the child to participate in special education and related services offered by the school. Federal restrictions limit use of public funds to special education and related services only; they may not be used for salaries, construction, permanent equipment purchases, or other expenses of private schools.

Other laws relevant to interagency cooperation are those that limit the legal function of each agency involved. Some types of programming will not be possible because of these regulations. All such restrictions should be understood before planning begins.

Rationale

The potential advantages of interagency cooperation are many and include: financial savings, elimination of duplication or gaps in services, improved or expanded services, more appropriate referrals, greater number of program alternatives, new delivery systems, better use of each agency's resources, opportunity to share and gain from others' experience and special expertise, greater program stability in times of funding cuts, and a broader base of support for special education.

Approaches

For interagency cooperation to be successful, principals must become familiar with agencies in the community, including state and local government offices, private charities, and any other organizations that provide services or resources to handicapped students. They must also identify areas of need and potential cooperation; emphasize common interests and areas of mutual benefit; consider the legal responsibilities, funding sources, and regulations of each participating agency (be realistic about barriers to cooperation); develop a clear agreement; and assign one individual to be in charge.

EFFECTIVE INTERAGENCY COOPERATION

COMMON CONTRACTS

Although state and local educational agencies retain responsibility for educating the children within their jurisdiction, they may not, in all cases, be the most efficient providers of every service the pupils need. As noted earlier, it is common for public schools, especially in rural areas, to contract with private schools, specialists, clinics, other private or public agencies, and even neighboring school districts, to serve very small populations of special needs children. In larger school districts, productive relationships have been forged between schools and other agencies to provide services to certain exceptional students on a continuing basis.

Vocational education programs, for example, have drawn together resources from the local school district, colleges and universities, state departments of vocational rehabilitation and developmental disabilities, federal programs under the U.S. Department of Labor, charity organizations, professional organizations, and private businesses.

THE BENEFITS OF COOPERATION

The benefits of such cooperative arrangements can be tremendous. There is great potential for saving the time and resources of all agencies involved and for sharing experience and expertise so as to eliminate costly and frustrating periods of trial and error. The results can include better, simpler, and more satisfying service delivery for students and their families as well as solutions to administrative nightmares of many kinds.

COMMON OBSTACLES AND CONCERNS

However, as anyone who has tried it knows, good potential does not guarantee successful cooperation. In fact, from any one agency's or staff person's perspective, there may seem to be more reasons not to cooperate than to give it a try. What reasons? Many agencies' funding is dependent on their client load. If they begin to share responsibility for clients, their budgets may be cut. In some cases, this has happened; it is, in many cases, a real concern. There are concerns about offering, or appearing to offer, services not mandated for the agency. Bookkeeping and auditing problems may seem too complicated to resolve and, again, there is the potential for loss of public funds.

Rarely do two agencies have the same approach, philosophy, or commitment. Frequently, there are long-standing antagonisms between them. A sense of competition and mistrust may make other problems appear even larger. Personal egos may be involved. If the question of "Who gets credit?" is not answered to everyone's satisfaction, a cooperative program may be blocked before it even gets started. So may the question, "Will all the extra meetings be worth it?"

WHAT'S IN IT FOR ME?

It is unproductive to enter the arena of potential cooperation without attention to these barriers. They are real. If they are not resolved, the program cannot be successful. The emphasis in planning must be on the real benefit to each participant, an answer to the question, "What's in it for me?" As is true in negotiation, cooperation is most effective when each party's interests are served.

With this in mind, this chapter explores difficult issues that cannot always be solved clearly, reviews cooperative efforts that have succeeded, and offers tips on what to do and what to avoid.

LEGAL ISSUES

The barrier to interagency cooperation in delivering services to handicapped children and youths has a legal basis: the authorizing legislation for handicapped programs and related regulations do not provide incentives for the various publicly funded agencies to cooperate in fulfilling their roles. The law or departmental policies could have included financial rewards, funding guarantees, or other explicit benefits for cooperative efforts, but they do not. In fact, regulations often make such arrangements quite ambiguous and difficult.

PROBLEMS WITH STATE AND FEDERAL LAW

There are other problems. Sometimes federal and state laws are awkwardly at odds with each other, and direction is unclear. Aid to private schools presents several examples. Federal law requires that handicapped students placed in private schools by their parents have access to special education and related services comparable to those received in public schools. The methods and settings for delivering these services include dual enrollment, educational radio and television, and mobile educational services. They are, as Shrybman (1982) points out, ''essentially the same as for educationally deprived children under Title I of the Elementary and Secondary Education Act'' (P.L. 89-10)(p. 453). Students in religious or sectarian schools are included. Yet several states have strict regulations against public funds' being channeled to religious institutions. In such states, the role of public education agencies is confusing.

Federal laws require that the level of benefits and funding of special education in public and private institutions be equal. This requirement poses special problems at a time when there are not enough funds to cover all mandated programs, no matter who might deliver them.

CONTINUING CLARIFICATION OF THE LAW

If parents themselves choose to place their child in a private program, when an appropriate public program is available, the schools are not legally required to pay for that placement. Yet many parents continue to demand such support, arguing that the schools should cover at least part of the expenses.

There also is a lack of clarity as to the responsibility of the school district to provide services in private institutions serving only the handicapped. These and related issues will continue to be treated in the courts.

APPROACHES

However great the problems, there also are successes. The following are a few notable examples from school districts around the country.

Mental Health

Many schools have joint arrangements with other agencies, organizations, or institutions in the area of mental health. In one district, a representative of the local publicly funded mental health agency sits on a school screening team helping to resolve cases of joint roles and responsibilities and offering consultation. The school, in turn, makes referrals to the mental health agency. Agency staff members (including college interns) are available to provide counseling to parents (and students) in afterschool hours. The system began with informal working relationships and evolved to its more formalized present status.

EXAMPLES OF SUCCESSFUL COOPERATION

Recreation

Scout troops, summer camps, and the YMCA, YWCA, YMHA, and YWHA are examples of community resources that can be mobilized to help meet the special recreational needs of handicapped students. In one town, the school cooperates with local (nonschool) recreational facilities by lending play equipment and providing training and consultation through the special education teacher. Begun as an afterschool program for handicapped students, it was expanded to include summer programming as well. By playing a key role in initiating the cooperative relationship, the schools have found a way to provide additional needed (although not legally required) services without spending additional funds.

Interagency Coordination of Services to Individuals

When many agencies are involved in service delivery, coordination can be a problem. In one district, representatives of the schools and six social service agencies meet on a regular biweekly basis to discuss services being provided to selected individuals. The group leader chosen for the meeting picks out one to three cases. By discussing these, members are able to clear up any misunderstandings, establish lines of communication, reduce overlap, and close any gaps in service.

Public Awareness

Another town sponsored a Special Education Awareness Month that included such activities as films, displays, press coverage, a special education open house, public programs, wheelchair basketball, and a panel discussion. Parents played key roles on the multiagency planning committee.

Vocational Education

A variety of resources, from businesses to charitable organizations to state agencies have figured productively in schools' vocational education programs for exceptional students. In one rural community, for example, the 4-H developed a curriculum for vocational education of the mildly mentally retarded and provided club members as volunteer tutors. In return, the special education teacher supervised the 4-H students, made arrangements with their high school for release time and credit, sent written reports to the school to form the basis for grades, and paid the costs of the students' transportation from district funds. The results were an adequate curriculum and tutorial assistance where none had existed before.

EXAMPLES OF SUCCESSFUL COOPERATION

Many special vocational education programs have involved agreements among the various public agencies with sometimes overlapping responsibilities for vocational training. Typically, these involve money-saving arrangements in which specialists from various fields (special and vocational education, for example) combine their expertise and the resources/facilities of their programs to meet the needs of a varied client population.

STEPS TO COOPERATION

Jan Baxter (1982) of the Michigan Department of Education offers the following key steps in developing interagency cooperation:

KEY STEPS IN INTER-AGENCY COOPERA-TION

1. identify needs for expanded or improved service
2. look around the community for agencies and organizations that might help
3. consider the needs, legal roles, and regulations governing each agency
4. develop a written agreement that satisfies the requirements of each agency
5. design a delivery system
6. analyze funding availability and constraints so that program costs can be billed to the most appropriate budget; conduct cost-benefit analysis.

Some options for encouraging continuing cooperative relationships include shared boards of directors and joint memberships, conferences, and publications.

THE SAME STEPS APPLY TO SCHOOLS

Guidelines to interagency cooperation also can be applied to internal cooperative agreements among the various departments and professions in the schools. There are obstacles here as well, including rigid curricula, credit hour requirements, differing philosophies, a history of isolation and competition, and so on. But when common interests can be identified and agreements made, the staff and students involved stand to benefit.

At any level, good communication is essential, as is an attitude of respect. There are many ways to kill cooperation; for example:

WAYS TO KILL COOPERA-TION

- We tried that six years ago
- We don't want to give up control.
- You can't trust them.
- That's our job.
- Somebody might think we are doing less.
- I wouldn't work with that guy.
- They would take all the credit.

The principal who hears such remarks should challenge the person, proving the critic wrong by showing that cooperation does work—especially for the students served, which after all is the real bottom line

LOCATING ADDITIONAL RESOURCES

HOW TO FIND ADDITIONAL SUPPORT

Many more organizations may provide assistance in the education of handicapped children in addition to those mentioned here. A search for those available in the community might begin with an agency that frequently makes referrals, including the school district, welfare office, public hospital, or other social services. Private organizations can be approached, as can church and charitable groups and other organizations. Knowledge of the community and its resource potential will be helpful.

There also are national organizations that operate as advocacy/support groups for various disabilities. They can be useful for parent referrals and may have several other services available (e.g., Brailled books or special equipment to lend, speakers, information on the handicapping condition, etc.). Several listings of these groups are available. The one in Appendix 19-A is taken from Carol Michaelis's (1980) *Home and School Partnerships in Exceptional Education*. The telephone directory or referrals listing for local branches can be checked.

REFERENCES

Baxter, J.M. (1982). Solving problems through cooperation. *Exceptional Children, 48*(5), 400–407.

Michaelis, C. (1980). *Home and school partnerships in exceptional education*. Rockville, MD: Aspen Publishers, Inc., pp. 288–291.

Shrybman, J.A. (1982) *Due process in special education*. Rockville, MD: Aspen Publishers, Inc.

Appendix 19–A

Disability Support Organizations

Autism

National Society for Autistic Children
1234 Massachusetts Avenue, N.W.
Suite 1017
Washington, D.C. 20005

Blind

American Council of the Blind
1211 Connecticut Avenue, N.W.
Washington, D.C. 20036

American Foundation for the Blind
15 West 16th Street
New York, N.Y. 10011

National Association for Visually Impaired
305 East 24th Street
New York, N.Y. 10010

National Federation for the Blind
655 15th Street, N.W.
Suite 300
Washington, D.C. 20005

Cerebral Palsy

United Cerebral Palsy
66 East 34th Street
New York, N.Y. 10016

Deaf

Alexander Graham Bell Association for the Deaf
3417 Volta Place, N.W.
Washington, D.C. 20007

National Association of the Deaf
814 Thayer Avenue
Silver Spring, Md. 20910

Deaf-Blind

National Association of the Deaf-Blind
2703 Forest Oak Circle
Norman, Okla. 73071

National Deaf-Blind Program
Bureau of Education for the Handicapped

Donohoe Building
400 6th Street, S.W.
Washington, D.C. 20202

Emotionally Disturbed

National Mental Health Association
1021 Prince Street
Alexandria, Va. 22314

Epilepsy

Epilepsy Foundation of America
4351 Garden City Drive
Landover, Md. 20785

Health Impairments

Allergy Foundation of America
801 Second Avenue
New York, N.Y. 10017

American Cancer Society
777 Third Avenue
New York, N.Y. 10017

American Heart Association
7320 Greenville Avenue
Dallas, Tex. 75231

The Candlelighters Childhood Cancer Foundation
2025 I Street, N.W.
Suite 1011
Washington, D.C. 20006

Cystic Fibrosis Foundation
3379 Peachtree Road, N.E.
Atlanta, Ga. 30326

Juvenile Diabetes Foundation
23 East 26th Street
New York, N.Y. 10010

National Hemophilia Foundation
25 West 39th Street
New York, N.Y. 10018

National Kidney Foundation
Two Park Avenue
New York, N.Y. 10016

Learning Disabilities

Association for Children with Learning Disabilities
4156 Library Road
Pittsburgh, Pa. 15234

The Orton Society, Inc.
8415 Bellona Lane
Suite 115
Towson, Md. 21204

Mental Retardation

Down's Syndrome Congress
1802 Johnson Drive
Normal, Ill. 61761

National Association for Retarded Citizens
2709 Avenue E East
P.O. Box 6109
Arlington, Tex. 76011

Physically Handicapped

Arthritis Foundation
3400 Peachtree Road, N.E.
Atlanta, Ga. 30326

Little People of America
P.O. Box 126
Owatonna, Minn. 55060

Muscular Dystrophy Association, Inc.
810 Seventh Avenue
New York, N.Y. 10019

National Multiple Sclerosis Society
205 East 42nd Street
New York, N.Y. 10017

National Spinal Cord Injury Foundation
369 Elliot Street
Newton Upper Falls, Mass. 02164

Spina Bifida Association of America
343 South Dearborn Street
Room 319
Chicago, Ill. 60604

Speech Impairments

American Speech-Language and Hearing Association
10801 Rockville Pike
Rockville, Md. 20852

All Disabilities

Association for the Severely Handicapped
1600 West Armory Way
Garden View Suite
Seattle, Wash. 98119

American Coalition of Citizens with Disabilities
1200 15th Street, N.W.
Suite 201
Washington, D.C. 20005

National Easter Seal Society for Crippled Children and Adults
2023 West Ogden Avenue
Chicago, Ill. 60612

National Foundation–March of Dimes
1275 Mamaroneck Avenue
White Plains, N.Y. 10605

National Tay-Sachs Foundation and Allied Diseases Association
122 East 42nd Street
New York, N.Y. 10017

Source: Adapted from *Home and School Partnerships in Exceptional Education* (pp. 288–291) by C. Michaelis, 1980, Rockville, Md.: Aspen Publishers, Inc. © Copyright 1980 by Aspen Publishers, Inc.

Chapter 20

Staff Relationships and Staffing Patterns

SUMMARY

Statement of the Problem

Meeting the needs of handicapped students in integrated classrooms demands cooperative efforts among regular and special educators and other professionals. Such cooperation often is made difficult, however, by the traditional separation of these professional disciplines and by associated attitudes of suspicion, competition, and exclusivity.

Legal Issues

P.L. 94-142 calls for interdisciplinary input at several points in the special education process. Evaluations, according to the act, must be performed by "a multidisciplinary team or group of persons, including at least one teacher or specialist with knowledge in the area of the suspected disability" (Sec. 121a.532(e)). Placement decisions must be "made by a group of persons, including persons knowledgeable about the child, the meaning of the evaluation data, and the placement options" (Sec. 121a.533(3)). And the IEP meeting must include at least the child's teacher and "a representative of the public agency, other than the child's teacher, who is qualified to provide, or supervise the provision of, special education" (Sec. 121a.344(a)(1)). Interdisciplinary cooperation is further implied by the requirement to provide "related services" such as physical therapy, audiological exams, psychological services, transportation, etc., that are necessary for the child to be able to profit from the special education programs (Sec. 121a.13(a)). The list of covered services is so broad as to imply the potential involvement of a great number of specialists in any given school.

Rationale

Cooperative professional arrangements often are not only the most efficient means of carrying out special education laws, they are also the most child-centered and humane, since (unlike the completely separate educational environments of past programs) they can allow handicapped students to learn in the most normal possible environment. Professional commitment to pursue what is best for the child should therefore engender a commitment to cooperation.

Approaches

The principal should model and encourage a positive approach toward the presence of special students in the school; encourage regular teachers to use specialists as resources; encourage specialists to be flexible, tolerant of teaching differences, and nondogmatic; distribute attractive physical space and time schedules, as well as nonacademic tasks/responsibilities, equitably among regular and special education staff members; and provide adequate time for planning and coordination among staff.

If possible, the principal should consider cooperation and communication skills when hiring staff members. Taking funding requirements into account, the principal should consider expanding the duties of special educators to include additional services to regular teachers and/or regular students (e.g., consultation on materials and curriculum modification and consultative help for all students, not just those identified for special education).

PROBLEMS IN STAFFING RELATIONSHIPS

In schools where special and regular educators are working together for the first time, complaints such as the following may be all too familiar to administrators:

"I have 28 students in my class already. Why should I have to take in *your* students, especially when you only have to deal with five or six at a time?"

"If regular class teachers had better attitudes toward kids with disabilities, if they individualized their teaching in the first place instead of expecting all students to learn in the same way . . . if they just had more commitment, there wouldn't *be* so many special students."

"I'm tired of so-called experts coming in and telling me how to run my class. Half the things they tell you to do don't work anyway."

ATTITUDINAL BARRIERS TO COOPERA-TION

"In a regular class, my students don't get the acceptance and understanding they need. It's a continual experience of failure, instead of a chance to find out what they really can do."

The educational philosophy embodied in P.L. 94-142 (especially the least restrictive environment aspect) relies on cooperation between regular classroom teachers and a variety of specialists; yet attitudes such as those just cited seem to make that cooperation impossible, or at least highly difficult, to achieve. Such complaints and prejudices may not actually be verbalized. They may emerge as avoidance (failure to contact a specialist for advice, for example), as subtle assertions of power (use of professional jargon that others do not understand, refusal to acknowledge the opinion of a colleague from a less statused profession), the waste of valuable meeting time in petty disputes, and so on.

ORIGINS OF THE CONFLICTS

Although frustrating and obstructive, such attitudes do have understandable historic origins. After all, educators' training most likely has been oriented toward producing autonomous experts, individuals in control of their own office, clinical setting, or classroom. There has been additional, pronounced separation between the disciplines of regular and special education—different training, different educational philosophies, different working conditions and populations of students.

The result has been an educational environment based on a notion of "my" students versus "yours" and accompanying attitudes of suspicion, defensiveness, and intimidation. Despite the demand for cooperative efforts imposed by P.L. 94-142, clear roles and structures have been slow to evolve. Furthermore, as a result of escalating community demands in a variety of areas, teaching has become a more and more stressful occupation (and still commands lower salaries and less status than other professions with comparable responsibilities). To some extent, conflicts over special education are outlets for broader based frustrations.

WHAT PRINCIPALS CAN DO

Principals cannot be expected to work miracles, to erase decades of isolation, suspicion, and turf protection with a wave of the hand. But they can make a difference. As one analysis puts it, "It is the principal who can encourage and reward teachers for working collaboratively . . . it is the principal who can make scheduling changes so that teachers can observe each other, coteach a lesson, and provide in-classroom help and assistance to each other" (Johnson & Johnson, 1980).

Principals can model interest and acceptance of all students, staff, and programs in the school; they can distribute space, schedules, and resources so as to minimize conflict; they can structure new roles and new formats in which staff members can work together supportively. Even when options are severely limited by such factors as budgets, personalities, and lack of maneuvering room within district policies, the principal is in a better position to improve staff relationships than any other individual in the school.

This chapter offers information on four useful aspects of those relationships: (1) collaboration and cooperation, (2) possible new roles for the professionals involved, (3) multidisciplinary teams, and (4) the consultation process.

Collaborative Roles

2-BOX MODEL VS. CONTINUUM OF SERVICES

The old approach to education of the handicapped often is called the "two-box" model (Reynolds & Birch, 1977); a student was assigned either to regular or to special education, one or the other, without overlap. Staff members in one "box" had no particular reason to talk with those in the other. Today, schools are required to provide a continuum of educational placements to ensure that each handicapped student is served in the most normal environment possible and in the company, to the greatest possible extent, of nonhandicapped peers. That continuum generally includes arrangements of the following types:

- special schools for the severely handicapped, with an effort to arrange some type of contact with nonhandicapped peers
- special classes in the regular schools with shared nonacademic activities—art, music, physical education, lunchtime, and assemblies, depending on the population involved
- regular class assignment with special class placement for some subjects or parts of the day
- full-time regular class placement with assistance to the teacher
- full-time regular class placement with temporary interventions either in or outside the classroom.

LEVELS OF COOPERATION AMONG PROFESSIONALS

Although the level varies, each type of arrangement requires some measure of cooperation among special educators and other professionals. At a minimum, there is a need to coordinate schedules. Beyond that, there are almost limitless possibilities for sharing knowledge in ways that benefit handicapped students directly and also result in increased acceptance and understanding on the part of others. For example, through joint planning a resource teacher can schedule remediation or skills development work to complement lessons in the regular class and regular class teachers can learn to monitor and reinforce students' progress on these skills. A special educator in a consulting role might offer help in anything from individualizing lessons or locating appropriate materials to creating an accepting social environment among nonhandicapped classmates.

STAFFING MODELS AND THEIR ADAPTATIONS

Some standard collaborative models (such as resource, consulting, and diagnostic-prescriptive teachers) are described in Chapter 6 on Placement. Each model has been used effectively in many schools. These descriptions should be viewed, however, as starting places, rather than as restrictions or endpoints in the process of developing constructive cooperation among personnel. Within their basic structure, these models can and should have room for individual initiative, experimentation, and problem-solving. Although much has been learned, there still are many difficulties to be worked out and there still is great need for exploration of new approaches.

New Roles for Special Educators

Where history and tradition have bred an environment of isolation, unfamiliarity, and suspicion, the first step toward cooperation is to build trust. A number of innovative ideas have been proposed for redefining the roles of special educators in mainstreamed schools, with increased trust from regular teachers as one of the primary goals. Ideas for principals to consider on possible new roles for special educators include:

NEW ROLES FOR THE SPECIAL EDUCATOR

- team teaching combined classes where one regular and one special education teacher are jointly responsible for all students
- providing certain consultation and training services for all students, including, for example, consulting with regular teachers on all pupils with learning problems, whether or not identified for special education; and training all students in social skills, communication skills, the nature of handicapping conditions, and other areas of special expertise or benefit to assist in the successful integration of new, handicapped students into regular class settings
- consulting on the grading of special students
- leading inservice seminars and/or parent meetings
- sharing equal responsibility for supervision of lunchrooms, playgrounds, etc.
- supporting regular teachers in parent meetings
- providing occasional activities for gifted and average students (this can help remove the stigma from resource rooms and special programming)
- sharing responsibility with regular teachers for planning and development of school policies as well as individual programming.

The Principal as Agent of Change

Because the principal is the chief agent of change, new conceptions of the administrator's role also must be developed. In the area of improving staff relationships, the principal might begin the process with self-evaluation along such lines as:

SELF-EVALUATION ISSUES FOR PRINCIPALS

- Have I really accepted the special education students and teachers here?
- Have I demonstrated that acceptance before all faculty members (in meetings, newsletters, special programs, etc.)?
- Have I shown unfairness or favoritism in the treatment of either group of teachers (regarding room assignments, time schedules, other indications of status, etc.)?
- Have I seen to it that special students have had access to status roles and activities?
- Have I provided the support necessary to make it possible for mainstreaming to succeed (planning time, inservice training, aides, etc.)?
- Are both regular and special educators convinced that I understand their problems (and their contributions) and that I am committed to the best possible use of school resources to bring needed improvements?

DIFFICULTIES OF CHANGE

Adjustments in the roles of building staff are not straightforward and simple to bring about. They are hardest, say Brown and Wood (1978), "where responsibility for the problem or credit for the solution is not shared mutually, or where solving the problem involves changes in the behavior of school personnel, whether regular or special" (p. 57). While they caution against expecting too much of the human beings who happen to be professional educators, they, like other authors, believe that innovations in such areas as joint long-range planning and improved professional training will reduce tensions in the future.

The Multidisciplinary Team

USES OF MULTIDISCIPLINARY TEAMS

Many schools use a permanent multidisciplinary team to coordinate and carry out key phases of the special education process, including preliminary screening, formal evaluation, placement decisions, developing the IEP, and amending programs when problems arise. They may bear different names, such as Child Study Team or Evaluation and Placement Committee, and may vary in the number and professional specialty of members. (For several examples, see Oliver, 1982.) But they all are similar in function. A standard arrangement is to meet weekly for a set, limited time or number of cases.

The role of the principal on such teams may vary from observer to active team leader. According to Lietz and Towle (1982), it generally includes such administrative responsibilities as:

THE PRINCIPAL'S ROLE IN THE TEAM

- scheduling meetings
- sending reminders to all participants, including parents
- acting as liaison between staff members and other participants (parents, community agencies, etc.)
- taking responsibility for due process requirements
- supervising staff performance.

The potential benefits of such a team structure include increased efficiency, greater accuracy in assessment and placement decisions, and fruitful and creative exchange of ideas, values, and knowledge. However, the potential problems also are numerous. Critics of the multidisciplinary teams have cited such shortcomings as ambiguous decisions, unsystematic approach, inadequate involvement of parents and regular education teachers, lack of clarity of purpose, unclear role distribution, rivalry and lack of trust between specialists of different disciplines, inefficiency as a result of too many or too few team members, and lack of needed expertise that stalls progress.

BENEFITS AND PROBLEMS OF TEAM STRUCTURE

The central factor in resolving many of these problems is the successful negotiation of roles and responsibilities. The authors of *The Interdisciplinary Team: A Handbook for the Education of Exceptional Children* (Golin & Ducanis, 1981) suggest the following four steps for such negotiations:

NEGOTIATING ROLES AND RESPONSIBILITIES

1. clarifying role perceptions and expectations
2. identifying professional competencies
3. examining overlapping roles
4. renegotiating role assignments.

They also recommend giving all professionals on the team an opportunity to share information about their specialties and to structure time for discussing perceptions of their own performance and that of other members of the team. The result of negotiations should be roles that are not too rigidly defined (it may be expedient and productive for members to trade responsibilities at some points, for example) but clear enough to minimize instances of overlap, power struggles, incomplete information, and so on.

THE CONSULTATION PROCESS

Since many of the professional relationships among regular class teachers and specialists are consultative, the following is summarized from Joel Myers's (1982) publication, *Consultation Skills: How Teachers Can Maximize Help*. He identifies four levels of consultation:

4 LEVELS OF CONSULTATION

1. Direct Service to the Student: The consultant observes and assesses the child and prescribes an intervention that the teacher carries out.
2. Indirect Service to the Student: Similar to Level 1 except for lack of direct contact with the student; someone other than the consultant gathers assessment data. This can be a highly efficient use of the consultant's time.
3. Service to the Teacher: At this level, consultation is oriented toward changing the behavior of the teacher, rather than of the student.
4. Service to the Organization: Altering organizational practice is the most indirect means of delivering service to the child, but the most appropriate in some situations.

KEYS TO SUCCESS

If any of these consultations is to be successful, the relationship must be conceived of as a collaborative, joint effort on the part of equals. The teacher receiving consultation must maintain ownership of the problem being discussed, must be actively involved in the problem-solving process, and must feel free to accept or reject the consultant's advice. Participants can help build trust in one another by listening attentively and nonjudgmentally; reflecting empathy, respect, and acceptance; being genuinely themselves; and generally displaying cooperative (as opposed to competitive) behavior. Specific steps in consultation are to:

STEPS TO FOLLOW IN CONSULTATION

1. Identify the Problem: Both participants should agree on the level of consultation most appropriate to the situation and have some agreement on the roles that each will play.
2. Define the Problem Clearly and Specifically: The consultant should explain the conceptual framework to be used. Both participants should cooperate in clarifying the problem and should reach a consensus on a definition.
3. Devise Intervention Strategies: This stage too is most effective when developed with teacher input. The teacher should feel free to ask for more than one possible approach.
4. Evaluation: It can be productive to have the teacher be the one to collect evaluative data on the student's performance.

REFERENCES

Brown, V.I., & Wood, F.H. (1978). A partnership between regular and special education: From adversaries to advocates. In J.B. Jordan (Ed.), *Exceptional students in secondary schools*. Reston, VA: The Council for Exceptional Children.

Golin, A., & Duncanis, A. (1981). *The interdisciplinary team: A handbook for the education of exceptional children*. Rockville, MD: Aspen Publishers, Inc.

Johnson, D., & Johnson, R. (1980). *Promoting constructive student-student relationships through cooperative learning*. Washington, DC: American Association of Colleges for Teacher Education.

Lietz, J.J., & Towle, M. (1982). *The elementary principal's role in special education*. Springfield, IL: Charles C Thomas.

Myers, J. (1982). *Consultation skills: How teachers can maximize help*. Washington, DC: American Association of Colleges for Teacher Education.

Oliver, T. (1982). Administrative systems for service delivery. In R.C. Talley & J. Burnette (Eds.), *Administrators' handbook on integrating America's mildly handicapped students*. Reston, VA: The Council for Exceptional Children.

Reynolds, M. & Birch, J. (1977). *Teaching exceptional children in all America's schools*. Reston, VA: The Council for Exceptional Children.

Chapter 21

Student Relationships

SUMMARY

Statement of the Problem

While P.L. 94-142 requires that handicapped students be educated "to the maximum extent appropriate" in the company of their nonhandicapped peers, simply placing the two groups in physical proximity will not in itself create attitudes of acceptance and, in fact, may reinforce previously learned negative stereotypes.

Legal Issues

For a complete description of the least restrictive environment regulations, see Chapter 6, on Placement.

Rationale

Handicapped individuals deserve to live as normal a life as possible. To this end, the public schools have a responsibility not only to provide such children with an appropriate education but also, in support of this goal, to combat negative attitudes and to create an atmosphere of acceptance and appreciation in which handicapped and nonhandicapped students can form a variety of positive relationships. Social factors are as important as academic ones in preparing students for an active and satisfying role in the adult community.

Approaches

Principals should model positive, accepting, nonjudgmental attitudes toward special students and their teachers and provide equal opportunities for status within the school to special students and their programs, classes, and instructors. Principals should stress the importance of peer relationships and encourage teachers to structure cooperative learning experiences in which handicapped students, under reasonable expectations for their performance, can work interdependently with nonhandicapped peers. They must be aware that successful mainstreaming requires active efforts to create receptive attitudes by regular students.

PEER INTERACTIONS

Most educational theory and research focuses on child-adult (teacher, parent) relationships. If such authors talk about peer interaction at all, they are most likely to approach it as a problem of off-task behavior and classroom disruption. Parents, for their part, also are likely to take a negative tack, worrying about peer influence in such areas as drugs, disobedience, and sexuality. But those concerns, however important, are only one facet of the complex and vital role that peer relationships play in a child's learning.

PEER RELATION-SHIPS ARE IMPORTANT

It is through interactions with their friends and classmates that children practice and learn socialized values, control of aggressive impulses, empathy for others, sex role identity, and social skills. The peer environment also shapes their educational goals and attitudes and serves as a predictor of adult mental health (Johnson, 1980; Schmuck, 1971). Johnson cites several studies that reveal a significant correlation between poor peer relationships and "destructive social conduct in adolescence and psychological pathology in adulthood" (p. 127).

The lack of friendships is one of the most serious problems confronting the handicapped, especially in adolescence, and can have deleterious effects on the individuals' self-image, psychological adjustment, and vocational skills.

If handicapped individuals (like everyone) are to lead productive and satisfying adult lives, they must have had a variety of interactive experiences and must have found acceptance, inclusion, and bonds of friendship among the acquaintances of childhood.

Controversy

SOCIAL ARGUMENTS FOR AND AGAINST MAIN-STREAMING

Some would say that all this is an argument for mainstreaming, others that it is an argument against. In a special school, the latter group argues, children are not judged inferior by their able-bodied classmates and are not as susceptible to teasing and exclusion as they are in an integrated class. In addition to the academic advantages of smaller, more homogeneous special classes, the partisans say, there are social advantages as well. In a school where all children are handicapped, there is widespread understanding, acceptance, and lack of prejudice; there are similar modes of communication (e.g., signing among deaf students) and similar constraints and needs—all of which foster an experience of equality and make the development of friendships less difficult.

ATTITUDES CAN BE CHANGED

Proponents of mainstreaming, on the other hand, emphasize the necessity not of evading situations laden with potential problems and prejudices but of confronting them and working for change. Certainly, stereotyping and prejudice exist, the mainstreaming advocates acknowledge; but these never will disappear if the non-handicapped population never has an opportunity to interact with disabled individuals, to exchange those one-dimensional stereotypes for the richer experiences of personal contact. For the information gleaned from such experiences to be received clearly, the contacts must begin in childhood. Advocates point to researchers such as David Johnson (Johnson, 1980; Johnson & Johnson, 1980) who offers assurances that social attitudes can be changed, and backs up the assertion with a variety of success stories.

Current Realities

SUCCESSES AND FAILURES

This has been the controversy: What is the current status? Is mainstreaming meeting its social goals? The results, like those of racial integration programs such as busing, are a resounding yes and no. Which is to say:

- It is no longer a question of whether to integrate; the laws have clearly mandated such a change, and it is being carried out.
- On a social level, too, there have been some successes, cases in which integrated placement has indeed resulted in greater respect and understanding among people of different groups.
- There also have been failures: educational integration of the disabled, as with different racial/ethnic populations, has been known to increase existing prejudices and antagonism rather than to dissipate them and also to contribute negatively to handicapped students' self-image.
- Integrated education per se and, more specifically, the means of bringing it about, still are the subject of controversy.

In short, the need for positive social interactions in childhood is great and sometimes is difficult to meet in today's heterogeneous classrooms. Principals and other educators, although they have little voice in the matter of heterogeneity, have an obligation to recognize both the benefits and the obstacles to such interactions and to work conscientiously to foster them.

SETTING THE TONE

THE ROLE OF THE PRINCIPAL

The principal is in a position to have a great influence on the quality of student attitudes and relationships in a mainstreamed school. Enthusiasm and commitment on the part of the building administrator will be translated through teachers to the students served. To model and communicate a positive attitude, principals should:

WHAT THE PRINCIPAL CAN DO

- see that special students have the same access to status activities as other students (working in the office, carrying messages, appearing in school newsletters, bulletin boards, assemblies, and so on)
- get to know the students, call them by name, model acceptance and interest
- encourage activities in which special students can participate and play prominent roles
- encourage awareness and efforts to foster productive social relationships among students

- make sure that separate special classes/resource rooms and separate special education staff members, if they exist in the building, have equal access to the same pleasant physical accommodations and desirable schedules (lunchtime, for example) as do other classes/professionals
- provide the fullest support possible (clerical and logistical help, materials, planning time, inservice classes, etc.) needed to make special education programs successful
- remove stigmas from special programs through techniques such as renaming a resource room the activity room, stocking it with interesting resources and activities and setting hours each day when it is open to all students and faculty members for browsing and exploring; also, send gifted students to the room for occasional special activities.

COOPERATIVE ACTIVITIES

What, exactly, can principals ensure that teachers do help promote positive peer interactions? Like several other authors, Johnson (1980) proposes that the most effective means is through structured, cooperative activities:

CREATION OF COOPERATIVE ATTITUDES

> In order for peer relationships to be constructive influences, they must promote feelings of belonging, acceptance, support and caring. In order to promote constructive peer influence, therefore, teachers must first ensure that students interact with each other and, second, must ensure that the interaction takes place within a supportive and accepting context. In other words, teachers must control the group dynamics affecting student-student interactions (p. 132).

He suggests that such control should be directed toward structuring cooperative, as opposed to competitive (spelling bees, grading on a curve) or individualistic activities (such as giving the special student an alternative lesson to sit and work on alone). One example would be assigning a research topic to a small, heterogeneous group. Each student could be responsible for checking a particular source or for contributing one element of the group's report. The essential characteristics of effective cooperative learning experiences are that:

CHARACTERISTICS OF COOPERATIVE LEARNING ACTIVITIES

1. Students in the learning group are interdependent and must work together in order to reach a goal.
2. Roles are clear and each individual is accountable for fulfilling an assigned task and/or for mastering the information in the lesson.
3. Work is evaluated based on the whole group's performance, and each group member gets the same grade.

Adjustments for handicapped students can be made in the type of role assigned, the portion for which they are held responsible, and the grading of their work. It is essential to set reasonable expectations for these students so that they are challenged but not frustrated and so that other group members are not penalized for their difficulties. Special educators can be consulted for assistance in making these adjustments. (Special educators also can help by training all students in cooperative social skills.) The role of the regular teacher in setting up these activities includes:

STRUCTURING GROUP ACTIVITIES

- specifying, as far as possible, the instructional objectives
- selecting the group size most appropriate for the lesson
- assigning students to groups (common practice is to maximize heterogeneity)
- setting up an appropriate physical arrangement of the classroom
- providing appropriate materials
- explaining the task and cooperative group support
- observing the student-student interaction
- intervening, as consultant, to help students solve problems and learn interpersonal skills and to see that all members are learning
- evaluating group products (Johnson & Johnson, 1980).

BENEFITS OF THE COOPERATIVE APPROACH

Studies are proving the benefits for all students of substituting structured cooperative formats for traditional competitive or isolated individualistic approaches to learning (Johnson, 1980). These benefits include greater self-esteem, higher achievement, increased motivation, more liking for other students and school personnel, and greater seeking and exchanging of information.

In close, interdependent settings, students not only develop more positive attitudes about themselves and their peers, they also become more realistically aware of the nature of handicaps and their effects on the individual. The handicapping condition then takes on a dynamic (as opposed to static, stereotyped) meaning, and students become more able to perceive the disabled as unique and worthy individuals. As Johnson and Johnson (1980) point out: "It is when handicapped students are liked, accepted, and chosen as friends that mainstreaming becomes a positive influence on the lives of both handicapped and normal-progress students" (Appendix B, p. 2).

ATTITUDE CHANGE PROGRAMS

Should mainstreamed class teachers devise and present special curriculum units on handicaps as a means of changing student attitudes? The research suggests a cautious affirmative. Some program components that appear effective with mainstreamed classes include:

ELEMENTS OF SUCCESSFUL UNITS

- opportunities to interact with handicapped adults
- information sufficient to dispel fears and promote understanding
- sanctioned opportunities for staring (either at individuals or at media representations)

- opportunities to discuss feelings and beliefs
- simulations (e.g., blindfolds, one hand behind back) and an opportunity to explore and experiment with assistive aids and devices such as crutches, hearing aids, and so on.

TUTORING PROGRAMS

BENEFITS OF STUDENT TUTOR PROGRAMS

Peer/cross-age tutoring is another constructive, organized student activity that not only can promote friendships and understanding among handicapped and nonhandicapped students but also can help principals and teachers meet the needs for individualizing instruction. Properly structured student tutorials have proven as effective as tutoring by adult aides, and there are added potential benefits for those involved.

For tutors, these include increased academic and social maturity as well as self-confidence and improved attitudes toward school and toward individuals different from themselves. For pupils there are academic gains, self-confidence, and positive social experiences. Other students in the class frequently benefit, too, as a peripheral effect of the teacher's work in task analysis and individually designed programming.

These benefits are addressed by Joseph and Linda Jenkins (1982) in *Peer and Cross-Age Tutoring,* which also offers guidelines to setting up successful tutorial programs. The necessary elements, they write, include:

ELEMENTS OF SUCCESSFUL PROGRAMS

- a highly structured lesson format (steps include selecting skill or content and outcome desired, analyzing and sequencing the tasks, stating them as measurable learner performances, then modifying teaching tasks to fit the ability level of the tutors)
- tutorial content related to the pupils' curriculum
- mastery learning (working on one skill until mastery is achieved, then going on to the next)
- short (about one-half hour) daily session schedules
- tutor training in skills such as giving clear directions, confirming correct responses, praising appropriate behavior, making nonpunitive corrections, monitoring, recording results, redirecting off-task behavior, holding friendly conversation before and after tutoring session; special training for skills and content can be given to some extent as the tutoring goes on; tutorials could be scheduled four days a week, with the fifth day reserved for conferencing tutors
- active supervision, monitoring the first session closely and giving the tutors feedback and assistance periodically throughout the program.

CHOOSING STUDENT TUTORS

Good tutors, according to Johnson and Johnson, are generally dependable, responsible, sensitive, caring, students—or those likely to develop these traits. They must have the required academic competence and the time to spare. It is important, however, to be cautious about possibly exacerbating existing social and racial tensions. For example, principals or teachers should not consistently choose able-bodied white males as tutors for members of all other groups. It may be possible to find tutoring roles for some handicapped students. Girls may respond better to female tutors and minority students to tutors of their same racial and ethnic group. Many students have an easier time accepting tutors who are at least somewhat older than they. This will not be true in every case, of course; the choices demand sensitivity on the part of the teacher(s) involved.

REINFORCEMENT FOR TUTORS

Some students have participated as committed tutors for two or three years. To combat potential boredom or loss of motivation in long-term tutorial arrangements, principals or teachers occasionally can change tutor/tutee pairs, providing reinforcing events for both members of the dyad, and help make tutoring a prestigious activity in the school.

REFERENCES

Jenkins, J.R., & Jenkins, L.M. (1982). *Peer and cross-age tutoring*. Washington, DC: American Association of Colleges for Teacher Education.

Johnson, D. (1980). Group processes: Influences of student-student interaction on school outcomes. In J. McMillan (Ed.), *The social psychology of school learning*. New York, Academic Press.

Johnson, D., & Johnson, R. (1980). *Promoting constructive student-student relationships through cooperative learning*. Washington, DC: American Association of Colleges for Teacher Education.

Schmuck, R. (1971). Influence of the peer group. In G. Lesser (Ed.), *Psychology and educational practice*. Glenview, IL: Scott, Foresman.

Chapter 22

Teacher Evaluation

SUMMARY

Statement of the Problem

As a result of recent changes in educational philosophy, many school principals trained in the supervision of regular class teachers are now being asked to evaluate the performance of special education and mainstreamed class teaching as well. The situation creates new demands and many potential tensions.

Legal Issues

Although not required of building principals by P.L. 94-142, this extension of their responsibility is an outgrowth of the concept of least restrictive environment mandated by that act and other legislation. Specific regulations, requirements, and format for teacher evaluation vary, of course, from one state and school district to another.

Rationale

In the past, special and regular education tended to be separate systems. There were separate staffs, each with full responsibility for separate populations, with resulting attitudes of "my students" versus "yours." In contrast, current legal and policy changes are aimed at creating an environment of coresponsibility for all of "our" students. A key facet of those changes is the effort to educate as many handicapped students as possible in their neighborhood schools. Since principals are charged with overall responsibility for those schools, it thus follows that they should play a major role in evaluation of teachers and programs serving the handicapped, as well as the nonhandicapped, students in their buildings.

Approaches

The same general techniques and policies that make any teacher evaluation productive apply when evaluating special educators. Among these are: reaching a prior, clear understanding among all school staff members on what will be evaluated, how, and for what purpose; selecting a fair and appropriate evaluation instrument; and establishing a relationship of support and trust. Two specific suggestions for the meaningful evaluation of special education/mainstreamed teachers are for the principal to: (1) hold a preevaluation conference; that is, sit down and discuss with the teacher the special needs of the students and the goals and strategies for meeting them; or (2) put together an evaluation team that includes specialists with relevant expertise. It is essential for the evaluator, whomever that may be, to develop some knowledge of appropriate curricula and teaching techniques.

THE PRINCIPAL'S ROLE IN EVALUATION

There are times when the shifting currents of educational policies can leave an experienced professional feeling like a beached whale, tossed ashore on an alien shore with no means of returning to the familiar systems that had been mastered so well. It is one of those times, quite likely, when a conventionally trained and experienced principal is told to walk through the door of a special education classroom to evaluate the teacher in charge there.

INHERENT TENSIONS

Evaluations always are vulnerable occasions, to which both parties bring their own assortment of fears and anxieties, goals and beliefs. All the tensions already inherent in the situation are exacerbated when the teacher (reasonably or not) believes that the evaluator is not qualified for the task. (In the situation considered here, the traditional separation of regular and special education may generate distrust in any case.)

From the principal's point of view, the task may be unsolicited, unfamiliar, and at least mildly intimidating. Problems abound. There are risks associated with negative evaluations and dangers in overrating or ignoring poor performance in order to avoid confrontations. Because the situation is new, assistance in navigating through these shoals is hard to come by.

This chapter pulls together some of the most useful ideas from the very limited literature available. It includes a few writers' guidelines to effective evaluation programs, a summary of proposed basic competencies, suggestions for critical skills to observe when evaluating mainstreamed/special education teaching, and notes on the role of the principal and other possible evaluation staff persons.

THE EXPERIENCE OF ONE STATE

One of the few published articles on the evaluation of special education teachers (Moya & Gay, 1982) concerns a survey of school districts in California, where a statewide uniform evaluation system has been mandated by law since 1972. Of the school districts responding to the survey (77 percent of a selected 190), 87 percent reported that they used the same evaluation criteria for both regular and special educators. Those that had different criteria for special education varied in their approaches. These included:

EVALUATION CRITERIA USED IN CALIFORNIA

- criteria used for regular teachers plus the ability to write and follow through on an IEP
- criteria used for regular teachers plus the ability to communicate with other teachers
- evaluations based on specific job descriptions.

Districts responding affirmed that the principal was the primary person responsible for performance evaluation; 10 percent reported that the principal had assigned this responsibility to another individual, usually the director of special education or the vice principal. Most districts sampled used a preevaluation conference and both verbal and written reports of results.

Moya and Gay note that it still is unknown whether the evaluation methods and criteria used for special educators are effective. They suggest as steps toward improvement that administrators:

RESULTS AND RECOMMENDATIONS OF A STATE SURVEY

1. clarify a basic philosophy of teacher evaluation at the district level, considering community priorities
2. develop clear job descriptions for special educators that specify differences in responsibility between regular and special teachers. (Optimally, this should be a collaborative process involving both teachers and supervisors.)
3. inform the evaluator and teachers through inservice training, a handbook, or other method of the criteria for evaluation
4. find the evaluation techniques best suited to the school system. (For example, the survey found one school that used a combination of trained evaluators, peer evaluation by teachers from different schools, and teacher evaluation of administrators.)

EFFECTIVE EVALUATION PROGRAMS

KEY ELEMENTS OF ALL EVALUATION PROCEDURES

Because there is great potential for resentment and conflict, it is especially important, when evaluating teachers of exceptional students, that principals follow a sound, rational, planned approach. It is important to know what is being evaluated and to select instruments and procedures that will yield appropriate information; that the evaluation criteria be fair, relevant, and clearly understood by all staff members; and that the evaluation take place, to the greatest extent possible, in an atmosphere of support and trust.

Two Approaches

MEASURING METHODS VERSUS OUTCOMES

There are two basic approaches to evaluating teachers. The first involves measuring methods (the quality of teacher performance) and the second outcomes (the amount of student improvement). Most educators would agree that the ultimate goal of teacher evaluation is to optimize student learning, but in fact (and this is the problem that underlies all others in this area), the relationship between teaching methods and student achievement is hard to prove.

There are (1) a multitude of factors affecting a child's learning, (2) little ethical possibility of controlling them in order to pinpoint the role that teachers play, and (3) tremendous differences of opinion as to what constitutes good teaching. So while it is important to understand which approach has been chosen (methods or outcomes), it also is essential to recognize that present means of measuring either the quality of teaching or the rate of learning cannot give rigorously accurate, nonsubjective results.

Judging the Evaluation Instrument

There are several other factors to consider when selecting or designing an evaluation form. These include:

SELECTING A PREPARED EVALUATION INSTRUMENT

- Validity: Does it really measure what it says it will?
- Reliability: Does it yield consistent results over time, with different evaluators, etc.?
- Relevance: Does it measure factors that are really important?
- Utility: Does it provide information that is useful in improving teaching, eliminating incompetence, or other defined use?
- Fidelity: Does the evaluation really reflect actual performance?
- Ease of Administration: How practical is it?

Useful Guidelines

Ross (1981) proposes the following steps for administrators to use in developing their own evaluation program:

DEVELOPING YOUR OWN EVALUATION PROGRAM

1. establish criteria on which teachers will be rated (for example, classroom management, communication skills, compliance with school policies, and so on)
2. establish three to six specific characteristics for each criterion
3. develop a standard classroom observation form
4. submit the form to other staff members for review
5. establish an evaluation timetable
6. hold inservice training for both teachers and evaluator(s).

Both Ross (1981) and Weisenstein (1976) also offer useful suggestions for steps that can help improve the interpersonal dimension of evaluation procedures. Principals are advised to:

STEPS TO MINIMIZE TENSIONS

> assure that evaluation planning has been extensive enough so as to allow participation by staff members at all levels and to assure that the plan for evaluation is . . . understood by each staff member . . . ; that the evaluation instrument used generates data free from bias and misinterpretation; that the evaluation process is carried out in a friendly atmosphere in which personalities and assignments are considered, and professional improvement is emphasized; that the evaluator is to the point and honest, relating to the evaluatee both strong and weak areas and giving the evaluatee ample opportunity to appraise his/her own performance; that resources for change are provided if change is recommended; and that the degree and direction of change be determined jointly by the evaluator and evaluatee (Weisenstein, p. 18).

Ross lists six rules to minimize tensions between teachers and the principal as evaluator. The principal should:

1. keep evaluation criteria in mind when selecting and employing new staff members
2. explain the evaluation process during yearly inservice sessions
3. establish a regular pattern of classroom visits
4. document everything
5. enforce school policies consistently
6. provide opportunities for teacher self-evaluation.

PROPOSED EVALUATION CRITERIA

What, then, are the criteria on which to base an evaluation of mainstreamed/special education teachers? What are the competencies they ought to have attained? The skills listed next represent one comprehensive attempt (Reynolds, 1980) to answer these questions and to identify the basic "clusters of competencies" that all teachers should have in order to prepare them to teach in today's integrated classrooms:

PROPOSED COMPETENCIES FOR MAINSTREAMED CLASS TEACHERS

- Curriculum: Acquaintance with the general curriculum and an ability to design, develop, and modify the curriculum to meet individual needs.
- Basic Skills: The ability to teach basic literacy skills (e.g., word attack, reading comprehension, spelling, and study skills) through the fifth grade level, to teach maintenance and personal development skills, and to relate these skills to the academic curriculum; teachers also should be able to relate course information to career implications.
- Class Management: Skills in general class management procedures, including group process, applied behavior analysis, crisis intervention, and group approaches to creating a positive affective climate.
- Professional Interactions: Proficiency in consultation, communication, interprofessional planning and negotiations.
- Teacher-Parent-Student Relations: Skills and sensitivity in dealing with parents and siblings of students, particularly with families of handicapped and minority students.
- Student-Student Relationships: Skills in managing relationships among students, such as generating cooperative, mutually helpful behavior; developing cooperative and tutorial group activities; and giving increasing responsibility to students in managing their educational and social environment.
- Exceptional Conditions: Basic knowledge of exceptional conditions and educational modifications for each; knowledge of key terminology and familiarity with the functions of specialists.

- Referral: Skills in making and recording systematic observations of students, familiarity with referral procedures and available resources, and commitment to use such resources as a means of bettering the education of individual students.
- Individualized Teaching: The ability to carry out individual assessments, to identify students with special needs and learning styles, and to modify instruction to meet individual needs; familiarity with due process requirements and the writing of IEPs.
- Professional Values: Commitment to the primary importance of individual students' rights to a free appropriate public education; familiarity with relevant laws, regulations, and professional ethical codes.

OTHER SUGGESTIONS FOR EVALUATION FOCUS

In districts in which such competencies have been adopted or specific job descriptions have been developed, the evaluator will already have a clear sense of what skills to observe. In other districts, the following suggestions may prove helpful. Four of the most important skill areas to evaluate are:

FOUR SKILL AREAS

1. Physical Environment: Has the teacher adapted the physical environment of the classroom to meet the needs of special learners? (See Part II for specific suggestions related to each handicapping condition.)
2. Individualizing Instruction: Does the teacher demonstrate ability to modify the curriculum, materials, and/or instructional style to meet the different needs of individual students?
3. Classroom Management: Does the teacher have enough understanding of applied behavior management techniques to make appropriate selections and to use reinforcement in the classroom?
4. Student Assessment: Can the teacher identify student needs and devise fair and appropriate grading/evaluation methods?

TASK ANALYSIS AND TIME USE

Fredericks, Anderson, and Baldwin (1979) studied special educators and found that the two factors contributing most to teacher effectiveness with this population were: (1) how well the teachers used instructional time, and (2) the level of skill at performing task analysis on the curricula.

A third list of factors especially important to special educators is found in *The Elementary Principal's Role in Special Education* by Lietz and Towle (1982):

KEY ATTRIBUTES, SKILLS, AND KNOWLEDGE

- Attributes: Dependability, cooperation, adaptability, open-mindedness and imaginativeness, an understanding of and tolerance for other staff members, initiative, interest and enthusiasm, perceptiveness, assertiveness, independence.
- Skills: Communication and interpersonal skills including interviewing and counseling parents and working with community groups.
- Knowledge: Working knowledge of specific tests and measurement concepts for use in testing and test interpretation; knowledge of the characteristics, curricu-

lum, and instructional techniques for their own exceptionality, plus a rudimentary knowledge of other exceptionalities.

THE ROLE OF THE PRINCIPAL

While principals are automatically involved in evaluation as part of their overall responsibility for school programs, and while it is they who must take leadership in developing and carrying out the teacher evaluation program, it is not necessary or always appropriate for them to bear the entire evaluation burden alone. There are a number of variations in the nature and extent of the roles that principals may play. These include:

VARIATIONS ON THE PRINCIPAL'S ROLE

- the principal as sole evaluator with little or no input from staff
- an evaluation team of which the principal is one member
- the principal as the overseer of teacher self-evaluation
- the principal's assignment of all evaluating tasks to other staff members
- the principal as evaluator, with assistance from district special education personnel.

ALL MODELS HAVE STRENGTHS AND WEAKNESSES

Each model has advantages and weaknesses and is more or less effective in different instances. The third format, for example, seems most productive when the goal of evaluation is teacher improvement. The fourth is sometimes expedient, but should not be overused, since it weakens the principal's essential involvement in school programs.

The team format is helpful in rounding out or filling gaps in the professional knowledge and experience of the chief administrator. It is a good approach to the problem of evaluating special educators. Other team members might include department heads, curriculum consultants, teachers, specialists, and so on. The chief disadvantage, or potential problem, is the tension that may rise when the same person acts as both adviser and evaluator of teaching staff.

THE PRE-EVALUATION CONFERENCE

The preevaluation conference is a useful technique that borrows, in a sense, from several of the formats discussed. As used with a mainstreamed/special education teacher, it might involve talking over with that person the special educational needs of individual students in class and the types of modifications being made to accommodate them. Reviews of the students' IEPs and periodic visits to the class at other than evaluation times would be helpful additions.

In summary, there are both practical and philosophical reasons for building principals to take responsibility in evaluating special education programs in their schools. Clear planning and communication and shared knowledge can help alleviate the problems that threaten to arise.

REFERENCES

Fredericks, H.D., Anderson, R., & Baldwin, W. (1979). Identifying competency indicators of teachers of the severely handicapped. *AAESPH Review, 4*(1), 81–95.

Lietz, J.J., & Towle, M. (1982). *The elementary principal's role in special education*. Springfield, IL: Charles C Thomas.

Moya, S., & Gay, G. (1982). Evaluation of special education teachers. *Teacher Education and Special Education, 5*(1), 37–41.

Reynolds, M. (1980). *A common body of practice for teachers: The challenge of P.L. 94-142 to teacher education*. Washington, DC: The American Association of Colleges for Teacher Education.

Ross, V. (1981). Here's how teachers should be evaluated. *American School Board Journal, 168*(8), 25–27.

Weisenstein, G. (1976). *Teacher evaluation: The principal's role*. Salem, OR: Oregon School Study Council.

Chapter 23

Working With Parents

SUMMARY

Statement of the Problem

P.L. 94-142 requires parents' participation in several aspects of their child's education, but a number of factors may affect the parent-school relationship negatively, including previous unpleasant experiences with schools and other institutions involving the treatment of their child; teacher reluctance, resistance, and/or lack of training in working with parents; and numerous related stresses affecting the persons involved.

Legal Issues

P.L. 94-142 guarantees several rights to the parents of handicapped children, (or to the legal guardian, persons acting as parents, or appointed surrogates), including:

- Their consent is required before initial evaluation and placement can take place.
- They must be notified in advance (in their native language or mode of communication) each time the school proposes or refuses to initiate or change the child's identification, evaluation, program, placement, or free appropriate public education.
- They may contest any school decision they feel inappropriate or not in keeping with the law, and they have the right to call for an impartial due process hearing to resolve disputes.
- They are expected to participate in preparing the child's IEP.

- All special education and related services spelled out in the IEP must be provided at no cost to the family.

Parents may also request an independent evaluation of their child and review and challenge any item in the school records. The school district is required to notify parents of these rights.

Rationale

Because they have the greatest overall responsibility, parents are automatically involved in and concerned with their child's education and deserve the right to help make decisions about it. Further, their special knowledge and commitment can make them valuable partners in that education.

Many of the problems associated with present school-parent relationships should improve as community and professional attitudes change, in part under the impetus of P.L. 94-142, toward wider acceptance of the handicapped and their families, and thus toward greater possibilities for mutual trust.

Approaches

Principals should make certain that they themselves and teachers in their building accept parents as equal partners in the education of the child, ask them for information they have that may be helpful, listen nonjudgmentally, ask if the school can be of help to them, maintain frequent positive communication (about school events, the youngster's progress, and other topics of interest), avoid waiting until there is a problem, be aware of legal requirements for parental notice and participation, and develop appropriate forms and procedures to ensure that these requirements are met.

Special parent services such as discussion groups, workshops, and forums can be beneficial, but educators must be cautious. Experience has shown that only a relatively small percentage of parents will attend such events, speakers/leaders should be chosen carefully, parents will not benefit from advice unless they are ready for it, and too many services can be a burden.

THE ROLE OF PARENTS

FAMILY STRESSES: FACTORS TO TAKE INTO ACCOUNT

Giving birth to and raising a handicapped child can be an extremely stressful experience, replete with grief, guilt, fears, family disruptions, financial strains, and relentless hard work. The families of the handicapped, just as surely as the handicapped themselves, need help and support—yet it is striking how often they do not get it.

Almost every family with a handicapped child has its own accumulation of bad experiences: neighbors and even family members who rejected them and their child; a doctor who distorted or evaded truth in diagnosis; specialists who offered contradictory explanations in language they could not understand; a religious leader who played on their guilt and implied it was their own fault; a teacher who was insensitive, disapproving, unapproachable, or frighteningly uninformed.

By the time the parents reach their first or second or tenth school conference, they may have good cause to be suspicious or defensive. There are three factors in particular to which educators should be sensitive:

1. Parents' stresses in raising a handicapped child
2. Parents' previous bad experiences with professionals
3. Parents' fears about school, based either on their own bad experiences or on the expectation that the schools as they knew them would be unable to accommodate their youngster (fears that their child will be teased and rejected, that the teacher will set unfair expectations and scold the child for not living up to them, or that the child will not be understood and appreciated).

EDUCATORS OFTEN CONTRIBUTE TO THE PROBLEM

Like the parents, educators deserve understanding and respect for the stressful conditions of their own jobs. But it cannot be denied that many educational professionals have contributed to the problem. For a variety of understandable reasons, they may exhibit:

- a lack of commitment to least restrictive environment (mainstreaming)
- a lack of knowledge or training
- a resistance to sharing decision-making responsibility with parents.

Any of these can be perceived by parents and will have a negative effect on their relations with the school.

By setting a tone of cooperation, empathy, and respect for parents and by providing committed leadership in meeting the practical and philosophical goals of P.L. 94-142, the principal can bring about significant improvements. This chapter, after covering related legal issues, provides specific suggestions for further improving school-parent relations. These are designed to build better communications both in conference situations and on a continuing basis. They also constitute guidelines on providing additional parent services.

LEGAL ISSUES

Parent Surrogates

As noted throughout this handbook, parents are legally involved in every major phase of a handicapped child's education. What happens when the parents are not available? P.L. 94-142 assigns parental responsibilities in such cases as follows:

To Guardians

Persons acting as parents of the child (grandparents, neighbors, etc., who are acting with permission of natural parents or guardians) or the child's legal guardian can carry out the rights and responsibilities given to parents under P.L. 94-142, unless the guardian is the state or its appointed representative. In that case, a surrogate parent must be appointed.

GUARDIANS AND SURROGATE PARENTS: DUTIES AND DEFINITIONS

To Surrogates

A surrogate parent is a person appointed to represent the child in matters related to identification, evaluation, placement, and provision of a free, appropriate public education. (All other parental rights and duties remain with parents, guardians, or other custodians.) Surrogates must be appointed, according to the law, if a "reasonable effort" to contact the parents or guardians has failed. (In some states, natural parents may request the appointment of a surrogate for educational purposes.) A person appointed and paid by the state to serve as the child's guardian cannot also act as the surrogate parent, except that foster parents may be trained for and serve in this role, provided they have no conflict of interest.

The means of appointing, monitoring, training, and setting the terms of surrogate parents are state decisions. Surrogate parents may be removed and their qualifications may be challenged in due process hearings.

Student Records

The confidentiality and fairness of information that the school keeps on students is protected by the federal Family Educational Rights and Privacy Act, 20 U.S.C. 12326, commonly called the Buckley Amendment (as well as by P.L. 94-142). These regulations apply to all students, not just the handicapped.

PARENT RIGHTS REGARDING STUDENT RECORDS

According to the law, parents (and their chosen representatives) have the right to inspect and review any files kept on their child. The school district must comply with a request for review as soon as possible and no later than 45 days after it is made. Parents also have a right to request that information in the files be deleted or changed if they feel it is inaccurate, misleading, or in violation of the child's rights. If the school representatives decide to refuse to make the requested change, they must inform parents of their right to call for a due process hearing to review that decision.

Lietz and Towle (1982) in *The Elementary Principal's Role in Special Education* elaborate on these rights:

FURTHER RIGHTS AND REGULATIONS ON STUDENT RECORDS

> Individuals over eighteen and parents of public school students have the right to see, correct, and control access to all nonexempt records. Parents have a right to examine the records personally in the principal's office, and the principal is in violation of the law if he/she agrees only to read to the parents from the records. Parents have a right to have any aspect of the records explained or corrected if it is false or misleading. Schools may not destroy embarrassing items from the records after they have been requested. Parents may obtain copies of the records when they are transferred to third parties, including another school. School officials in the school district to which a child intends to transfer may be sent a child's records without parental consent, but only after the parent has had an opportunity to request a copy of the records and to challenge their contents.
>
> Other people who may use a child's records without parental consent are school officials in the same district, those with court orders, [and] various state and national educational, accreditation, and research organizations.

Other important requirements of the laws related to student records include:

- Parental consent is required before information that can be identified as personally involving a specific child is released to persons other than those mentioned earlier or for purposes other than the regular ones of the school.
- A record must be kept of each access to student information, including the date, purpose, and name of the person gaining access.
- Parents who are unsuccessful in their efforts to have the child's files amended may write a statement, comment, or reason for disagreement that then becomes part of the permanent record.
- One person in the school must have responsibility for enforcing the regulations, and all those collecting or using the information must be trained in related state policies.
- Information no longer needed must be destroyed at the request of the parents, except for permanent records of the student's name, address, phone, grades, classes, attendance record, grade level, and year completed.

IMPROVING COMMUNICATION

The essence of productive school-parent relationships is good communication. As one parent, now a professional in the field, has put it:

PARENT ATTITUDES TOWARD THE SCHOOL

> A parent does not measure the school system by the impressive grouping of buildings and lists of degrees of teachers and administrators but by how well the school helps the child with what the parent thinks the child needs. To a large extent, the parent feels that the child's needs are being met if someone at the school listens and responds when the parent wants to talk about the child's needs (Michaelis, 1980, p. 38).

Under the general heading of improving communication come a number of techniques and skills. This section addresses three topics: methods, educators' attitudes, and conferencing skills.

Methods

TIPS FOR BETTER COMMUNICATION WITH PARENTS

How often do principals and teachers communicate with parents? What methods are effective? A teacher whose communication goes no farther than necessary paperwork and crisis calls to discuss misbehavior can expect parents to build up negative associations with school contact, which are hardly conducive to a good cooperative relationship. Parents of exceptional children need to know that their youngsters are welcome in the school, as is their own involvement. A much better climate is created if communications with parents are frequent and if they stress positive, not just troublesome, aspects of the child's school experience. Some examples (especially for elementary school level classes) include:

- a letter of introduction to parents before the school year begins and a handbook of school/class policy sent home the first week
- contact with parents early in the year to see if they have any skills they would like to share or ways they would like to help (a questionnaire is useful)
- daily or weekly report cards under certain conditions
- a notebook that the student carries daily between school and home, in which either teacher or parents can send messages
- awards and/or acknowledgments of positive behavior and achievements
- periodic newsletters for all parents and students (each student must be recognized at some point over the course of the year)
- telephone calls or conferences to share positive information about the student
- a stated time when parents are especially welcome
- invitations to parents to come see new or special projects
- notifications to local news media about activities of special interest
- school programs and workshops scheduled at times when all parents could be invited to attend
- a policy of sending all school communications home with the students each Monday; this provides time until Friday for parents to return necessary papers and offers the school an opportunity to send home positive news each week.

Educators' Attitudes

IMPROVING EDUCATORS' ATTITUDES

To be effective in communicating with parents, educators must be attentive to their own honest attitudes toward the students and their families. Successful cooperation requires attitudes of trust, respect, acceptance, and sharing. School-parent relationships are not helped when educators view parents as (1) clients or patients, (2) the cause of the child's handicap, (3) adversaries, or (4) intellectual inferiors. Educators who view the parent conferences as an opportunity only to deliver information—as opposed to sharing with equals—can expect problems. The fact is, each participant does have valuable knowledge to share. Carol Michaelis (1980) suggests the following lists:

What Educators Know Better Than Parents	*What Parents Know Better Than Educators*
Child development	Developmental history
Evaluation techniques	Medical history
Behavior reinforcement	Social and educational history
Medical and educational terminology	Favorite toys and activities
Rules and policies of the school	Amount of sleep and rest
Problems at school	Medication and diet

Conferencing Skills

How are an educator's supportive attitude and information conveyed effectively? The following is a list of useful techniques and behaviors, many of them offered by Richard Simpson (1982) in *Conferencing Parents of Exceptional Children*. Principals (and teachers) should:

KEYS TO SUCCESSFUL PARENT CONFERENCES

- return calls promptly
- schedule meetings at a convenient time and place for both parents (not necessarily at the school, which may be intimidating)
- be aware that the parents may have values very different from those of the educators, the mother and father themselves may differ on wishes and needs, and single parents face special problems and stresses
- arrive at the conference calm, relaxed, prepared
- ask parents about the child
- listen with warmth and respect, nonjudgmentally; parents often are not seeking advice, just empathetic attention; encourage them to share their feelings
- share positive information about what the child can do and help parents see this too; do not create a false sense of progress (be truthful) but do not discourage goals that may be beneficial to the pupil

- do not use jargon or technical terminology that parents may not understand
- help family members anticipate problems they may experience and look at alternatives for the future
- encourage parents to develop their own interests apart from those related to the handicapped child and to be attentive to the needs of their other children
- encourage parents to take responsibility for their child; share ways they can help the youngster reach agreed-upon educational goals
- share information about helpful community resources
- be willing to go over issues that were discussed previously.

PARENT SERVICES

WAYS THAT SCHOOLS CAN HELP

In spite of problems they may have had with the schools, whether as students themselves or as participants in their children's educational experience, parents are likely to look to the schools as an important—perhaps the most important—source of help in raising their children. In addition to scheduling conferences to discuss individual needs, many schools offer more intensive services and structured parent activities, including family counseling and referrals, parent advisory committees, parent-to-parent support groups, training programs and workshops, and so on.

CAUTIONS REGARDING PARENT PROGRAMS

Such programs can be of value to many parents and certainly can help build trust and involvement in the schools. However, a caution is sounded again and again by experienced educators: Parents have different expectations and different needs. Their ability to cope is affected by a myriad of factors, including the temperament of the child, their own attitudes toward the youngster, their social involvement and support system, their ability and willingness to seek and use help, the ages of other children, discipline, the parents' personality and time-management skills, and the extent of agreement between them on child-rearing values.

DIFFERENT PARENTS HAVE DIFFERENT NEEDS

Parents must be respected as individuals. Educators cannot expect all of them to want to participate equally or to take advantage of all the services the school has arranged, particularly if it does so without asking parents what help they feel they need. Until they perceive a need for advice or assistance, the parents may not listen; furthermore, too many offers of help can be overwhelming and a burden in themselves.

Parents' varying relationships with the schools have been conceptualized in terms of a Mirror Model of Parent Involvement. Figure 23-1 is one version of the model (Kroth & Krehbiel, 1982).

NOTES ON THE MIRROR MODEL OF PARENT INVOLVEMENT

The levels above the center line refer to needs, those below to contributions. Some key points that Kroth and Krehbiel make in their discussion of the model include:

- It is important that schools be systematic in informing parents of their child's program and of their rights in the special education process. (If educators have relied on written communications, they may want to check to be sure they have been understood.) Regular communications about school events can help build

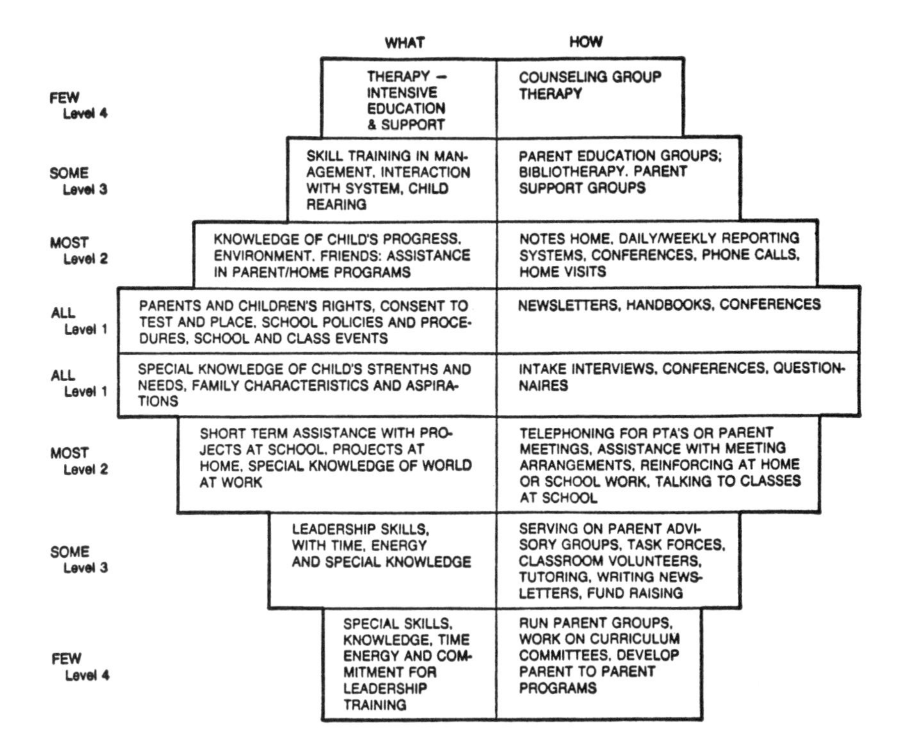

Source: From *Parent-Teacher Interaction* (p.12) by R. Kroth and R. Krehbiel, 1982, Washington, D.C.: American Association of Colleges for Teacher Education. Copyright 1982 by American Association of Colleges for Teacher Education. Adapted by permission.

---

trust and acceptance. So will frequent notice of the pupil's accomplishments and progress.

- Much attention is paid to parent training activities but relatively few parents (20 to 40 percent, according to Kroth and Krehbiel) in any population are likely to take advantage of such aid.
- The school psychologist probably is the person to take charge of service and/or referrals for Level 4 needs.
- All parents have special knowledge of their child that can be highly useful to educators, including effective reinforcers, health needs, and so on.
- Some kind of training generally is important if the program is to make the best use of parent volunteers.
- Parents themselves often are the most effective aids to other parents and advocates for the school. Finding, training, and encouraging those few parents willing and able to take on leadership roles can have great benefits for all involved.

PARENT MEETINGS

TYPES OF PARENT MEETINGS

Parent meetings may take many forms, including informal sessions planned and run by parents in their homes, PTA events, formal hearings, schoolwide conferences organized by administration to inform parents of policies and/or solicit their help in developing such policies, and special interest groups small enough to encourage parents to speak and share.

The two general topics of most importance to parents are how to help their children progress and how to be effective parents (Michaelis, 1980). In discussing such meetings, Michaelis offers several useful suggestions. The principal and/or the teacher(s) must:

TIPS FOR SUCCESS

- choose the group leaders carefully; it is best if their own life experiences are close to those of parents participating
- make the environment as nonthreatening and comfortable as possible; for example, mark building entrances clearly or, better yet, station one host at each entrance to receive guests and direct them to the meeting room; be sure the room is an appropriate size, with adequate seating; provide refreshments; vary the format occasionally
- provide printed programs and name tags for larger meetings
- involve students in the program in some way, from making the invitations or program covers to staging a musical, dramatic, or other performance
- pick a convenient time and organize the program well so that goals can be accomplished quickly and efficiently
- treat parents as peers, not as students.

Parents are critical to the success of any educational program. With handicapped students, services to and involvement of parents deserve special attention and commitment.

REFERENCES

Kroth, R., & Krehbiel, R. (1982). *Parent-teacher interaction*. Washington, DC: American Association of Colleges for Teacher Education.

Lietz, J.J., & Towle, M. (1982). *The elementary principal's role in special education*. Springfield, IL: Charles C Thomas.

Michaelis, C. (1980). *Home and school partnerships in exceptional education*. Rockville, MD: Aspen Publishers, Inc., p. 38.

Simpson, R. (1982). *Conferencing parents of exceptional children*. Rockville, MD: Aspen Publishers, Inc.

Index

E

F

H

I

J

M

R

S

T

U

V

W

Z

About the Authors

Greg R. Weisenstein

Dr. Greg Weisenstein is Coordinator of Vocational and Secondary Special Education Programs at the University of Washington and a member of the President's Committee on Employment of the Handicapped. A frequent lecturer and author on educational administration, mainstreaming, special education and vocational education, his past positions include international president of the Council for Exceptional Children's Division on Career Development, co-chair of two international conferences, and coordinator of research and training projects on mainstreaming in the University of Washington Teacher Certification Program.

Ruth Pelz

Ruth Pelz' writing credits in the field of education include three elementary and secondary textbooks and various curricula, staff and teachers' manuals, research reports, and other publications. She has served as publications specialist for a number of special education programs at the University of Washington, including the Dean's Grant on Mainstreaming, Western States Technical Assistance Resource, Specialized Training of Educators Project, and other mainstreaming and transition studies, and as curriculum developer for Seattle Public Schools and the State of Washington. This *Administrator's Desk Reference* is one of a number of publications on which Weisenstein and Pelz have collaborated.